Southern Literary Study

PROBLEMS AND POSSIBILITIES

Southern Literary Study

PROBLEMS AND POSSIBILITIES

EDITED BY

Louis D. Rubin, Jr.

AND

C. Hugh Holman

THE UNIVERSITY OF NORTH CAROLINA PRESS

CHAPEL HILL

Library of Congress Cataloging in Publication Data

Main entry under title :
Southern literary study.

   Proceedings of a conference sponsored by the English
Department of the University of North Carolina, held
Nov. 30-Dec. 2, 1972, at Chapel Hill.
   1. American literature—Southern states—History and
criticism—Congresses. I. Rubin, Louis Decimus,
1923- II. Holman, Clarence Hugh, 1914-
III. North Carolina. University. Dept. of English.
PS261.S528   810'.9'975   75-11553
ISBN 0-8078-1252-8

This book is dedicated to

JAY B. HUBBELL

as pioneer and leader
in the field of southern literary studies

Table of Contents

Preface   *ix*

Papers

1. *Southern Literature and Southern Society*
   NOTES ON A CLOUDED RELATIONSHIP
   by Louis D. Rubin, Jr.   *3*

2. *Early Southern Literature*
   PAST, PRESENT, AND FUTURE
   by Richard Beale Davis   *21*

3. *Dim Pages in Literary History*
   THE SOUTH SINCE THE CIVIL WAR
   by Arlin Turner   *36*

4. *The South's Reaction to Modernism*
   A PROBLEM IN THE STUDY OF SOUTHERN LETTERS
   by Lewis P. Simpson   *48*

Discussions

5. *Colonial Southern Literature*   *71*

6. *Nineteenth-Century Southern Literature*   *102*

7. *Twentieth-Century Southern Literature*   *133*

8. *The Continuity of Southern Literary History*   *165*

9. *Thematic Problems in Southern Literature*   *199*
   EDITOR'S NOTE   *222*

Appendix

A List of Topics Suggested for Further Study   *227*

Preface

The study of southern literature has been going on for a long time . . . for almost as long as there has been a recognizable and identifiable American South. It has served many ends; not only the understanding of the region through its literary imagination and the relationship of the novels, poems, stories, and other writings of southerners to the life and thought of the region, but also those of self-identification, community defense, regional pyschoanalysis, and even chauvinistic patriotism. Someone ought one day to write a book about the history of southern literary study; among other things it would tell us much about the South's intellectual life.

With the rise of what has been called the Southern Literary Renascence of the 1920s, 1930s, and 1940s, the study of southern literature also had a kind of awakening. It became less defensive, less adulatory, more critical—perhaps both because the work of some of the major twentieth-century southern authors stood in no great need of defense, and because the South itself lost some of the strong sectional consciousness that had contributed so greatly to the passion with which southerners identified their own situation with that of their region. Indeed, the two developments are more than a little related. And there was also the renewed impetus to look back at the literature of an earlier South critically and imaginatively, in order to understand how the contemporary South and its literature came to be what they were. Scholars such as Jay B. Hubbell and critics such as Allen Tate led in what has been in effect a concerted effort to understand the South through its literature and the literature through the society from which it evolved.

In any event, the universities and colleges offering graduate and undergraduate study in southern literature—and by no means all of them are located in the southern states—are numbered in the hundreds. In 1967 the Society for the Study of Southern Literature was formed to help stimulate and guide the study of southern writing. A bibliographical guide to the field has been compiled under its aegis. Other such projects are under way. Two journals— the *Mississippi Quarterly* and the *Southern Literary Journal*—are devoted exclusively to the publication of scholarship in southern writing. An up-to-date census of dissertations and theses has been prepared and is presently being readied for publication. The *Mississippi Quarterly* publishes an annual critical checklist of scholarship in southern literature.

It was with a view toward providing direction and coherence in the field of southern literary scholarship that in 1972 the English department of The University of North Carolina at Chapel Hill undertook to convene a working conference, whereby many of the leading scholars in the subject might be assembled to discuss problems, possibilities, and future directions in southern literary study. Since the early 1900s, when C. Alphonso Smith, one of the first scholars to work in the subject, was a member of the English department faculty, the university has been one of the more active centers for southern literary scholarship. For many years Addison Hibbard and Gregory L. Payne were teaching and directing research. The University of North Carolina Press has been one of the most active presses in publishing work on southern literature and culture. The work in history, sociology, and economics at the university by such scholars as Howard W. Odum, Rupert Vance, Guy Johnson, George Tindall, Fletcher M. Green, and George Mowry has served to keep the interest in the South free of the excesses of regional piety and sectional self-congratulation that have marred much southern scholarship. There has been a long and fruitful tradition in creative writing at the university, and various southern authors have been among its graduates.

Because of its long tradition of work in the field and its continuing involvement in the study of southern literature, The University of North Carolina at Chapel Hill felt obligated to take the lead in making possible a fresh look at what has been done and what needs to be done, by some of the scholars who have been most deeply involved. Through the generosity of the National Endowment for the Humanities, a grant was secured whereby some two dozen scholars could be invited to Chapel Hill for a three-day conference. It was also possible to commission certain scholars to prepare papers setting forth their thoughts on the problems and possibilities for future study. Each participant was asked to submit in advance a list of topics that might profitably be investigated by future scholars. Tape recordings were made of each of the five discussion groups which were held during the conference, and the proceedings transcribed and edited.

The conference was held on November 30 and December 1 and 2, 1972. The participants were:

Cleanth Brooks, Yale University, New Haven, Conn.

Norman D. Brown, University of Texas, Austin.

Philip Butcher, Morgan State College, Baltimore, Md.

Richard J. Calhoun, Clemson University, Clemson, S.C.

George Core, University of Georgia, Athens.

Charles T. Davis, Yale University, New Haven, Conn.

Richard Beale Davis, University of Tennessee at Knoxville.

Carl R. Dolmetsch, College of William and Mary, Williamsburg, Va.

John C. Guilds, University of South Carolina, Columbia.

M. Thomas Inge, Virginia Commonwealth University, Richmond.

Robert D. Jacobs, Georgia State University, Atlanta.

Lewis Lawson, University of Maryland, College Park.

Rayburn S. Moore, University of Georgia, Athens.

Charles A. Ray, North Carolina Central University, Durham.

Paschal Reeves, University of Georgia, Athens.

Lewis P. Simpson, Louisiana State University, Baton Rouge.

Walter Sullivan, Vanderbilt University, Nashville, Tenn.

Arlin Turner, Duke University, Durham, N.C.

Floyd C. Watkins, Emory University, Atlanta, Ga.

Thomas Daniel Young, Vanderbilt University, Nashville, Tenn.

These were joined by the following members of the English and history faculties of The University of North Carolina at Chapel Hill:

Robert A. Bain
C. Hugh Holman
Blyden Jackson
Lewis Leary
Louis D. Rubin, Jr.
George Brown Tindall

The pages which follow consist of the proceedings of that conference. Unfortunately the paper prepared by Professor Philip Butcher could not be made available for the published proceedings. Throughout, no attempt has been made to regularize or render more formal the actual language used in the discussion, beyond the elimination of obvious conversational awkwardness and imprecision arising from the nature of the medium; the objective has been to present, as faithfully as possible, what the assembled scholars had to say about southern literary study. It will be seen that the participants in the several discussion groups interpreted their tasks differently; some of the groups tended to concentrate on the specific needs for scholarship in a given area, while others focused their attention upon themes and problems that future scholars might take into consideration in approaching southern literary study. The chairman of the session on Thematic Problems in Southern Literature has felt that because of the range and variety of the subject matter discussed in that session, it was useful to append to the transcript a note indicating specific topics that might be investigated.

There was one scholar absent from the proceedings of the conference who should have been there. Jay Broaddus Hubbell, professor emeritus of English at Duke University and for many decades the leader and moving spirit of scholarly inquiry into the literature of the South, was unable to attend. He was, however, well represented by various of his former students, now in turn engaged in passing on to new generations the devotion and zeal for southern literature he had kindled in them.

Publication of the proceedings of this conference, as an aid to scholars and potential scholars in southern literature, has been made possible by a grant from the Faculty Research Council of The University of North Carolina at Chapel Hill.

Planning, convening, conducting, and summarizing the proceedings of a conference such as this is a complicated undertaking, and the editors of this volume, who were coordinators of the conference, are indebted to many persons for help in making the venture both possible and successful. These include: Ronald Berman, William R. Emerson, David J. Wallace, and Miss Sherolynn Maxwell of the National Endowment for the Humanities; Dean George R. Holcomb and W. W. Fulk of the administration of The University of North Carolina at Chapel Hill; James R. Gaskin, William R. Harmon, Lewis Leary, Siegfried Wenzel, C. Carroll Hollis, and Martha J. Cook of the faculty of the Department of English; Matthew Hodgson and Malcolm M. MacDonald of The University of North Carolina Press; and Karin Gleiter, Jeanne Nostrandt, Mary Flinn, Beverly Miller, and James L. Zachary.

L. D. R.
C. H. H.

PAPERS

1. Southern Literature and Southern Society

NOTES ON A CLOUDED RELATIONSHIP

by Louis D. Rubin, Jr.

I should like to address my remarks to a specific aspect of southern literary study: the relationship between southern literature and the South. I do so not merely because it has often been talked about, though seldom analyzed, and not merely because I find it fascinating, but also because I believe that one of the most important roles of imaginative literature is that of knowledge, and that literature can instruct us about society in ways that nothing else can, and that, in the case of southern literature, relatively little use has been made of it for that purpose. It is not the only purpose of literary study, it may not even be the most important purpose, but surely it is a legitimate purpose, and one that I assume we are all concerned with.

When we take the adjective "southern" and we place it before the noun "literature," what we have is the study of literature in a particular place and a particular time. The place is the American South, the time is the period from the beginnings of English settlement in that place up to the present. We thus accept for our objective the study of the writer *in* and *of* the South, and that of the South *in* and *of* the writer. If we will conduct our study with imagination and with thoroughness, we should be able to find out something about both.

All of this seems obvious, as indeed it is. But if obvious, it is not simple. To do it properly requires an ability to read a work of the literary imagination, one with a logic and with dynamics that are internal and governed by its artistic needs and objectives, and also and equally an ability to understand the detailed complexities of a society that has evolved and changed in time, which has existed politically, economically, racially, socially, culturally, geographically. Between the work of literature and the society there can be an intense and creative relationship. The writer's effort to perceive order and meaning in life through language, his attempt at representation of reality, takes its form and its meaning from the institutions, artifacts, attitudes, and concerns of the life that he has known, which means that to the extent that the writer is part of and a product of his society, the stories and poems that he writes will draw on the nature of that society for their human image.

The difficulty lies in the nature of the relationship—between the southern writer and the South out of which he writes. It is not a one-for-one relationship; it does not involve anything like simple cause and effect. For the relationship is transmitted through the medium of art, and so by means of an image. And the image is a manifold thing, a mass of properties, a variety of surfaces, a complexity of structure. Without the image, literature is nothing at all, and thus without our approaching it through the image and in terms of the image, the work of literature will have little or nothing to say to us about the society out of which it evolves. What it has to tell us about the work will mean nothing unless we can recognize how it serves in the composition of the image. In other words, to learn about the South through its literature we have got first to understand it as literature, and to learn about literature through the South we have got to understand that the impact of the South upon the literature will manifest itself in literary ways.

Unless the nature of this relationship is understood, and the central position of the literary image as the expression of the relationship is recognized, then southern literature will have nothing of importance to tell us about the South, nor will we be able to learn very much about southern literature from what we know of the South. We have got to know the work of literature, and we have got to know the South, and we have got to understand *how* the one affects and is affected by the other. This I presume is one goal of southern literary study, at least to the extent that it is *southern* literary study.

I say we have got to. I do not think it has been done very often. Consider, for example, the fact that while we are all pretty much in agreement that there is something known as southern literature, we are quite at variance on what is southern about it. When I was in graduate school in the early 1950s, I proposed to write a doctoral dissertation on the subject of Thomas Wolfe as a southern writer. But the distinguished scholar to whom I made my proposal informed me that this would be out of the question, since Thomas Wolfe was not a southern writer at all, but properly belonged with the midwestern writers such as Dreiser and Lewis. Obviously the scholar in question had in mind a definition of southern literature that involved a certain kind of attitude and a certain kind of subject matter into which Thomas Wolfe did not fit. His particular idea of what was southern, I fear, was bound in with the southern plantation myth; according to this standard, William Faulkner was a southern writer, all right, and Robert Penn Warren and Sidney Lanier were southern writers, but not a garrulous plebeian like Thomas Wolfe. (I might add that I wrote the dissertation anyway, with a French phenomenological literary critic filling in as director.)

What lies at the root of the problem is that in a very real sense there is more than one South, and each of us has his own version in mind. I like the answer that my colleague Hugh Holman made at a symposium a few years ago when someone in the audience asked him how he could possibly consider Thomas Wolfe a southern writer, coming as Wolfe did from Asheville, N.C., a cosmopolitan mountain center, and also since Wolfe never spoke of southern institutions except in terms of contempt, and left the place as soon as he could. Holman replied—the reply is so apt that I will quote from the exchange in *Southern Fiction Today* at some length—that "in order to say what you are saying, you have made an assumption that there is *a* South. I don't know which one you are assuming, but it sounds to me a little bit as though it is located in the Tidewater or low country, and that the South of the Piedmont region is not really a South. Now I would argue that, in actuality, there are many Souths . . . that there is a variety of experience in the South. Atlanta is certainly not the South of even Milledgeville, Georgia, or certainly not the South of the country around Augusta at the time that Caldwell was writing about it, or Judge Longstreet, for that matter. And these sections are all a part of this entire region, and I think that your question serves as a warning to us that we have . . . been discussing in our own ways and within our own limits our own quite limited concepts of what the South should be."

My point here is not whether or just how Thomas Wolfe was a southern writer, but rather that despite all the work that has been done on southern writers, and despite the fact that for almost 150 years now we have been referring to something known as a southern literature, we not only are not in general agreement about what the term means, but as Holman indicates, actually we haven't even thought about the problem enough to recognize, except in odd moments, that there *is* a problem. In short, in this as in other instances there has been little or no effort to define many of the primary terms and premises of our common endeavor. To be sure, I am aware of the noted southern abhorrence of theory and the pure idea, but really, this is carrying things too far.

You might ask what we are to do about it. Well, one thing we might do is to encourage our students to attempt a few of those searching, conceptualized thematic studies such as get written about the literature of New England and other places. Consider, for example, a book such as R. W. B. Lewis's *The American Adam*. I myself don't like much about the book, but it has the merit of looking at the assumptions behind a complex body of literature, and pointing out important relationships, patterns, similarities. Or consider Leo Marx's *The Machine in the Garden*, which though also unsatisfactory in parts is in many respects a brilliant use of literature to understand culture, and of culture to delineate literature. *The Machine in the Garden*—it sounds like a book about the New South, doesn't it? Is Thomas Sutpen a machine in the plantation garden? Is Flem Snopes? Or the tractor that kills Mr. Guizac in "The Displaced Person"? Why hasn't anyone written that kind of book about southern writing? Offhand I can think of only one book that attempts anything of the sort, and it doesn't in my opinion succeed very well.

One of the things that we are told is a key attribute of southern literature is the devotion to place. One very important southern author, Eudora Welty, has even written a little monograph on it. We constantly hear this advanced as an essential characteristic of southern writing. And I agree. But what exactly does it mean? What has it meant to various southern writers? Has anyone ever really tried to see what place is made to signify in southern writing? Cable describes New Orleans, Faulkner northern Mississippi, Ellen Glasgow Richmond, Elizabeth Madox Roberts Kentucky, of course; we know that, though I can think of a few people who continue to tell us about it as if it were a breathtaking discovery. But what does the sense of place symbolize aesthetically, socially? How do the southern writers *use* place? Clearly the matter has social, political ramifications. Edward King, for example, noted in 1875 that the southerners he had seen in his tour of the region were extraordinarily bound to certain parts of the South. The late Frank Owsley contended that the Confederate States of America died of States' Rights. Surely history is tied in with it. But in what ways? Why does Joe Christmas come back to Jefferson and Yoknapatawpha County? Why does Cass Kinsolving come back to Charleston? It seems to me that the matter could do with a little investigation, by someone with imagination enough not to stop where the travel guidebooks usually do, which is to say, at mere cumulative description, but to go on and think about what functions place—more properly, *places*—serve in the dynamics and the meaning of important works of southern literature. But if someone does wish to attempt it, he will get nowhere merely by isolating the fictional and poetic descriptions of places and comparing them with the actual places the author is writing about. This is the level on which all too much southern literary study has been conducted, and if this is all that our scholar does, he will have nothing to tell us that any social scientist can't tell us much more authoritatively and precisely. Instead, he must read the poems and stories as works of literature, and proceed to his job of studying place through what place is made to signify and symbolize in the artistic dynamics. Only then will the southern literary imagination unfold itself to reveal what it, uniquely, can reveal: what things mean.

Or consider another of the commonplaces of southern scholarship, which has to do with caste and class. The southern legend had it that in the Old South there were three classes: planter aristocracy, poor white dirt-eaters, and black slaves. Historians have long since proved that this was not so, and that the antebellum South, like the twentieth-century South, was predominantly a middle-class affair. We all know this, and on occasion we like to point it out. But what happens to this relationship in southern fiction? I have noticed several things. In much antebellum fiction, there is almost a kind of class war between the Cavalier myth and the middle-class circumstance. In *The Yemassee*, for example, Simms puts the lieutenant governor of Carolina, Lord Craven, on the frontier in disguise as Captain Harrison, to rally the settlers and save the colony from the Indians. It is supposed to be the Cavalier nobility of Lord Craven that enables him to lead the settlers. But it isn't; it's the fact that as a backwoodsman and a frontier fighting man he is the best of them all, and he leads them to their successful defense against the Yemassees because he can think better and faster in the field and can more accurately figure out what the Indians are up to. He is indeed a split personality, and the Captain Harrison part is far more convincing than the Lord Craven part. Simms has to yank the adventure plot back into pure romance in order to reconvert his hero into an authentic Cavalier lord at the end, and his most convincing scenes throughout are those involving middle-class folk. In Kennedy's *Horseshoe Robinson* we get more of the same. The middle-class Sergeant Galbraith Robinson takes over completely once the action starts, and the aristocratic officer, Major Arthur Butler, must spend a goodly part of the time kept safely out of the way in a Tory prison so that Sergeant Horseshoe Robinson can go ahead and win the Revolutionary War in the South. The aristocratic figure is essential only to the romance, the love story, and not to the fighting, at which the middle-class Horseshoe Robinson is the expert. Yet oddly enough, when the hard work is done and the romance can resume, Kennedy doesn't seem to have a role for his middle-class sergeant any more. We learn that he never married and died childless. Now perhaps this involves the influence of the celibate Natty Bumppo on historical romance, but I think there is more to it than that.

As for the twentieth century, if we take the same situation and project it into Faulkner's *Absalom, Absalom!* for example, we get a different emphasis. In a very real way Thomas Sutpen behaves like Horseshoe Robinson; that is to say, unencumbered by too much gentility, he gets the job done. But with Faulkner the democratic admiration has turned into amazement and dismay. Quentin Compson, as Faulkner says, is appalled to realize that a man like Sutpen, without gentility or breeding or ideals, could be what he is and do what he does. Faulkner's view of the matter, you might say, is, in a tragic vein, rather more like that of those Whig humorists of the Old Southwest contemplating the amorality and cleverness of the Simon Suggses and Ovid Boluses, looking down at their rustic crudeness yet with a sneaking envy of their superior grip on reality. In terms of caste-and-class role, Quentin Compson is Faulkner's young aristocrat, his Lord Craven and Major Butler and the superior effectiveness, in the real world, of the non-aristocratic figure, whether he be Dalton Ames in *The Sound and the Fury* or Thomas Sutpen in *Absalom, Absalom!* drives him to despair. Only Jason Compson can cope with a world of lower-caste Snopeses—by turning into one.

Now what does all this mean? I am not sure. But I do know this: it is worth looking into. We have spent considerable time trying to make the fiction of William Gilmore Simms into something better than it is, and very little time trying to use it as it is, to help us understand the antebellum South or, for that matter, William Gilmore Simms. Nobody has really examined the class-and-caste relationships in southern fiction, whether antebellum, postwar, or twentieth century, to see what they may show about southern life or about the southern literary imagination. In this respect a historian, William R. Taylor, comes closest to dealing with the antebellum picture, in his book *Cavalier and Yankee*, though he is out after different game. Taylor, for example, does point out the interesting fact that neither Simms nor Kennedy was an aristocrat by birth.

It seems to me that there is a wealth of material here, if only we will use it. But by and large we have ignored it, and spend our time attempting to prove that Henry Timrod is a Metaphysical poet like John Donne, that Simms's Captain Porgy is funny, that *Absalom, Absalom!* is or is not a parable of southern history, and so on. Please do not misunderstand me; I do not say these are not interesting things to do. I have spent considerable time on the matter of *Absalom, Absalom!* and southern history myself, and am probably not done. But I would suggest that instead of more arguing back and forth whether *Absalom, Absalom!* is or is not "about" the South (and what it usually comes down to is sectional self-defense against the enemy Yankees, however we may disguise it—disguise it to ourselves most of all), we might assume that if William Faulkner sets out to write a novel set in nineteenth-century Mississippi and dealing with race relations, that novel couldn't *help* being about southern history, and go on from there to see what he has to tell us about it.

I do not advance such conjectures as hypotheses to be followed; as generalizations they are all too tentative and too hasty. But I do think they illustrate what *kind* of discovery might be possible to the scholar who will approach southern literature to see what is there, and who is willing to examine the dynamics of the work, think about the human relationships it embodies, and look beyond the surface of so many of the customary assumptions and commonplaces made about it. The literature seems to me to offer an unusually rich field for imaginative thematic criticism. There are so many notions that might be tested out: the presence of Calvinism and its ramifications in the society, for example; the function of southern literature as pastoral for an urbanizing society uneasy about its new values; the continuation, into new forms and into a new day, of sectional self-defense; the insistence upon community identity; and so on. Such inquiries, if developed imaginatively and not merely as the framework for cumulative tabulation, could tell us much about the South and its history, and also about the nature of the southern literary imagination. Perhaps we might then be able to identify, with more authority and agreement than we now can, what that imagination is and what are its distinguishing qualities.

But this kind of thematic study, in which recurrent themes, motifs, and situations are developed through the investigation of a complex body of literature, is only one way whereby the relationship between southern literature and southern society can be approached. To study one writer it is not, after all, always necessary to compare his work with that of others, or to concentrate on recurrent themes and patterns. We can take the story or poem itself, for its own sake, and see what it has to tell us, as a story or poem. We need not stop there, of course; we can go into and out of biography, history, as we wish; but the story or the poem is our starting point and our returning point.

Thus far I have said nothing at all about what U. B. Phillips and others have referred to as the central theme of southern history: race. I should now like to speculate a bit how it might be possible to understand this great problem, in part at least, through the study of the South's literature. One point at issue in southern history upon which an imaginative reading of southern literature ought to be able to throw some light is that of the extent to which the slaveholding South supposedly felt secret guilt over its "peculiar institution." This has been argued back and forth by historians and others. Part of the difficulty, of course, is that from the vantage point of the twentieth century, we feel certain that the antebellum southerner *should* have felt guilty, and so when in his printed records he defends slavery or, even more pointedly, fails to seem perturbed over being a slaveholder enough to bother to defend himself, we conclude that the guilt must surely have been repressed. Our present attitudes also affect our reading of the past, in that if we are on the side of civil rights, we will feel better if we can believe that the antebellum South was secretly guilty over slavery, because it is analogous to our own guilt over continued racial segregation. So we try to read behind or between the lines of the memoirs, letters, documents, journalism, public pronouncements, and so forth, of the antebellum South, hoping to find more unease than seems to be there over the ownership of human beings as property.

It is well known, of course, that very little antebellum southern literature deals with slaves and slavery. This gives us very little evidence from which to work. We can try the analytical hypothesis known to scholars as the Sherlock Holmes opening: "Is there any point to which you would wish to draw my attention?" Inspector Gregory asks. "To the curious incident of the dog in the night-time," Holmes replies. "The dog did nothing in the night-time," Inspector Gregory objects. "That was the curious incident," declares Sherlock Holmes. In other words, we can point to the almost total exclusion of any consideration of the moral right or wrong of slavery in important antebellum literature, and see this as a confession of helplessness and guilt. But although this is not without importance, it is a rather negative way of getting at the ties between southern literature and southern life. Recently I read an essay on *The Yemassee* in which the author takes what Simms has to say about Indians, and interprets it psychologically as demonstrating his suppressed feelings of terror and shame about slavery. This is an approach to the matter, but it leaves me rather unconvinced, for from what I know of Simms, the psychology thus implied is too subtle to fit his case. Rather more to the point is Simms's treatment of the slave, Hector, in that novel. That redoubtable black is so clever and so self-reliant as an Indian fighter that after the Indian attack has been foiled Lord Craven feels impelled to give him his freedom; whereupon, in one of the earliest of those famous "dis ole darky don't wanna be free" scenes that were so much a part of post-Civil War literature, Simms must have his slave say, in contradiction to his whole characterization up until then, that he wishes to remain a slave because as a free Negro he could not fend for himself. This scene is significant, I think, but it also goes against too much evidence elsewhere in Simms's life to be very conclusive. In general Simms would seem not to have seen slavery as an evil, and not to have been very concerned over his failure to do so.

To find, in the southern literary imagination, more convincing evidence of what the antebellum southern writer thought about slavery, I think, it is more profitable to examine writing of the local color period. For these writers were not dealing with a politically tabooed subject. They could discuss slavery in the public print, provided that they did not insist that it was too bad that it had been discontinued. Most of the leading local color writers had grown up under slavery, and they knew the attitudes of slaveholders in their own experience and from knowledge of themselves. They were usually defensive about it, of course, since the racial issue was still very much under debate even though slavery was done. This was the period when the plantation novel came into full flower as a literary subgenre. Writers such as Thomas Nelson Page portrayed plantation life as an idyllic Eden destroyed by the might of the industrial North. As Jay B. Hubbell says, Page "looked back upon the old regime as a near approach to the Golden Age and regarded Reconstruction as a betrayal of the state and the social class to which he belonged." It was Page who led in popularizing the use of Negro dialect to tell stories of gentle ladies, noble masters, and faithful retainers back before the Fall.

Now ordinarily the fiction of Thomas Nelson Page might be the last place anyone would think to look for critical insights into what the antebellum South really thought about slavery, since Page's whole literary career would appear to have been based on the uncritical, eulogistic defense of the Old South. But Page was a writer, and what writers know, they know best *in* their fiction, not in what they say about what it means. "Never trust the artist," as D. H. Lawrence puts it. "Trust the tale." In the 1880s Page tried his hand at what then was a popular magazine genre, the ghost story. He wrote one entitled "No Haid Pawn," and included it in his first book, *In Ole Virginia*, the volume that includes those classic and beautiful eulogies of the old regime, "Marse Chan" and "Meh Lady." The ghost story was based on a legend current in the antebellum Virginia neighborhood of Page's boyhood at Oakland. It involved a long-deserted plantation home in a swampy neck along the river. The slaves throughout the neighborhood were quick to tell how the old place was the abode of ghosts and spirits of various sorts, including those of a number of slaves who were stricken with typhus malaria and were buried, while still alive, alongside the pond, on which it was their wont at night to float in their coffins. None of the white children ever dared venture into the swamps and bogs of the abandoned place, where the ghost of a former owner was said to prowl. This man, who had come from the West Indies, had been a person of brutal temper and ungovernable passions, and his slaves had been very much afraid of him. Finally he had on one occasion hacked the head off a slave and displayed him before an open window to his terrified slaves. The authorities had intervened, the man had been arrested, tried, and sentenced to death, and hanged just at the rear of his own mansion, within sight of his crime. At the hanging something especially gruesome happened: the man's head was severed from his body. From that day onward, nobody went near No Haid Pawn. It was, Page says, "invested, to us, with unparalleled horror; and thus to us, no less than because the dikes had given way and the overflowed flats had turned again to swamp and jungle, it was explicable that No Haid Pawn was abandoned, and was now untrodden by any foot but that of its ghostly tenants."

Having set the scene, Page begins the ghost story proper. The narrator describes how he as a youth, home from boarding school, determined to go duck hunting in the No Haid Pawn area, and how as night approached the onset of a furious storm forced him to take shelter in the old mansion. He found an ancient bed and a fireplace, though he had no matches with which to start a fire. The storm raged on, and eventually he fell asleep. Several hours later he was awakened by a very peculiar sound, "like a distant call or halloo." Presently, hearing it come closer, he looked outside at the canal, and saw a boat, coffin-like, with a man standing upright in it and something lying in a lump or mass at the bow. Then as he waited, he heard the ground-floor door pushed open, and "a string of fierce oaths, part English and part Creole French," and then the sound of someone dragging a body up the steps and flinging his burden on the floor with a strange wild laugh. Then,

> For a moment there was not a sound, and then the awful silence and blackness were broken by a crash of thunder that seemed to tear the foundations asunder like a mighty earthquake, and the whole house, and the great swamp outside, were filled with a glare of vivid, blinding light. Directly in front of me, clutching with his upraised hand a long, keen, glittering knife, on whose blade a ball of fire seemed to play, stood a gigantic figure in the very flame of the lightning, and stretched at his feet lay, ghastly and bloody, a black and headless trunk.
>
> I staggered to the door and, tripping, fell prostrate over the sill.

With that the story "No Haid Pawn" ends, though a postscript informs us that the house, struck by lightning, burned to the water's edge and the river later reclaimed the spot and "all its secrets lay buried under its dark waters."

The ghost, of course, is supposedly the ghost of the West Indian owner who had decapitated the slave and had himself been hanged and decapitated, and in true "House of Usher" style the dead had come to life and the mansion had been destroyed. But Page was writing his story in the 1880s, when the old-fashioned pure ghost story, as Henry James later remarked in his preface to *The Turn of the Screw*, was no longer in fashion. So Page must have a rational explanation for what happened at No Haid Pawn, and he sets one up just before the narrative proper begins. The neighborhood had been disturbed at the time, he says, by the presence of Abolitionists. More than the usual number of slaves had run off until the Abolitionists had been discovered and had fled. All the slaves had been caught or had returned except for one, a Negro of brutal character, brought from the lower Mississippi, and who cursed in a strange dialect and laid claim to voodoo powers. Even so his owner had kept him because he was an expert butcher and first-rate boatman. It was suspected that many a missing hog in the neighborhood had found its way to his cabin. It turned out that this slave had been the leader in the secret meetings with the Abolitionists, and had disappeared for good when the intruders fled.

So what really was happening out at No Haid Pawn that night, we are supposed to infer, was that it was no ghost carrying a murdered human corpse who had reappeared in the haunted mansion, but the fugitive slave from the lower Mississippi, who had been living out there by himself all the while, subsisting on what he could find, depending on the place's reputation for his safety; and the "black and headless trunk" he carried in that night was that of a stolen hog.

There is not time here to do more than to suggest what this story can be made to reveal about the Old South and slavery. Page himself obviously sensed the connection. Of the appearance of the Abolitionists in the neighborhood he writes:

> It was as if the foundations of the whole social fabric were undermined. It was the sudden darken-

ing of a shadow that always hung in the horizon. The slaves were in a large majority, and had they risen, though the final issue could not be doubted, the lives of every white on the plantations must have paid the forfeit. Whatever the right and wrong of slavery might have been, its existence demanded that no outside interference with it should be tolerated. So much was certain; self-preservation required this.

The very image, "foundations of the whole social fabric were undermined," is interesting. In the story he makes a point that the old house had been built by the slaves, that one of them "had been caught and decapitated between two of the immense foundation stones," that the rumor was that under the house were "solid rock chambers, which had been built for dungeons, and had served for purposes which were none the less awful because they were vague and indefinite." Before the young man enters the haunted mansion for shelter he finds himself standing under the very crossbeam from which the owner had once been hanged. It is important that the owner had not been from the neighborhood, but was from the West Indies, where slave revolts had wiped out the French planters, and that the fugitive slave was from the lower Mississippi. For whatever slavery might have been in Virginia, however much it may have been gentled there, nevertheless in the deep South it could be something horrible and very brutal, without any of the mitigating mildness that, as Page so often insisted in his other stories, characterized it in Virginia. The point is that the possibilities were always there in the institution, that it was only local custom that made of it in Virginia something more palatable than in the Deep South, and that even there it was possible, on a remote plantation, for a slaveowner to exercise "a brutal temper, inflamed by unbridled passions," for "a long period of license and debauchery." No matter what the daylight justification of slavery might be, there was, back there in the darkness, that awful knowledge. And always, in the background, was that fear of revolt and massacre.

In "No Haid Pawn" Page clearly tells more than he means to. For a ghost story requires horror, and Page had a ready-made subject. The picture that he gives of the white children growing up among the slaves on the plantation is not that of gentle old darkies telling quaint tales of the days when the animals talked like folks. He describes how the slaves would inform the children about evil spirits, ghosts, frightening and terrible things. Concerning the malaria that wiped out the slaves on the nearby plantation, the children were told of "the horrors of the pestilence of No Haid Pawn as a peculiar visitation," of "with bloodcurdling details the burial by scores, in a thicket just beside the pond, of the stricken 'befo' dee *daid*, honey, befo' dee *daid*!' " And more than that—I am not a psychologist and can only barely suggest what I feel is there—the story is an initiation story, in which a youth, coming toward his manhood, ventures out of the known into the darkness of a swamp blocked by vines and tangled branches, "a mire apparently bottomless," and stands under the gallows, "a heavy upright timber with an arm or cross-beam stretching from it, from which dangled a long chain, almost rusted away." This house was the place where "a long period of license and debauchery" had once taken place—perhaps you see what I am getting at.

Furthermore, it is important, I think, that as the boatman outside the house neared the building he gave a call. Here Page clearly means to suggest that not only was the fugitive slave hiding there in the swamp, but that he was signaling to someone. The inference would seem to be that other slaves were taking care of him. There was a possibility of a union between this man and the supposedly docile and contented slaves back on the plantations. In another piece of writing Page describes how the Southside Virginia insurrectionist Nat Turner hid out for several weeks before he was discovered; he remembered being told the story, he says, as a child, by one who had been there. The experience of "No Haid Pawn" comes from just that period in his life.

I shall speculate no more. Here is the story, "No Haid Pawn," set in the middle of a book of stories which otherwise glorify the joys and delights of plantation life before the war, and which are designed to show how the black slaves were perfect retainers, humble, loyal, gentle, content with their lot, devoted to their owners. As for the owners, we are given for model the Ole Marster in "Marse Chan," who "didn' like nobody to sell niggers, and knowin' dat Cun'l Chahmb'lin wuz sellin' o' his, he writ and offered to buy his M'ria an' all her chil'en, 'cause she hed married our Zeek'yel." It is Thomas Nelson Page's tribute to the golden days before the Fall. But in it, seemingly unrelated to the life described in all the other stories, is this terrible tale of horror, guilt, fear, and depravity. *"In Ole Virginia,"* one commentator has written, "is pre-eminently the Virginia classic. Anyone who wants to understand the Virginia mind, and the persistence of certain attitudes into the twentieth century, should read it." And so they should, but along with "Marse Chan" and "Meh Lady" and "Unc' Edinburg's Drowndin' " they should read "No Haid Pawn," for it has something to tell that none of the other stories has.

I have spent a long time, perhaps too much, on this one, lesser-known story by Thomas Nelson Page. My point is that there are many others like it, stories and poems by southern authors that are potential sources for better understanding of the society and culture out of which they were written. Page's fiction is not, perhaps, in the first rank even of southern literature, but it is the work of an honest and dedicated artist who wrote with skill and perception. And there are others like him. If only we will read their work imaginatively, and give to them the careful attention that we might not under other circumstances hesitate to give to other kinds of southern studies, we can learn a great deal about the society in which they lived. But we have to read them *as* stories and poems, as works of literature, if they are to instruct us with any authority.

My quarrel with so much of the scholarship expended upon southern writing is that it is too literal, too unimaginative, and too often uncritical. Too frequently the southern literature scholar displays his own limitations by trying to "prove" that mediocre work by southern writers is better than it is, or by attempting to enhance the stature of such work by likening it to stories by Hawthorne or James or other major writers, supposedly elevating the southern writer by demonstrating that the two were attempting to do the same thing. I quote from an essay published in 1923: "O. Henry's humor has been acclaimed by a world of grateful readers because, like the humor of Shakespeare, Molière and Cervantes, it rises naturally and spontaneously from the situation in which his characters are placed." Well, that may be how O. Henry's humor rises, but it does not do it quite like Shakespeare's does. Here is a more recent comment on Mary Johnston's Civil War work: "Although Mary Johnston expressed contempt for the theology of *Paradise Lost*, this work of hers is closer to Milton's poem than it is to the Prophetic Books of Blake. . . . " Perhaps so, but it is also at a pretty far remove from either of them. There seems so little purpose in this sort of thing, when Mary Johnston's work is perfectly well worth reading in its own right without anyone's having to pretend that it is like *Paradise Lost*. If we will only read Mary Johnston, and Thomas Nelson Page, and other writers like them, for what they are, not for what they are not, and if we will do so with care and with imagination, we have available to us a large, and still mostly unexplored, resource for understanding the South and its writers. The literary imagination, through its imagic representation of reality, can afford a unique view of human experience. From its beginnings the South has been rich in writers, and never more so than in our own day. Surely one of the goals of southern literary study ought to be the making available of this resource. It is an exciting prospect, and the job is ours to do. Let us get on with it.

2. Early Southern Literature

PAST, PRESENT, AND FUTURE

by Richard Beale Davis

Perhaps the major relevant question, but certainly not the only one, regarding early southern literature is that raised by nineteenth- and twentieth-century historians and critics regarding early New England: is the colonial Puritan writing, or a consideration of it, essential to an understanding of the intellectual flowering of that region in the mid-nineteenth century? The New England question has never, in my opinion, been satisfactorily answered, despite the valiant efforts of a number of able men. As southern literature from the beginning of the third decade of the twentieth century has at least equaled that of our northeastern neighbors of a century ago, a vital question is whether or not there is a continuity and growth in our writing from the seventeenth and eighteenth centuries until the first great flowering in our time. Is there in Faulkner and Welty, Styron and Warren, Tate and Brooks and Dickey and scores of our other friends and acquaintances, theme and attitude, even form, which may be traced back to the written (and oral) expression in our first settlements and societies? So far we may have done no better in covering the question than those who have pondered Puritanism in its relation to Emerson-Hawthorne-Thoreau-Lowell-Dickinson, but we have probably in the last few decades done just as well.

Nearly or equally as significant is the question, which nineteenth-century critic-historians answered almost unanimously in the negative, as to whether or not there ever was genuine literature (in the artistic if not purely belletristic sense) in the colonial

South. Step by step, sometimes painfully, the materials which might suggest or prove that there was have been or are being assembled, edited, and assessed by competent scholars, perhaps already enough to show that there was a southern literature from Roanoke Island to Yorktown or the adoption of the Constitution or the Treaty of Ghent in 1815. Some of its characteristics have been drawn into a fairly clear outline of an image. But to cover the dry bones with flesh, to use in paraphrase a William Byrd expression concerning his work on the *Histories of the Dividing Line*, to see its contours and even its basic form unblurred or undistorted, much yet remains to be done. Much can be done by the generation now alive. Some must extend into the future. One should again be reminded that the form and significance of Puritan writing is still in dispute, and that the rough portrait drawn in the mid-nineteenth century of Puritan expression is being altered and reinterpreted from day to day.

Perhaps in attempting to answer the two questions just noted and other corollary or concomitant inquiries it is best to begin with a glance at what has been accomplished in the past few decades. Then one should note trends and some specific instances of work in progress, and finally, attempt to indicate what will remain to be done, what directions must be taken.

One perhaps obvious but necessary observation. The literary and intellectual historians of New England discovered long ago that the writing of that region could not be assessed only per se, that economics, politics, science, fine arts, above all religion, had to be taken into consideration. You will recall that *usually* Samuel Eliot Morison, Perry Miller, Edmund S. Morgan, Alan Heimert, Norman Grabo, Sacvan Bercovitch, and Robert Middlekauff have discussed literature in a context of other matters. Most southern critics of the early period have come to work in much the same way. "Bacon's Epitaph by His Man" may with profit be analyzed as an example of a certain tradition in the elegy, and Byrd's *History of the Dividing Line* as mock epic, but fully to be appreciated as art they must be studied more in their social and political setting than does a poem of Donne's or even of Edward Taylor's.

Before 1940 early southern writing as any sort of art received scant attention. Parrington, Trent, and Wertenbaker touched upon it, the *Library of Southern Literature* included a few "representative" examples, Moses and Baskervill and Mims were among those who noticed it in anthologies or literary histories, but only Moses Coit Tyler knew much of it (and his gaps are glaring) and gave it some extensive attention. J. Franklin Jameson's *Original Narratives of Early American History* (1906-17, 1952-59) and Peter Force's *Tracts and Other Papers Relating [to] the Colonies of North America* (1836, 1966) included prose documents of the early South which are in many instances good literature, and there were single-province collections such as Susan M. Kingsbury's *Records of the Virginia Company of London* (4 vols., 1906-35) and W. K. Boyd's *Some Eighteenth Century Tracts Concerning North Carolina* (1927). These and the Evans, Sabin, and single-colony bibliographies such as William Clayton Torrence's for colonial Virginia were not only to prove of immense value when the time and opportunity for serious study came, but also offered useful models for later similar work.

The thirty-year generation 1940-70 marked perhaps the beginning of comprehensive and perceptively critical studies of early southern literature. Important if occasionally somewhat naive appraisals of John P. Kennedy, William Wirt, and Hugh Swinton Legaré came at the beginning of the period. And also in 1940 appeared the still-to-be-reckoned-with *Mind of the South* of Wilbur J. Cash, that masterly study of the nonintellectual side of the region's character with which none of us can fully agree or fully ignore. Cash's book, in many ways anti-intellectualism at its peak (in its portrayal of the southern mind as a replica of what Henry Adams found in Rooney Lee), devotes not too many of its earlier pages to the first South but implies the continuity of certain cerebral characteristics from colonial Tidewater to his own time and region. He failed to see, in the very pages and faces he scanned to find far different facts, that from simplest yeoman to most sophisticated landowner white southerners loved and read and owned books, employed as acute perceptivity in laying out gardens or designing houses (large and small) as the Puritan did in digesting his morsel of Calvin, developed an all-level and in theory all-embracing scheme of education, and in his observations and collection of plants, animals, and minerals broadened the base of scientific knowledge in the Western world. And he was oblivious to the fact that the early southerner composed verse and essay and history and even drama not occasionally but by the time of the Revolution fairly regularly.

The forties also saw other studies in intellectual history which opened the way to examinations of literature. Louis B. Wright's major work, *The First Gentlemen of Virginia: Intellectual Qualities of the Early Colonial Ruling Class* (1940) with its companion volumes continuing to the present; Joseph T. Wheeler's several essays on early Maryland books and reading; Frederick Bowes's *The Culture of Early Charleston* (1942); Brydon and Sweet on religion; Wesley F. Craven's *The Southern Colonies in the Seventeenth Century* (1949, 1970) will remain useful. Gregory Paine's *Southern Prose Writers* (1947) joined its companion volume Edd Parks's *Southern Poets* (1936) as a remarkably able critical, bibliographical, and well-selected anthology. Louis Wright's chapter on early southern literature in volume 1 and some materials in bibliographical volume 3 of the *Literary History of the United States* offer only a little to the interested southern student. Howard Mumford Jones's *The Literature of Virginia in the Seventeenth Century* (1946, 1968) is one of the earliest comprehensive surveys of a segment of colonial writing as art, though it is replete with the factual errors one might expect from a scholar working in relatively unfamiliar territory. Perhaps it is most important in its suggestiveness of one of the sorts of critical procedures that should be followed. And the forties saw competent editions of at least two early journals, Bridenbaugh's of Dr. Alexander Hamilton and Farish's of Philip Vickers Fithian.

The fifties showed more. For our earliest period Jay B. Hubbell's monumental *The South in American Literature, 1607-1900* (1954) unearthed dozens of forgotten figures, analyzed them and certain better-known authors, and included magnificent annotative bibliographies. He expanded, corrected, and at times contradicted Moses Coit Tyler's studies of southern men and movements. His leads on writers and books of the early period are in many cases still to be followed. His critical vignettes are often the best accounts in existence of scores of southern books, essays, pamphlets, and poems—with their authors.

In the sixties, impelled in part by the research-production attending the 350th anniversary of Jamestown in 1957, Hubbell's book just mentioned, and the organization of the early American Literature Group in the American Literature section of the Modern Language Association and the founding of the Society for the Study of Southern Literature, there was a tremendous surge forward in the study of early southern writing, perhaps a proportionately greater surge than that in any other branch of American literature. Anthologies for general survey use began to include more than William Byrd and Thomas Jefferson, or at best John Smith and/or Ebenezer Cook added to these two, though one anthology of *southern* literature in its second edition cut down on the amount and number of early figures represented. The blazed trail toward future critical assessment became a clear road in the sixties through a remarkable series of critical editions of unfamiliar southern writers, biographies of some of the same and others who had been unfamiliar, and bio-historical studies of phases of southern life and thought. The classic example of the last is J. I. Waring's *A History of Medicine in South Carolina, 1670-1825* (1964), for his running history of medical practice and theory is accompanied by sketches of the physicians who were belletristic as well as scientific writers, and of their poetic, dramatic, and manners-essay composition which suggests further investigation of each. Then there were *The Three Worlds of Captain John Smith* (1964), by Philip L. Barbour, which may have answered once and for all the impugners of its subject as man and as writer; the lives of the two scientific John Claytons by Edmund and Dorothy Berkeley (1963, 1965) and the Berkeleys' life of Dr. Alexander Garden (1969); S. G. Culliford's *William Strachey* (1965), slightly outmoded even as it appeared; and Robert C. McLean's *George Tucker: Moral Philosopher and Man of Letters* (1961). Every one of these widens the avenue of approach to an important and characteristic southern writer and his circle. There were good editions, varying in commentary and annotation, of George Percy, John Rolfe, and William Strachey (*two* of the last), all in attractive paperbacks; of John Lederer (actually 1958) in the standard Cumming-Rights edition; *The Journal of John Harrower* (1963), by Ed. M. Riley and *The Diary of Landon Carter of Sabine Hall* (1965), by Jack P. Greene, the latter two taking places beside Farish's *Fithian* and Wright and Woodfin's Byrd *Diaries* as most significant southern autobiographies. In these printings, most from original manuscript, lies irrefutable evidence that the early southern mind could be as religious, as philosophically alert, as attentive to books in depth and breadth, and in the Carter (along with the 1972 *Letterbook of Eliza Pinckney*) instance as introspective as the Puritan mind of a Mather or an Edwards and as down-to-earth and practical as a Benjamin Franklin. Moses C. Tyler knew none of these. And in this decade Hugh Lefler gave us a beautiful and ably edited edition of John Lawson (1967); the University of Georgia Press began publishing in the Wormsloe Foundation Series the Urlsperger Tracts and Henry Newman Salzburger Tracts (1966-67); the University of South Carolina, Hamer and Rogers's *The Papers of John Laurens* (1968-) and Richard Walsh's *The Writings of Christopher Gadsden* (1966); and Philip Barbour for the Hakluyt Society *The Jamestown Voyages under the First Charter, 1606-1609* (1969), a new and perceptively edited text of Smith, Percy, and others which will remain the standard resource for students of the period and the authors represented.

Though it is concerned primarily with a slightly later era, W. R. Taylor's *Cavalier and Yankee: The Old South and American*

National Character (1961) offers some stimulating and fresh cri-
tiques of the earlier period. My own *Intellectual Life in Jefferson's
Virginia, 1790-1830* (1964) attempts to show, among other things,
how wrong Henry Adams was about the limitations of the southern mind. This compilation-cum-commentary should be, Russell
Nye declares in John Garraty's *Interpreting American History*,
the sort of thing which must be done for each southern area and
time period before more specific evaluation can be undertaken. In
the late sixties the general early American anthologies of Kenneth
Silverman and Harrison T. Meserole are remarkable both for
what they omit and (especially in the case of the former) the
egregiously incorrect conclusions drawn concerning early southern literary characteristics even from the evidence (selections)
they themselves present. Most important of all, 1969 saw the publication under the general editorship of Louis Rubin of *A Bibliographical Guide to the Study of Southern Literature*. For early
writing, Lemay's chapter on "The Colonial Period" and the necessarily condensed bibliographies of more than a dozen early figures are invaluable—even though John Taylor was overlooked.
And Leo Lemay's appendix, "Sixty-Eight Additional Writers of
the Colonial South," includes the names and rudimentary bibliographies which must be investigated and developed in the next
few decades.

A glance at 1970-72 early southern bibliographies, books, and
reviews indicates what is now going on. The "Special Southern
Issue" of *Early American Literature* (1971) presents a variety of
approaches to writers known and unknown. J. A. Leo Lemay's
"Robert Bolling and the Bailment of Colonel Chiswell," so long
that it had to be carried over into the next issue, has been assessed
by one Virginia scholar-editor as the single most significant essay
for both history and literature in the Old Dominion to appear in
this century. I would suggest that you all have a look at it.

Perhaps one should turn at this point to a phase of southern
writing not yet touched upon—Black or Negro. Though for the
past decade I have scanned or read almost everything that has

appeared in this country on early Black writing, I have found little that is genuinely southern, though one may well argue that some of that written in the north is southern in theme, style, and language. As far as I can tell, it was not until 1971, in Dorothy Porter's *Early Negro Writing, 1760-1837*, by a veteran bibliographer of Black writing, that there existed any real anthology for the period, and one finds in it only Benjamin Banneker representing the South before 1800 (his piece is dated 1792). The recent discovery and use of the Banneker papers in a biography of that remarkable man by Silvio Bedini (1972) would seem to suggest that there may exist other writing by other Black authors as yet unknown. Further search is in order, especially in South Carolina, Virginia, and Maryland, where there were schools before the Revolution which many Negroes attended, schools sometimes Black and sometimes integrated.

In the past three years Barbour has continued his study of Smith and his friends in *Pocahontas and Her World* (1970), a somewhat misleading title; and Everett Emerson's *Captain John Smith* (TUSAS, 1971) is the most useful study since Barbour's biography in assessing its subject as writer and editor. One may conclude the attention to Smith by noting that now Philip Barbour is officially appointed (by an influential organization) editor of the complete works. An authoritative edition may be expected.

Pierre Marambaud's *William Byrd of Westover, 1674-1744* (1971) is a fresh look by an outsider who knows his way around in eighteenth-century Virginia. It is short on biography and long on cultural backgrounds, and is a comprehensive survey of Byrd's writing. The Southern Indian authority Louis De Vorsey, Jr., has edited (1971) *De Brahm's Report of the General Survey of the Southern District of North America*, written originally in the early 1760s, adding a delightful and informative volume to the impressive shelf of early southern historical literature. In connection with it should be pointed out the several recent publications of Indian writing and writing concerning the Indians, from the new facsimile edition of James Adair to the three volumes edited

by William S. McDowell of *Documents Relating to Indian Affairs
. . . in Colonial Records of South Carolina . . . 1710 . . . 1765*
(1955-70), both rich collections of Indian-White oratory and rhetoric, correspondence, proclamations, creation-stories, and other
matters.

What else is being done? Professor Carl Dolmetsch is having his
M.A. students edit one by one the unpublished essays of St. George
Tucker, and it is to be hoped that he and they will go on into
poems and plays and that eventually he will be the general editor
of a collected edition. What early southern subjects your students
are working on, you here today will have to mention. I can note
only some of my recent dissertations: William H. Castles, Jr., on
the *Virginia Gazette* (1962); Wilbur H. Ward "Bacon's Rebellion
in American Literature" (1971), especially perceptive critically in
its chapters on the seventeenth- and eighteenth-century accounts;
Lynn Hogue, "The Juridical and Philosophical Essays of Chief
Justice Nicholas Trott of South Carolina" (1972), a competent
edition of an unpublished manuscript by a major mind of the
colonial South; Jack D. Wages's "The Southern Elegy to 1763: A
Critical Anthology" (1968), a study which refutes some of Silverman's generalizations about southern verse; Homer D. Kemp,
"The Pre-Revolutionary Virginia Essay: The Pistole Fee and the
Two-Penny Acts Controversy" (1972); and (hopefully by next
week, the final version of) Charles J. Churchman, "Samuel Davies
as a Representative Eighteenth-Century Anglo-American Poet."

Lemay has significant work in progress in his census of all
colonial printed poems to 1800, of which volume 1 has recently
appeared, and in his edition of the prose and poetry of Robert
Bolling, Jr., of Chellowe, Buckingham County, Virginia, the
publication of which may place Bolling alongside Alexander
Hamilton and William Byrd as the major literary figures of the
eighteenth-century South. Lemay's *Men of Letters in Colonial
Maryland* is just out. Robert Bain is preparing a much-needed
new edition of Hartwell-Blair-Chilton's *Present State of Virginia
and the College* and Professor David C. Skaggs is editing from

manuscript the really remarkable sermons of the Maryland parson Thomas Cradock. You must know of much more.

From my point of view—that is, after thirty-nine years of research and reading and writing in early southern literature, what remains to be done? The answer is, so much that I cannot even name all of it here, much less amplify or exemplify everything. Some of what seems vital—and perhaps for some of you most obvious—I will attempt to note in conclusion.

Perhaps the first need—for everything else depends upon it—is for a series of scholarly editions and authoritative texts (as I feel sure Barbour's *Smith* will be) of every major and most minor early southern writers. I will touch upon only a few major ones, or potentially major. What Lemay is doing for Robert Bolling's writings may or may not raise him to the colonial intellectual and artistic peerage, but it will certainly mean that hereafter no real consideration of southern verse may be made which does not bring his work into the discussion. The poems and plays of St. George Tucker, as I have just mentioned, should be edited along with his essays, and the general editor must be, in my opinion, a mature scholar who is already well acquainted in the intellectual climate in which Tucker worked.

There should be either variorum editions, or at least authoritative text editions of such major writers as Dr. Alexander Hamilton of Annapolis and William Byrd of Westover. My own collection of photostats of all known versions of the *Histories of the Dividing Line* and of two of the reports on which they were based (all from manuscripts scattered between London and California) shows me that there must be a new collated edition of both *Histories*, for there are a number of interesting variations which not even Wright's 1966 Harvard edition has attempted to show. Though Byrd is already acknowledged as a major early American author, there needs to be made a collated authoritative-text edition of Dr. Alexander Hamilton's "Minutes," "Record," and [mock] "History" of the Tuesday Club, no one ever published except in a few snippets, to establish Hamilton as Byrd's peer among southern authors—though I am not yet ready to join Lemay in proclaiming the Maryland physician as the single ablest writer of the colonial South. In the instances of both Byrd and Hamilton, there must also be the redemption of their fugitive pieces from newspapers and journals, and the bringing of these together with unpublished manuscripts of minor works, perhaps even with their fascinating letters.

These men are by no means alone among significant figures who must be edited and published before there can be any accurate appraisal of the character and quality of our early literature. The manuscripts and printed works of Governor Arthur Dobbs of North Carolina (including philosophical and religious writing, speculative voyage literature, and poems) should be brought together. The fugitive pieces and even rare-book poetic volumes of Dr. James Kirkpatrick of South Carolina should be edited. His poems, narrative and occasional and scientific, should probably be published along with his remarkably able scientific essays.

These are among the men and works I should like to see edited if I had another fifty years. Along with them must go book-length biocritical studies of versatile loyalist Parson Jonathan Boucher, rationalist-political pamphleteer Richard Bland, poet-satirist-essayist-lawyer John Mercer, and the completed study by Joseph C. Robert of William Wirt.

These are individual and particular instances. To study a literature (indeed for writing to become literature) it must exist in print, and the editions of known figures and acknowledged art-writing is not enough. To go back to beginnings, as perhaps I should have done in the first place, I would see to it that the inventory of every book collection of every county of every colony was put into print, one or more large volumes to a province. Recent studies such as Caroline Robbins's (1959) and H. Trevor Colbourn's (1965) of books in relation to ideas in seventeenth- and eighteenth-century England and America, especially Colbourn's examination of the nature and content of private libraries in relation to American pre-Revolutionary thinking and writing, may well be imitated in attempting to determine what and how much the books they read may have influenced the writing of Daniel Dulany or Maurice Moore or Richard Bland or Landon Carter. It is not without significance that Dulany, Jefferson, Madison, Bland, Mercer, Dobbs, Peyton Randolph, and many South Carolinians and Georgians active in early American English-Constitutional controversies and in the Continental Congress owned large and usually the largest book collections in their communities. And it is not without significance that even a sampling in each province reveals the omnipresence of Algernon Sidney, John Locke, Shaftesbury, Molesworth, Trenchard and Gordon, and other Whigs or demi-republicans and that they are frequently referred to in newspaper essays, political pamphlets, satiric verse, and provincial as well as continental legislative debate. Ideas spring from ideas. Other things in their libraries too we must allow all to see—e.g., Aristotle and Ramus, Cicero and Quintilian, Addison and Bysshe. The editions of Palladio and Vitruvius, of herbals and garden manuals, give us clues to their thinking and fashioning or creating in terms of their natural surroundings. This paper might well have been devoted to what may be learned of the early southern mind and writing from libraries alone. But if it were, it would only place the footings for the foundations of our literature.

There must be separate in-depth-and-breadth studies, as partially suggested above, of every colony, perhaps for chronological periods. There should be studies of the city and town literary and social circles as inciters to thinking and writing. It is not for nothing that there is varied and sometimes exciting literary material in the gazettes of these colonies, and it is clear that at least some of it sprang from the Meddler's Club in Charleston or the Annapolis Tuesday and Homony groups, the Wirt circle in Richmond or the Delphian Club of Baltimore, even a group of kindred spirits in frontier Winchester in Virginia. The town intellectual groups' influence in southern literary production has never been really explored. Yet one knows or can guess that Hugh Swinton Legaré, George Tucker and William Wirt, John Pendleton Kennedy and other Baltimoreans were as writers influenced in the convivial circles of their friends.

There must be particular and general studies of southern historical writing, from John Smith through Beverley and Jones and Stith to David Ramsay and Edmund Randolph, perhaps something kin to Peter Gay's *A Loss of Mastery*, the analysis of early New England history. Actually Gay himself has said he was interested in exploring early southern historical expression. There should be a critical study of southern verse from 1610 to 1815, an expansion, perhaps in new directions, of the earlier part of the introductory critique in Edd W. Parks's *Southern Poets*. The early and continuous development of various forms of satire, suggested by current forms in Great Britain but coming to possess what may be some peculiarly southern characteristic traits in theme and dialect and other qualities, must be examined. Somewhere in the process one may come face to face with William Faulkner or Robert Penn Warren or James Dickey, or reminders of them, including some interesting uses of irony.

The nature of Indian-White literature is a study in poetry, forensics, dramatic ritual, rational argument, and picturesque imagery, from Captain Smith's conversations with Powhatan to the dialogues during the Augusta Treaty of 1763. Dozens of entrancing questions present themselves: for example, how does the education and personal background of the interpreter-intermediary affect the style and quality of recorded discourse? Is there a gradual but decided change in red rhetoric from Powhatan to the chiefs questioned by James Adair, or does the style of two centuries have much in common? And does Indian speech influence southern rhetoric at all? Remember that Jefferson knew or created Logan's soliloquy, that Simms and Faulkner and others have used real or imagined Indian imagery in their creative fiction.

The comprehensive and variegated anthologies which must be published must be preceded by genre compilations. Among these must come volumes of letters, perhaps the richest and most abundant literary expression of the early agrarian South. From John Pory to John Randolph there are still in each colony-state thousands of letters buried in public and private repositories. And one hopes that Louis B. Wright will soon be able to bring out his long-researched volumes of the epistles of the three William Byrds. A beginning of letter editing has been made in state archival publications, historical journals, and occasional book form, but it is only a beginning and is not genuinely systematic.

There should be volumes of writings on politics and economics in the seventeenth century for the Chesapeake colonies, probably much but certainly not all of it now in print too often in obscure places and garbled form. For the eighteenth century there must be separate volumes for each colony, for the expression will never be seen in its full significance until it is so brought together. Included among them would be scores of southern colonial newspaper essays, equally as important as privately or publicly printed pamphlets. Introductions should indicate the intellectual and immediate local-action origins of these pieces, and their value as art and as propaganda.

The southern colonial sermon has never received its due as religion or as art, and rarely recognition that it even exists or ever did. Though only two are known for the seventeenth century, for the eighteenth, hundreds in manuscript and print exist in repositories from Maine to California and in Great Britain. There are several great collections which cry out for new printings, preferably new editions, as the gathered sermons of James Blair and Samuel Davies, and of Samuel Quincy and the Reverend Alexander Garden. Prolific sermon writers whose work has never been collected include at least a dozen in Maryland (as Cradock and Bacon and Sterling); several in Virginia (as Maury and Stith and Paxton); and others in South Carolina (as Isaac Chanler and Josiah Smith). These range from orthodox and deistic Anglicans to fiery nonconformist supporters of Whitefield. With them should be published the southern-delivered discourses of the Quakers Thomas Story, William Edmundson, and George Fox. Together, with scattered theological tracts, they show that the early southerner was in his way as religious as his northern contemporary. James Blair's preface to his collected edition and Thomas

Cradock's joyous festival sermon on the harmless pleasures of wine and music show one facet of the southern mind in literature. The Calvinist militancy of Davies and the powerful defenses of Whitefield by Josiah Smith represent other facets. Plain-style, with doctrine at a minimum, these Anglican and Presbyterian homilies may remind us of contemporary southern writing on religion.

Histories of the *Gazettes* of each colony are needed, and studies of the written expression of early concepts of southern womanhood. Was the lady on a pedestal in the pages before 1800? The matter of domestic dramatic production and of plays authored locally or in Britain by provincials has been touched upon by Rodney Bain and in Dolmetsch's recent essay on Byrd as dramatist. But there must be much more, which Rankin and Hoole and Willis and Shockley have not gotten into in their studies of the theater in the early South. Again, what fiction and narrative colonials read and its place in their thinking and expression before 1815, as in William Wirt and George and St. George Tucker, merits further investigation. For the southerner had Cervantes, Le Sage, Smollett, Fielding, Sterne, and Richardson in his library before Sir Walter laid aside his fishing tackle and wrote *Waverley*. And southern humor, in seventeenth-century lampoon, eighteenth-century Hudibrastic and scatalogical verse, in newspaper tales of Irish and Scottish immigrants who used homespun dialect and became enmeshed in ridiculous situations—does this lead to backwoods humor, A. B. Longstreet and Sut Lovingood and Mark Twain and William Faulkner?

These are a few of the things I would examine, or have others investigate if I had another half century to work. I hope that they will all be done in the next two decades so that the rest of America and the world can see now that there was an early southern literature, that its historical importance in politics and trade may be assessed. Above all, they should determine whether there is in it the seeds of the plant from which our recent literature has flowered. When this is done, I trust my spirit will be as content as now I think it will.

3. Dim Pages in Literary History
THE SOUTH SINCE THE CIVIL WAR

by Arlin Turner

It would be possible, I suppose, to speak of the American South and mean only a portion of the globe bounded by such and such coordinates of longitude and latitude. I sometimes say to a class or seminar in southern literature that the course owes its existence and its bounds to convenience only—that world literature, or American literature, cannot be studied in one piece, and that southern literature is a plausible unit for separate study. But the students realize soon, if not at once, that it is impossible, of course, to speak of the South, southern literature, or the society for the study of southern literature without meaning far more than a direction, or an area on a cartographer's grid. Literary works in particular are likely to be enshrouded in human and social implications, and literary discourse can be at best only an exercise in describing surfaces if it ignores the complex of forces that shape the mind and imagination of the author and determine the context in which the work is written. A comparable truncation or distortion or superficiality may result if the discourse moves to the opposite extreme and considers only the external, the public elements of the context. Not even Emily Dickinson's poems—and surely not Sidney Lanier's—can be extracted from the world that entered the poet's awareness, however restricted that world may have been. Nor can the works of Upton Sinclair or George W. Cable be read as no more than briefs in the social debates of their times.

Just as literary authors exist in a composite of time and place and attitudes and tastes, so do literary scholars and interpreters. Literary historians interpret and in a sense join their readers in recreating the literary past. The literary past thus formed will not have the same appearance it had in that past time or in any other time. We read, report, interpret, and evaluate earlier southern literature by our lights, and no one needs to be told that our lights today are not what they were five years ago. Literary historians of a future time will read the literary history and interpretation we write just as they read the novels and poems and plays of our contemporaries—will read them all as reflections of our time, and will judge them by their lights, not ours. That is to say that the literary history and criticism we compose today, no less than works in the main genres written at any time, is determined in large measure by the context from which it derives. The determining ingredient in the context for one work may be a view of man and God and the universe; or it may be for another work as minute and literal as the circumstances of publication. If you do not see what I mean by the second possibility, think of a reviewer in the *SAMLA Bulletin* or an alumni bulletin evaluating a book written by a friend of his—compare such a review as his with one written for the *Times Literary Supplement* of London, and published anonymously of course, not by such a magisterial British reviewer as would be assumed, but instead by an American scholar assessing an American book, or in the instance I have in mind, a gathering of American books, dealing with a controversial subject on which he has published firm convictions of his own.

It is not my intention, let me hasten to say, to remain in such generalities as these, but rather to leave the theoretical for the practical, after this reminder that any reference to southern literature implies an identifiable and a definable and presumably an understandable South, and further that literary study derives from its context no less, or at least little less significantly, than does literary composition. My main purpose is to touch on several matters of practical importance in such a study of southern literature as we concern ourselves with, and to indicate areas that seem to invite exploration and clarification.

For one thing, there are many souths, not one; and in some respects the differences among those souths are of greater consequence than the similarities. In the early South, regional identification was not prominent. Just as Americans anywhere found it difficult in the first decades of the new nation to put national allegiance above state allegiance, so the residents of Virginia, the Carolinas, Georgia, and also the newer states, apparently, were slow to acknowledge southern loyalties as distinct from state loyalties, even as sectional tensions increased before 1860, and even though the dimensions of the South, geographical and otherwise, were then much smaller than they would be later in the century. The Civil War yoked together, violently and in violence, it can be said, widely divergent regions and peoples. In a sense that would have been inappropriate before the war, Edward King, in crisscrossing the former Confederate States in 1873, could report on them as an entity in the "Great South" papers he published in the *Scribner's Monthly* first and separately afterward. He acknowledged the diversity of land and life in the region, but writing in the shadow of secession and the war and in the presence of the issues bequeathed to the new era, he wrote about one south, the Great South, a Paradise Lost, he said in his opening sentence, which might or might not become a Paradise Regained. Those issues, centering on the former slaves as citizens, so dominated southern history long after 1865 that a degree of unity could be assumed for the region.

Even so, there has been uncertainty at the edges, clearly apparent in the border states. And does the South start at the Chesapeake Bay or at the Potomac River; does it extend to the Mississippi River, or the Sabine, or the Colorado that divides East from West Texas, or the Pecos River? El Paso and Amarillo are cities in one of the Confederate States. What I want to suggest is the need to keep in mind the immense diversity within the South when we frame generalizations and sift for qualities that can be called essential and pervasive. I might suggest further that in view of the importance slavery and race (in their infinite ramifications) had in giving the South its identity and its distinctiveness, we must remain alert to the changes that may evolve as the issues related to race cease to be mainly southern and the prospect grows more likely that the seat of racial prejudice and the battleground for citizens' rights will shift out of the South.

Diversity in geography, climate, land, population, and means of livelihood is greater, surely, and culturally more significant in the South than in other sections of the country. It may be that Scottish, Italian, and Czech immigrants, together with the other nationalities that came in smaller numbers—it may be that in the South such immigrants took much the same route to naturalization and assimilation as elsewhere in America. But the French, Spanish, and Germans came in such numbers, represented each such a wide spectrum of society, and maintained—even close to the present time—their national and cultural identities so persistently that they require more than a passing reference in southern literary history. They became Americans with widely varying degrees of eagerness or reluctance, but in keeping alive the languages, the lore, and the traditions of their fatherlands, they all contributed variety and richness by their presence alone. We know them as subject matter in the local color writing of the 1880s and in the regional fiction of the 1930s. We are aware that much of their cultural history can be drawn from the many native-language newspapers they published. Such an awareness may be adequate for the German communities in Louisiana and Texas (the German Coast above New Orleans, for example, Fredericksburg, New Braunfels, Weimar, and Umbarger in Texas); it is less adequate for the Spanish, dating back to the earliest settlements and distributed from Florida to Texas—and of course on to California. Such an awareness is far from adequate for the French, who formed significant cultural islands in Charleston, Mobile, and elsewhere, and for almost two centuries maintained in New Orleans a full-round Latin civilization. The Creoles of New Orleans gave the opera and the drama their first significant beginnings in America; they maintained perhaps closer ties to current literature in their European fatherland than did any other segment of the American population; their newspapers during much of the nineteenth century found remarkably large space for literature and literary comment. The long history of the French-language newspaper in New Orleans, *L'Abeille—The Bee*, illustrates the in-and-out relations of the two peoples of the city—during part of its history, the paper was published in French only; in other parts it published parallel (but not always identical) French and English sections.

Charles Gayarré and Alcée Fortier were historians primarily, but both had considerable presence in literary quarters (Fortier was president of the Modern Language Association in 1898). George W. Cable and Lafcadio Hearn were fascinated students of the history, language, and lore of the Creoles. Edward Larocque Tinker in a later period was an earnest student of French Louisiana, as were also, to a degree, the novelists Roark Bradford and Lyle Saxon. Even so, the cultural history of French New Orleans is more remote from most of us than that of France. I am not sure the French Louisianians wanted to encourage *les Américains*—often the hated *Américains*—to explore their literary history any more than in the decades following the Purchase they relished the thought of losing their identity in the melting pot they saw the new nation to be. Literary history can learn a good deal from a full account of Gayarré's long life. (He was a dramatist and novelist.) By chance the half dozen or more letters William Gilmore Simms wrote to Gayarré, located at Tulane University, did not get into the edition of Simms letters, but no doubt they will be in a supplementary volume.

There is much more to be learned from the career of Grace King. An edition of her best stories would help, and a full biography would reveal much about the Creole-American relations in Louisiana, including literary relations, in the time of Cable and Hearn, Kate Chopin and Ruth McEnery Stuart. (An unpublished dissertation on Mrs. Stuart written at L.S.U. brings together the basic facts of her life and work.) Grace King's friendship with

Mark Twain, Howells, and others both in America and abroad can tell us more than we know about the literary lines from one remote region to the main literary centers. Someone needs to study in detail the portraits of Louisiana French characters drawn by Grace King, Kate Chopin, Lafcadio Hearn, and others, alongside the Creoles and the Cajuns of Cable's stories and novels. Such a study is invited by the Creole dissatisfaction with Cable's fiction when it appeared and by Grace King's avowal that her initial purpose in writing was to correct Cable's portraits. The apparent inconsistency in her published comments on Cable might be cleared away.

Let me mention in this connection one or two possibilities in what I suppose is the sociology of literature. In the early 1880s, George W. Cable visited in Cajun country, the prairie and bayou region west of the Mississippi, learning the speech and recording facts and observations and impressions for the benefit of the fiction he intended to write. His chief informant was Madame Sidonie de la Houssaye of Franklin, whom he asked from time to time to verify details in his stories. From her he had also some of the materials he put into the volume *Strange True Stories of Louisiana*. She was a writer herself, more devoted and determined than successful with the long romances, in French, employing but little from her abundant knowledge of the people Cable hoped to portray with accuracy and realism. Here would be evidence, if more were needed, on the contrasting views in the 1880s and 1890s as to the proper materials of fiction.

The fictional portrayal of the Creoles and the Cajuns suggests an aspect of all local color and regional writings that I believe needs more study—the relation of the author to his subjects. Some of the Creoles wrote in the newspapers vouching for the fidelity of Cable's Creole portraits. He had grown up among the Creoles and had warm friendships among them; he studied them in history and in his daily associations. Yet, he was an outsider, for all his knowledge, sympathy, and presumed understanding. Thad St. Martin, a physician in Houma, a town in southwest Louisiana, wrote *Madame Toussaint's Wedding Day*, a novel set among the simple Cajun folk on Bayou Lafourche. The work stood its own among the regional novels of the 1930s. When I met Dr. St. Martin once in Houma, he wanted to make sure that I not take him to be one of the Cajuns he had written about; he was a Creole, and he liked to spin yarns about those odd people, who were his patients, and whom he valued and loved. If one of his patients had possessed the ability to write about his own people, would he have written about Madame Toussaint, and the same kind of book Dr. St. Martin wrote? If he had, would the book have been one to please the readers of regional novels in the 1930s?

The same questions might be asked, I suppose, about other local or regional authors. Mary Noailles Murfree knew her Tennessee mountaineers from the summers she and her family spent in the mountains. O. Henry probably knew the mountaineers of his stories at no closer range. Jesse Stuart may be a good author to consider in this connection. A study of his works might suggest that in some regards and in subtle ways he has written as an outsider, his heritage and his residence in his native W-Hollow notwithstanding.

Members of one race drawing literary characters of another race are of course legion in southern literature and offer complex problems of interpretation and assessment. From Poe, Simms, and Kennedy to Irvin Russell, Thomas Nelson Page, Ellen Glasgow, Margaret Mitchell, Roark Bradford, and perhaps Eudora Welty, many authors have introduced Negro characters without giving the problem many troublesome variables. In the works of Joel Chandler Harris, Mark Twain, or William Faulkner, the complexity may derive mainly from confusion or uncertainty or changes in the author's mind. Such variations in the works of Negro authors have reflected additional complications: the paucity of models for such writings as their purposes might dictate, and the exigencies of being published and read in a literary world in some degree alien. The slave narratives had other purposes than character delineation, as did such writings as those of Mrs. Frances

Harper and others of the war period. The career of Charles W. Chesnutt is especially useful, I suspect, for the light it throws on the racial aspects of authorship in the decades following the Civil War. He resided in both South and North; he had sponsors among white authors of the time, including Cable; he submitted his stories to magazine editors at a time when they were growing reluctant to publish anything on the southern problem or the race question. With him, furthermore, characters of the two races presented separate but inseparable problems. Back of him, few members of his race had written stories or novels dealing with either race. As others present can say with more assurance than I, the debate over William Styron's *Nat Turner* has raised—perhaps has exacerbated and confused would be a better way to put it— the question as to whether a white author can portray a black satisfactorily (or the reverse, I suppose), or whether the attempt is even worth making. The contentions on this point seem to be more heated than logical. My only thoughts are that after a century or more in which aspects of race were in effect off limits for many authors, similar prohibitions dictated from a different quarter may have no better warrant. And further, we do not as a rule take our poets and novelists and dramatists to be promulgators of absolutes, to give us final words on the questions they raise. Don't we, rather, expect from them exploration, suggestion, speculation—the kind of insights and imaginative syntheses, under the spur of skeptical probing, which may aid finally to answer social, human, and moral questions?

We need to know more—and more of the subtleties—about southern authors in their relations to editors and publishers outside the region—and inside also. The discovery of Cable by Edward King and the editors of *Scribner's Monthly* has been told many times; the first national publication of works by Joel Chandler Harris, Thomas Nelson Page, Mary Noailles Murfree, Ellen Glasgow, and others have been recounted also. But there are other instances that may fill out our understanding. Within a few weeks after the surrender at Appomattox John Esten Cooke was publishing in New York the first in a series of biographical, historical, and fictional accounts based on his experiences as a Confederate officer. William Gilmore Simms was publishing in New York almost as promptly. Was it true, as has been said, that in the 1880s, and again in the 1930s, a southern book was easier to place with a New York publisher than a book from any other section? What were the results when editors and publishers outside the South urged southern writers (as they urged George W. Cable and Thomas Nelson Page) to give them romantic tales of the idealized Old South rather than the fiction of a different type they preferred to write? In the 1870s, 1880s, and 1890s some of the magazine editors in New York were ready to tell authors in the South what kind of fiction they would publish. One would like to know how generally such was the practice and what were the consequences, then—and in later times as well.

Let me name two areas where study is needed and where encouragement or exhortation may be required, or where there must be joint effort of the kind that a cooperative association might sponsor. I mean the study of lesser authors and lesser genres. There will be no shortage of new readings of "Ligeia" or "A Rose for Emily" or "Good Country People," or new evaluations of Huck Finn's decision to "go to hell, then," or new identifications of fertility symbols in Faulkner. Some of the lesser writers and lesser works are unexciting, to say the least. But if anyone is to read them and report on them, we homefolks will probably have to do it. William Tappan Thompson, Richard Malcolm Johnston, and Charles Henry Smith (alias Bill Arp) do not stand very tall in the era of Mark Twain, James, and Howells; but they continued to write well into that era, and in many ways that may be significant they brought the tradition of backwoods humor over from the 1840s and 1850s and at least helped prepare readers for the humor of Mark Twain, Joel Chandler Harris, and William Faulkner. We can speak with more assurance at this point when we have good biographies of these three men.

Literary history cannot chart only the highest peaks of achievement and let them stand as isolated, unexplained phenomena, like mountain summits above an expanse of clouds. The highest mountains grow from the lesser mountains around them and lean on them—to expand the same figure—and at times shifts in the supporting earth alter the relative or the absolute heights of the mountains. Herein lies a lesser but perhaps a sufficient justification for studying authors of the second or third or fourth rank.

Let me interject here a collateral question that may be worth exploring: How do we account for the number of books on southern literature published early in the present century? A list would include *Southern Writers*, by W. M. Baskervill and others, 1897 and 1902; S. A. Link, *Pioneers of Southern Literature*, 1899; C. W. Kent, *The Revival of Interest in Southern Letters*, 1900; Carl Holliday, *A History of Southern Literature*, 1906; Mildred L. Rutherford, *The South in History and Literature*, 1907; Kate Orgain, *Southern Authors in Poetry and Prose*, 1908; the section on literature in *The South in the Building of the Nation*, 1909; the seventeen volumes of *The Library of Southern Literature*, 1909 and afterward; and Montrose J. Moses, *The Literature of the South*, 1910. F. P. Gaines's *The Southern Plantation*, 1924, might be added, and also C. Alphonso Smith's *Southern Literary Studies*, 1927. Likewise the list might be extended backward to include a number of magazine articles published between 1880 and 1900; and possibly also the volumes of southern poetry, mainly war poetry, published after the Civil War, including one by Simms. It is worth noting also that Simms proposed soon after the close of the war to publish a multivolume series of southern authors. With a few exceptions these works do not contribute much to an understanding of southern literature; but they constitute something of a phenomenon and might be described and evaluated in a chapter on southern literary historiography in this period, comparable to the account of southern historiography published by Wendell H. Stephenson some years ago.

Along with literary history, strictly defined, attention might be given also to biography and autobiography and to letters and letter writing. We cannot expect other editions of letters to fill out and deepen our knowledge of literary history as much as the five volumes of Simms's letters have done, but the letters of Paul Hamilton Hayne already published suggest that a selection drawn from the total of Hayne's correspondence—if publishing the total is not feasible—that a generous selection would be invaluable to a study of the southern literary scene from the founding of *Russell's Magazine*, say, to Hayne's death in 1886. Couldn't much the same be said about the letters of John Esten Cooke and Thomas Nelson Page? And don't we need new biographies of Cooke and Page?

The literature of a new country or region particularly aware of its distinctiveness, or aware of a changing or uncertain status, is likely to be self-conscious. Such was true, surely, of writers for two or three generations after the American Revolution. Such self-consciousness is a handicap generally, until authors arrive on the scene with the talents and the independence of mind to escape the dominion of the local and the immediate and to bend those elements to their special literary purpose. Is it possible, I wonder, to observe in William Gilmore Simms the occurrence and the effects of a regional self-consciousness superseding an earlier national self-consciousness? No author in the South during the forty or fifty years after the Civil War could forget that he was a southerner, even though he might avoid the deprivations and pressures and prohibitions that generally prevailed. Hayne, Cable, Harris, Thomas Nelson Page, and Walter Hines Page come to mind. And of course Charles W. Chesnutt, for no Negro author in the South then—or today perhaps—could escape multiplied and disturbing forces on his pen. Mark Twain and Ellen Glasgow may have dominated their regional materials, partially at least, by achieving something of a literal distance and more of a figurative distance. But they escaped a hobbling self-consciousness only part of the time, as was probably true of William Faulkner also, and Thomas Wolfe. To my mind Eudora Welty is an author who has escaped or nearly escaped the limiting self-consciousness I have been talking about. She is as much at home in her region as the wisteria in her yard, and it is not easy to imagine her anywhere else—for long. Yet she sits aplomb, as Whitman might have said, self-assured and unperturbed. In those ways that are observable, Miss Welty has been as conscious of her region, as much bound up with it, I suspect, as any other of our authors. But the evidence is preponderant that she has remained serenely mistress of her own artistic destiny, that with her a full measure of self-consciousness—a full awareness, I would rather say—has been a major asset. What I want to suggest is that in noting the forces that have come to bear on southern authors, forces from inside the region or outside, exerted through the facts of publishing or in other ways— we must remain alert to the individual and subtle responses of each author to those forces. Thus, it seems to me, we will understand better the individual author and also the literary scene in its full spread and continuum; and we can hope not to mute the distinctive overtones of a literary work, however much it and its author belong to a particular time and place.

4. The South's Reaction to Modernism

A PROBLEM IN THE STUDY OF
SOUTHERN LETTERS

by Lewis P. Simpson

A controlling assumption among students of twentieth-century southern literature generally is that fundamentally and substantially it is a reaction to modernism. Although I do not question the overall validity of this attitude, I want to discuss the need for us to reconsider one of its prominent aspects. I refer to a particular version of the modern southern literary reaction that has prevailed widely among us—although not by any means with doctrinaire uniformity. If this version can be attributed to a single person, we may say that this is probably Allen Tate, whose brilliant critical work is so central to the field of southern literary studies that we cannot imagine it without him. I have especially in mind Tate's essay entitled "The Profession of Letters in the South," which was first published in 1935. I believe this essay can be taken as the beginning of the historical study of the literature of the South by the sophisticated modern literary intelligence. I sense a direct relation between it and our presence, nearly forty years after its publication, at this conference on the state of scholarship and criticism in southern letters.

I

At the end of Tate's essay we encounter an explanation of the twentieth-century flowering of writing in the South which has become classic:

[48]

From the peculiarly historical consciousness of the
Southern writer has come good work of a special
order; but the focus of this consciousness is quite
temporary. It has made possible the curious burst
of intelligence that we get at a crossing of the ways,
not unlike, on an infinitesimal scale, the outburst of
poetic genius at the end of the sixteenth century
when commercial England had already begun to
crush feudal England. The Histories and Tragedies
of Shakespeare record the death of the old régime,
and Doctor Faustus gives up feudal order for world
power.

Implicit in this famous observation is a refinement—a succinct
dramatization—of the relationship of the modern southern literary mind to the culture of the Old South which Tate had been
endeavoring to formulate for several years. In the excitement of
the days leading up to the organization and publication of the
manifesto of the Agrarians, *I'll Take My Stand* (1930), he had
written both to Robert Penn Warren and Donald Davidson advocating the founding of "an academy of Southern *positive* reactionaries." The academy was to have a signed "philosophical
constitution," setting forth "a complete social, philosophical, literary, economic and religious system." Such a program, Tate told
Davidson from Paris in 1929, "will inevitably draw upon our
heritage, but this heritage should be valued, not in what it actually performed, but in its possible perfection. Philosophically we
must go the whole hog of reaction, and base our movement less
upon the actual old South than upon its prototype—the historical
social and religious scheme of Europe. We must be the last Europeans—there being no Europeans in Europe at present." The
Academy of Southern Positive Reactionaries was not to become a
reality, but Tate's inspiriting concept of the European scheme as a
prototype of the South appears after a fashion in *I'll Take My
Stand*, notably in the essays contributed by John Crowe Ransom
and Tate. In Tate's essay, entitled "Remarks on the Southern Religion," in fact, the idea that Europe is the prototype of the South
is the basis for the distinction Tate draws between nineteenth-century New England and the nineteenth-century South.

The South could be ignorant of Europe because it *was* Europe; that is to say, the South had taken root in a native soil. And the South could remain simple-minded because it had no use for the intellectual agility required to define its position. Its position was self-sufficient and self-evident; it was European where the New England position was self-conscious and colonial. The Southern mind was simple, not top-heavy with learning it had no need of, unintellectual, and composed; it was personal and dramatic, rather than abstract and metaphysical; and it was sensuous because it lived close to a natural scene of great variety and interest.

Tate continues:

Because it lived by images, not highly organized, it is true, as Dogma, but rather more loosely gathered from the past, the South was a profoundly traditional European community. . . . The old Southerners were highly critical of the kinds of work to be done. They planted no corn that they could not enjoy; they grew no cotton that did not directly contribute to the upkeep of a rich private life; and they knew no history for the sake of knowing it, but simply for the sake of contemplating it and seeing in it an image of themselves. And aware of the treachery of nature, as all agrarians are, they tended to like stories, very simple stories with a moral.

Five years later when he published "The Profession of Letters in the South," Tate's conception of the history of the South had become more complex. But if he had become somewhat less certain about the simplicity of the Old South, he still interpreted it as a European community. In this essay the interpretation bears upon the problem of why the Old South failed to develop a literary profession, or even a literary tradition. Tate finds an answer in the aristocratic rule of the southern planter class, who had no real use for literature. The New England plutocracy had none either, although in and around Boston a marginal literary life did produce a few distinctive writers.

> But it is a sadder story still in the South [Tate observes]. We had no Hawthorne, no Melville, no Emily Dickinson. We had William Gilmore Simms. We made it impossible for Poe to live south of the Potomac. Aristocracy drove him out. Plutocracy, in the East, starved him to death. I prefer the procedure of the South; it knew its own mind, knew what kind of society it wanted. . . . It must be confessed that the Southern tradition has left no cultural landmark so conspicuous that the people may be reminded by it constantly of what they are. We lack a tradition in the arts; more to the point, we lack a literary tradition. We lack even a literature. We have just enough literary remains from the old régime to prove to us that, had a great literature risen, it would have been unique in modern times.
> The South was settled by the same European strains as originally settled the North. Yet, in spite of war, reconstruction, and industrialism, the South to this day finds its most perfect contrast in the North. In religious and social feeling I should stake everything on the greater resemblance to France. The South clings blindly to forms of European feeling and conduct that were crushed by the French Revolution and that, in England at any rate, are barely memories.

Both in "Remarks on Religion in the South" and in "The Profession of Letters in the South," as we can see, Tate takes the attitude that the Old South is the only part of America that has profoundly experienced the life of the traditional community as this life has been known in Western civilization. Elaborating on the implication of Tate's notion, we may say that the southern writer in the 1920s and 1930s, who consciously realized his inheritance, found himself in a world that had not only known but had lived traditionalist values. Among these are (to make use of a convenient list supplied by the distinguished historical sociologist,

Robert A. Nisbet, in his book *Tradition and Revolt*): "hierarchy, community, tradition, authority, and the sacred sense of life." The New England scene in contrast had been dominated by modernist values: "equalitarianism, individualism, secularism, positive rights, and rationalist modes of organization" (to make use of another list from Nisbet). The "peculiarly historical consciousness" of the southern writer at the "crossing of the ways" in the third and fourth decades of the present century consisted, Tate argues implicitly, in the knowledge that he descends from the "old régime." He has the feudal age in his bones.

In asserting a southern feudalism Tate's motive is by no means to confine the southern writer to a provincial status. Instead he intends to place him in the cosmopolitan mainstream of the modern literary sensibility. The modern southern writer has an intimate connection with the very source of the great modern Western literary renaissance; he is connected to the inspiring motive of Yeats, Joyce, Eliot, Valéry, and Mann. This is to say, he is a voice in that dialectic of modernist and traditionalist values which—generated and regenerated in successive waves of the traditionalist reaction to modernism in the aftermath of the French Revolution—is the substance of modern art and letters. Tate as a modern writer—as a writer educated in the literary world in which a reactionary poem like the *The Waste Land* had become the major cultural symbol—needed to believe in the legend of the South as a traditional European community. The need grew out of the literary drama in which he was involved; it was a requirement of the poetry of his role as a man of letters in the modern world.

But, I would suggest, we need to move to a perspective on the South and on southern literature different from that provided by the struggle between modernism and traditionalism. As a matter of fact, I think that, ironically, Tate felt this need even as he wrote his early essays on the South. In the total complexity of these essays, he places a heavy emphasis on the failure of the Old South as a feudal society. The South, he points out, did not have a feudal religion; it had Protestantism. It was a "semi-feudal society." The

Old South did not have a labor system that related the aristocracy to the soil as serfdom did; it had chattel slavery and the chattels were black and out of cultural origins completely alien to those of the masters. The Old South did not have a stable politics; it was "hag-ridden by politics" and thus always in a state of crisis. The Old South, Tate virtually says, could not under the circumstances of its actual existence have had an organic society in the feudal sense. What Tate did not see—we suspect, I think, that he did not quite want to see it, for he comes so close upon it—is simply that, although southerners appealed to the feudal image, it was because, save for the Greek and Roman worlds, they did not know what other historical image to appeal to. Since they did not have any possibility of living by what Tate calls "the higher myth of religion," they tried to live by what he calls "the lower myth of history." They endeavored to imitate historical forms of feeling and emotion. But in adapting the life of European traditionalism to their situation, the southerners succeeded only in being ornamental and meretricious. The southern feudal artifice rang as hollow as an empty armor.

II

What the southerners were really trying to be was something else. Something essentially not Grecian, not Roman, not feudal. They were never able adequately to express their aspiration, although they came close to it in some ways in the works of George Fitzhugh of Port Royal, Virginia, most expressly so in his *Sociology for the South* and in his *Cannibals All!* The South wanted a world in which chattel slavery was established beyond all doubt as the right and proper principle of the social relation, a world in which society was built, securely, permanently, unqualifiedly on the right of men to hold property in other men. The struggle of the Old South was not between a traditionalism rooted in European forms of feeling and emotion and an outside (or an inside) insurgent modernism. Under the historical circumstances it faced—

under the historical nature of its existence—the South's struggle
was between the rise of a unique slave society and the forces of
modernism.

Tate suggests that had the Old South had a literature, it would
have been unique in representing "the old régime" in modern
times. In its total expression, I believe, the Old South had a literature. We understand its nature and importance when we grasp its
inner irony. I mean when we see that it is a representation of the
novelty of the southern reaction to modernism.

Several months ago I fell one day to doing some rereading in
Henry James's *The American Scene*. Although I had gone to this
work specifically because I wanted to check on what James says in
it about his visit to Cambridge in 1905, I went on to the chapter on
Richmond, was drawn into it, and after a time discovered that—
together with the two chapters on Charleston and Florida immediately following—it affords for the literary student what well
may be one of the most significant essays on southern culture
written between the time of the Civil War and Tate's "The Profession of Letters in the South." I was sufficiently inspired by it to
write a note on James and the South as a preface to a number of
the *Southern Review* devoted to writing in the South I was then
putting together. Without repeating precisely what I suggest in
this comment, I'll try to adapt its import to what I am endeavoring
to say here. In doing so I'll quote a paragraph from James that I
could not get into the small space I had available in the magazine.
James is discussing the way in which the South conceived "of a
world rearranged" to accommodate the world to the "interest of
slave-produced Cotton."

> The solidity and comfort [of the South] were to
> involve not only the wide extension, but the com-
> plete intellectual, moral and economic reconsecra-
> tion of slavery, an enlarged and glorified, quite
> beatified, application of its principle. The light of
> experience, round about, and every finger-post of
> history, of political and spiritual science with which
> the scene of civilization seemed to bristle, had,

when questioned, but one warning to give, and appeared to give it with an effect of huge derision: whereby was laid on the Southern genius the necessity of getting rid of these discords and substituting for the ironic face of the world an entirely new harmony, or in other words a different scheme of criticism. Since nothing in the Slave-scheme could be said to conform—conform, that is, to the reality of things—it was the plan of Christendom and the wisdom of the ages that would have to be altered. History, the history of everything, would be rewritten *ad usum Delphini*—the Dauphin being in this case the budding Southern mind.

It strikes us that in these observations James essentially depicts the Old South as having reacted to modernity (that is, to the "reality of things," by which James meant nineteenth-century liberal humanism and the grand doctrine of the "century of hope," the "Progress of Civilization") not by any return to a medieval traditionalism but by proposing to establish itself on the basis of "an entirely new harmony," on a "different scheme of criticism." The South sought not to root the rationale of its difference from the modern world in the deep places of an old mind; but, to the contrary, to found its existence and establish its difference from modernity on a new mind. The mind of the Old South was a "budding mind." What would this new world the southerners wished to fashion have been like if the southerners had succeeded in making it? James does not pursue this question. He devotes himself to the barren cultural situation that the effort to make the new mind created in the South. The pursuit of the "Confederate dream" meant a drastic repudiation of the artistic and literary tradition of Western civilization. It "meant a general and permanent quarantine," James declares; "meant the eternal bowdlerization of books and journals; meant in fine all literature and all art on an expurgatory index." James continues:

It meant, still further, an active and ardent propaganda; the reorganization of the school, the college, the university, in the interest of the new criticism. The testimony to that thesis offered by the documents of the time, by State legislation, local eloquence, political speeches, the "tone of the press," strikes us to-day as beyond measure queer and quaint and benighted—innocent above all; stamped with the inalienable Southern sign, the inimitable *rococo* note. We talk of the provincial, but the provinciality projected by the Confederate dream, and in which it proposed to steep the whole helpless social mass, looks to our present eyes as artlessly perverse, as untouched by any intellectual tradition of beauty or wit, as some exhibited array of the odd utensils or divinities of lone and primitive islanders. It came over one that they *were* there, in the air they had breathed, precisely, lone—even the very best of the old Southerners; and, looking at them over the threshold of approach that poor Richmond seemed to form, the real key to one's sense of their native scene was in that very idea of their solitude and isolation. Thus they affected one as such passive, such pathetic victims of fate, as so played upon and betrayed, so beaten and bruised, by the old burden of their condition, that I found myself conscious, on their behalf, of a sort of ingenuity of tenderness.

Of course in these last remarks James becomes patronizing, and at the same time somewhat sentimental, about the meaning of the southern quest for an independent intellect. If he suggests graphically that the drama of the quest lay in its openness to novelty, he rather thoroughly undercuts the complexity of his suggestion.

Now the awareness I brought to the Jamesian discussion of the South when I came back to it last spring—the awareness both of its value and of its limitations—was more acute than what I had been able to bring to it in several prior readings. I think this may be attributed to my recently having read a good deal in the remarkable Marxist historian, Eugene D. Genovese. In two compelling works—*The Political Economy of Slavery*, and a sequel, *The World the Slaveholders Made*—Genovese, as we would suppose, insists upon the validity of a socialist class analysis of the Old South. But in spite of this insistence, Genovese impresses the student of southern culture not so much as an advocate of the Marxist doctrine of history as a rigorous historical actualist. He brings into focus a historically singular South, arguing cogently that the southern slaveholders conceived, and to some extent created, a unique historical community. Genovese presents the South that eludes Allen Tate in his attempt to define a feudal South, giving us one that lies more nearly within the Jamesian purview. It is a South which sought to realize itself not in the "institutional inheritance" of the old European régime but in "the plantation régime" as it actually was in the historical American South, with its existence established in "a patriarchal and paternalistic ethos" stemming from the rule of a "resident planter for whom the plantation was a home and the entire population part of his extended family." Genovese points to several critical aspects of the history of the plantation régime in the southern United States (in contrast to this régime in South America). One was the ending of the foreign slave trade at the moment the cotton South came into being. The slaveholding class, forced to rely primarily upon the development of a Creole slave population instead of a large importing of slaves as required, extended over the frontier a slave population which was encouraged to reproduce itself. However strong the purely exploitative motive in their use, southern slaves were thus necessarily accorded paternalistic treatment. They responded by being the only slave class in the New World to reproduce itself.

> The initial motivation [Genovese comments] to provide the slaves with adequate food, shelter, clothing, and leisure was of course economic, and the economic pressures for good treatment if anything grew stronger over time. It is nonetheless naive to leave matters there and to see economic interests and morals as discrete categories. Once extended over a generation or two, the appropriate standards of treatment became internalized and

part of the accepted standard of decency for the
ruling class. The growth of a creole slave population
narrowed the cultural gap between the classes and
races and prepared the way for those feelings of
affection and intimacy which had to exist if paternalism was to have substance.

Another crucial aspect of the history of slavery in the American
South, as Genovese interprets this, was the liberation of the
southern slaveholding class from England by the American Revolution. "If separation from England liberated a national capitalist
régime in the North," Genovese contends, "it simultaneously liberated a plantation slave régime in the South." The result was that
the southern ruling class, constrained by no power save a fairly
weak central government in Washington, was invited to assume
autonomous power over the region of the new nation in which
slavery was a primary institution. Such an invitation was not to
be neglected. The southern slaveholders soon moved toward
another critical turning point in their history. This was "the
formulation of the positive-good proslavery argument." Signaling "the maturation of the ruling class and its achievement of self-
consciousness," this argument was no mere apology for slavery.
On the contrary, "it represented the formulation of a world view
that authentically reflected the position, aspirations, and ethos of
the slaveholders as a class." In its "final formulation" this view,
as presented by the writer whom Genovese regards as the greatest
southern theorist, George Fitzhugh, set forth slavery as "the
proper relationship of all labor to capital." In Genovese's opinion,
such a conception of the link between slave labor and capital "had
no counterpart in the Caribbean or in Latin America."

Its development would have been especially difficult in Latin America since the Catholic tradition
. . . recognized slavery but declared it to be un-
natural. Paradoxically, it was precisely the most
originally bourgeois of the slaveholding countries
that produced a coherent defense of slavery as a
mode of production in its social, political, ideologi-

cal, and moral aspects. The paternalism at the core of the slaveholder's ideology rested primarily on the master-slave relationship but extended itself outward to encompass the white lower classes. As the régime developed, the plantations became increasingly self-sufficient and more enclosed as productive-consuming units. In the slave states as a whole . . . there was considerable progress toward regional self-sufficiency. Locally, this development meant the dependence of yeomen and poorer whites on the plantation market. . . . For the most part . . . planters do not appear to have exploited their economic opportunities with anything like ruthlessness but to have considered them part of a wider social responsibility. Many of the yeomen and even poor whites (that is, largely declassed freemen) were related to the planters. The local records of Black Belt counties make it clear that members of the same family occupied positions in all classes and income groups within the same county. The distinctly Southern sense of extended family cannot be understood apart from the social structure at the center of which stood the plantation, and it provided a powerful impetus for social cohesion, ruling-class hegemony, and the growth of a paternalistic spirit that far transcended master-slave and white-black relationships. There were undoubtedly powerful counterpressures, especially those associated with the egalitarian ethos, which would have to be given due weight in a full account. It is nonetheless clear that much of the political power of the planters and much of that oft-noted loyalty of the nonslaveholders to the régime derived from these semi-paternalistic relationships. . . . The slaveholders of the Old South . . . had inherited no hierarchical political principle to draw upon and had to develop this extended paternalism carefully, with full account of the contrary democratic and egalitarian attitudes residing deep in the lower classes. Southern paternalism developed in a contradictory, sometimes even hypocritical way, but the existence and force of the tendency among so egalitarian-

minded a people tells us a great deal about the character and power of the plantation system.

Reaching to fulfill its destiny, the southern slaveholding class
came eventually to the final turning point in its history. It was
impelled to secede from the nation-state which it had joined following the American Revolution and to stake everything on its
capacity to set up its own nation-state. But it was too late in history for this effort to be successful, for by this time the economic
and political goals of the southern slaveholding world were obso-
lete. A world marketplace had become the center of the economic
life of Western civilization and the principle of the sovereignty of
the people the center of its political life. The master class of the
South had no way effectively to cut the South off from the world
marketplace—could not envision doing so except in the austere
logic of a George Fitzhugh. Nor could the southern master class
perform—or envision performing save in a Fitzhugh's vision—the
logically necessary act of unifying the southern slave system by
enslaving the lower-class southern whites. In theory the master
class was not restrained by the unity of the white race from con-
verting all the available labor supply in the South—lower-class
white as well as free Negro—to the slavery system. Racism in the
old South was strong, but it was a result of special circumstances
and not an inherent part of the logic of the slave South. Slavery
remained always basically a class and not a racial ideology. In the
case of the lower-whites the master class confronted a segment of
the southern populace which had attained to an autonomous class
position and was potentially powerful enough to rise against the
master class and destroy it.

In summation, and I apologize for giving what is no doubt an
oversimplified resumé of his concepts, Genovese tells us that
antebellum southern society "is to be understood, not as a form of
capitalism, much less as a form of feudalism," but as a slave
society structured by class, although "deformed by internal and
external ties to the capitalist world and profoundly flawed by
racial caste."

III

If we accept Genovese's view of Old South history as a feasible one—or as being assuredly within the realm of possible and approximate interpretations of a complicated and paradoxical epoch in modern history—we are led to consider its bearing on the study of southern literature. I refer to the problem we commenced with: defining the reactionary nature of modern southern literature.

When we look at the Old South as a slave society, we realize the extent to which its literary expression in its entirety—the history of its literary life and the character of its literary expression in the varied forms of poetry, fiction, oratory, the social and political essay—constitute both the explicit and implicit record of the Old South's experience of its struggle for uniqueness in history. In contrast to the traditionalist intellectual of the post-French Revolution stamp, a Joseph de Maistre or an Edmund Burke, the nineteenth-century southern man of letters sought not to restore the sensibility of a European traditionalism but to encourage the building in the midst of modern history of not only a prebourgeois but a prefeudal slave society. He expected that somehow this society would accommodate itself to finance capitalism, industrialism, and a world market. In the final phase of the Old South, Henry Timrod, poet laureate of the Confederacy, dreamed that the southern society (in the form of the Cotton Kingdom) would become a redemptive world power, bringing the world general peace and prosperity; and in a more specific way redeeming the laborers of all nations from poverty. The vision which climaxes "Ethnogenesis" is well worth quoting:

> But let our fears—if fears we have—be still,
> And turn us to the future! Could we climb
> Some mighty Alp, and view the coming time,
> > The rapturous sight would fill
> > Our eyes with happy tears!
> Not for the glories which a hundred years

Shall bring us; not for lands from sea to sea,
And wealth, and power, and peace, though these shall be;
But for the distant peoples we shall bless,
And the hushed murmur of a world's distress;
  For, to give labor to the poor,
  The whole sad planet o'er,
And save from want and crime the humblest door,
Is one among the many ends for which
  God makes us great and rich!
The hour perchance is not yet wholly ripe
When all shall own it, but the type
Whereby we shall be known in every land
Is that vast gulf which laves our Southern strand,
And through the cold, untempered ocean pours
Its genial streams, that far off Arctic shores
May sometimes catch upon the softened breeze
Strange tropic warmth and hints of summer seas!

I know of no work by a southern writer which more poignantly conveys the singular isolation of the Old South from modern history than Timrod's "Ethnogenesis," his proclamation of the new southern nation. The literature of the Confederacy, a reading of this poem suggests, is not continuous with that of a southern society which assumes its existence is traditional; it is a development of expression in a society trying under great historical stress to make an image of itself and of its meaning in history. When we regard southern writings from the standpoint of the southern struggle for historical realization, we are likely to see how important it is to study all of the literary expression in the South, and not only a few novels and poems. We are the more likely to see how fundamental—in an age in western history when the use of letters was still the primary assimilating civilizational power— literary expression was in the Old South. And in this expression— from William Byrd II, through Thomas Jefferson, through Edmund Ruffin, who supposedly fired the first shot on Fort Sumter—we see the man of letters making himself at home as a master in a slave society (not, it may be added, as feudal landlord but as a plantation patriarch).

But the cost of making the man of letters *the southern man of letters* was his progressive removal from his proper home. He became an alien to the homeland of the man of letters which had developed with the decline of the universal Church, the realm of the cosmopolitan Republic of Letters. The man of letters as southerner also cut himself off from the shape and substance of modern literary history: the great dialectical process involving the reaction of traditionalism against modernism which commenced in the early nineteenth century. The writer of the Old South, after the Age of Jefferson at any rate, lacked the dialectical sense of past and present, of European tradition and American modernity, as Tate declares. Such a sense was vividly present in the New England writer like Emerson. "There are always two parties, the party of the Past and the party of the Future; the Establishment and the Movement," Emerson said in defining his age. "At times the resistance is reanimated, the schism runs under the world and appears in Literature, Church, State, and social customs." No southern contemporary of Emerson had such a vision of the mid-nineteenth century. It was not available to him; he was cut off from it. As I have argued elsewhere, it appears that in the Old South the realm of the State, in the interest of developing the ideology of slavery, virtually assimilated the realm of the Church and the realm of Letters. Since the early Renaissance at least the realm of Letters, the Republic of Letters, has been the homeland of the western literary mind. It has been the source of literary authority and fraternity. It has been in the Republic of Letters that the great debate between traditionalism and modernism has effectively taken place. The Old South in effect withdrew from this community, for the sake of seeking total social, political, and economic community. Its legacy to the South that came afterwards was in this sense largely negative; until the time when Tate and others, rejoining the literary community of western high culture that had been the intellectual homeland of Thomas Jefferson, began a poetic assimilation of the Old South to this community. Tate defined the "crossing of the ways" in the South, reinterpreting the history of southern literature and placing it in the dialectical drama of traditionalism and modernism. In so doing he at once fostered the legend of a traditionalism rooted in Europe as the integrating force in southern culture and obscured the assimilating power of the "peculiar institution" in the Old South world.

But if we accept the "peculiar institution" as the center of the world view of the Old South, we may well conclude that its influence on the southern mind was more responsible for "the peculiarly historical consciousness" Tate observed in the southern writer at the "crossing of the ways" than any world view derived from a European traditionalism. Understanding this we are possibly able to understand at the same time that the twentieth-century southern writer in a special way inherited from the Old South the chief issue in the dialectic between traditionalism and modernism: the nature of man in relation to community. Are we inescapably creatures of community, expressing ourselves properly and truly as men solely through a structured community, or are we truly ourselves as men only when liberated from the bonds of prescriptive community? In the Old South this issue did not take the form it did under European, or under New England, or under general American conditions. It took the uniquely intense historical form of the South's effort to achieve community through the development of a society founded on chattel slavery. This effort took the old southern civilization to the wall, and with its back to the wall it was destroyed. There was finally no southern willingness to compromise. The world the southern slaveholders made knew its own mind all right. It knew it better than some of its leaders, including Jefferson Davis and Robert E. Lee, knew it. Towards the end, as Robert F. Durden shows in his unusual compilation of documents concerning the Confederate debate on emancipation, both Davis and Lee were eager to accept slaves into the Confederate armed forces on condition of their freedom. If enough Confederate troops could have been mustered in this manner, the South might have had a chance for a negotiated settlement of the Civil War. But the Old South society preferred to go down as it was rather than compromise on slavery. And unless we grasp the intensity of its preoccupation with its vision of community, I doubt if we understand the presence of the Old South in the twentieth-century southern literary imagination. I am not necessarily saying with Quentin Compson, "You would have to be born there." (Eugene Genovese was born and raised in Brooklyn, incidentally.) I am saying that you have to know something about the special history of the American South to grasp the inheritance of the southern writer from "old slavery times."

From the complex frustration and defeat of the Old South's attempt to become a unique slave society, the modern southern writer inherited, as did no other American writer of his age, a compelling drama of man and community. There was available to the southern writer in story, in the silent artifacts of unspoken memory, and in the very silence of the South on some matters—in the gesture and style of the life around him—the experience of a people who had deeply lived the aspiration to community. They had lived it not only in the manners and conventions, ceremony and rituals, amenities and conflicts of the outward society, but in the goodness and evil, the nobility and depravity of the inner worlds of the individuals in it. They had lived it in the terrors and horrors of human nature and in the resistance to these; and, moreover, in the recognition that the intricate bonds of community may be as much of hate as of love. In other words, the South had experienced the life of community lived, as Faulkner puts it, out of "the heart's driving complexity." The historical experience of the southern quest for community was transmitted by the South of Reconstruction times and of the late nineteenth and early twentieth centuries into the 1920s. At this time it begins to emerge as the powerful imagination of community we know in Faulkner, Tate, Warren, Eudora Welty, Richard Wright, Flannery O'Connor, and William Styron. How this imagination is rooted in the deeper levels of the southern life is, I think, scarcely yet understood. I have been thinking since I came across it in George P. Rawick's recent study, *From Sundown to Sunup: The Making of the Black Community* (the book which serves as the introduction to *The American Slave: A Composite Autobiography*, the amazing compilation of narratives by ex-slaves collected by the WPA in the 1930s) that the imagination of community in the southern expression is nowhere more strikingly evidenced than in the recollection of William Colbert, born a slave in Georgia in 1844. Colbert tells a story that cannot be told other than in his own words:

> Nawsuh, he warn't good to none of de niggers. All de niggers 'roun' hated to be bought by him kaze he wuz so mean. When he wuz too tired to whip us he had de overseer do it; and de overseer wuz meaner dan de massa. But, mister, de peoples wuz de same as dey is now. Dere wuz good uns and bad uns. I jus' happened to belong to a bad un. One day I remembers my brother, January, wuz cotched over seein' a gal on de next plantation. He had a pass but de time on it done gib out. Well suh, when de massa found out dat he wuz a hour late, he got as mad as a hive of bees. So when brother January he come home, de massa took down his long mule skinner and tied him wid a rope to a pine tree. He strip' his shirt off and said:
> "Now, Nigger, I'm goin' to teach you some sense."
> Wid dat he started layin' on de lashes. January was a big, fine lookin' nigger, de finest I ever seed. He wuz jus' four years older dan me, an' when de massa begin a beatin' him, January never said a word. De massa got madder and madder kaze he couldn't make January holla.
> "What's de matter wid you, nigger?" he say. "Don't it hurt?"
> January, he never said nothin', and de massa keep a beatin' till little streams of blood started flowin' down January's chest, but he never holler. His lips was a quiverin' and his body wuz a shakin', but his moutf it neber open; and all de while I sat on my mammy's and pappy's steps a cryin'. De niggers wuz all gathered about and some uv 'em couldn't

stand it; dey hadda go inside dere cabins. Atter
while, January, he couldn't stand it no longer his-
self, and he say in a hoarse, loud whisper:
"Massa! Massa! have mercy on dis poor nigger. . . ."
Den . . . de war came. De Yankees come in and
dey pulled de fruit off de trees and et it. Dey et de
hams and cawn, but dey neber burned de houses.
Seem to me lak dey jes' stay aroun' long enough to
git plenty somp'n t'eat, kaze dey lef' in two or three
days, an' we neber seed 'em since. De massa had
three boys to go to war, but dere wuzn't one to
come home. All the chillun he had wuz killed. Massa, he los' all his money and doe house soon begin
droppin' away to nothin'. Us niggers one by one lef'
de ole place and de las' time I seed de home plantation I wuz a standin' on a hill. I looked back on it
for de las' time through a patch of scrub pines and
it look' so lonely. Dere warn't but one person in
sight, de massa. He was a-settin'; in a wicker chair
in de yard lookin' out ober a small field of cotton
and cawn. Dere wuz fo' crosses in de graveyard in
de side lawn where he wuz a-settin'. De fo'th one
wuz his wife. I lost my ole woman too 37 years ago,
and all dis time, I's been a carrin' on like de massa—
all alone.

In his study of the significance of the WPA narratives, Rawick
presses hard upon the thesis that the African blacks enslaved in
the Old South became an Afro-American people with their own
community and culture. They became so by heroic resistance to
the masters and to white racism pervasive in the South. In revising
our conception of the Old South to emphasize its character as a
slave society, certainly we cannot fail to take into account the rise
of the black community. But does the poetic tragedy of the quest
for community in the South lie any more purely in the black experience of the slave society than in the white experience of it? It is
of the utmost interest to all of us, black or white, who are students
of southern literature, that William Colbert of Georgia perceived
that it did not. He perceived this as clearly as William Faulkner of
Mississippi or Allen Tate of Tennessee. Probably he perceived

this more surely than they did. It may be that in some underlying process of carrying knowledge to the heart (to echo Tate's key phrase in "Ode to the Confederate Dead"), William Colbert taught them this. At any rate we need to learn more about the origins and the basic meaning of the knowledge—of the drama and the poetry—of community which has dominated the southern literary vision. A quest for this knowledge, it is hardly too much to say, brought the study of southern letters as we know it today into being. It is a quest opening yet before us in our inquiries into the present state of southern literary studies.

DISCUSSIONS

5. Colonial Southern Literature

MODERATOR:
Lewis Leary

PANELISTS:
Robert Bain, Richard Beale Davis,
Carl Dolmetsch, Lewis P. Simpson

LEARY: Richard Beale Davis this morning outlined pretty well what has to be done in studies in colonial southern literature. I have thought that perhaps the best way we could begin our discussion this afternoon would be to go around the table, calling on each one. Dick, I'd be curious to know what you are doing on your literary history, intellectual history, of the South. What are the problems that confront you as you get into it?

DAVIS: I should say first of all that my announced topic is "Intellectual Life in the Colonial South: 1585-1763," stopping at the Stamp Act.

LEARY: Do you find very much intellectual life as far back as 1585?

DAVIS: Well, yes. In John White and Thomas Hariot—a great deal. Actually I began this before I did the *Intellectual Life in Jefferson's Virginia.* Now I have been back at it for over ten years and I'm just on chapter 6 out of a projected ten. The chapters are running about 250 typed pages each. The five that I've finished are, first of all, "Promotional Literature," "History," and "Voyages." They look at America from inside and outside; they look at the South, and I've made some comparisons between the "southern paradise" and the "New England wilderness." One of the curious things I found was that the word "wilderness" occurs

[71]

relatively rarely in southern tract literature, but more frequently than not, as compared to even a *potential* paradise, in New England literature.

LEARY: Do you mean that the colonization of the South was very much less for religious than for economic reasons?

DAVIS: I think that's true, but that's not the point I'm making. The point I'm making is that this was a valley of plenty, a land of Canaan that the southerner was coming to. I'm putting aside religion for the moment. What I feel is that there was, in a sense, no "city on a hill," but a "vale of plenty," even from Captain John Smith's time on. Chapter 2 is "The White Colonist Looks at His Indian Neighbor," his image of the Indian. Indian rhetoric has fascinated me for a long time. Why did a colonial governor of South Carolina address the legislative assembly in the morning in one kind of rhetoric, and the Indian chiefs that afternoon in an entirely different kind of English, and what is the effect, if any, of the kind of English he used in addressing the chiefs? I find that up and down the coast. The conversations of Captain John Smith and Powhatan may be third-hand but there's something of the original stylistic qualities there. The animal imagery, and so on, the primitive, if you want to call it that, runs all the way through the period, from 1585, from Thomas Hariot and Ralph Lane. There are the two attitudes toward the Indian exemplified in Hariot and Lane—the only good Indian is a dead Indian, and the Indian as a noble savage—and toward the same chief. Actually the two attitudes are there from the beginning. Then I got into Indian ritual, which L. C. Wroth and others have written about. Wroth published an article on the Indian treaty as literature many years ago in the *Yale Review*. I found that all of the conventions hold for the South that held for the North and even a few more, and that 1763 is an excellent cutoff date for the Indian because that was the year of the Treaty of Augusta which opened the Southwest and the West to the southerner, and the text contained the chain of friendship, all the other speeches and gifts and dances and songs, and so on. And then the southern observers at the Treaty of Albany and the Treaty of Lancaster and various other things, which were essentially southern treaty groups. These records are all from the white man, so it's the white man still looking at the Indian, but he's getting something there that he continues. William Parks, or perhaps one of his successors, printed the 1744 treaty, and it's a very different version from the one that Benjamin Franklin printed in Philadelphia.

LEARY: What you're dealing with is what you might call "unself-conscious" writing, without any attempt at conscious style. These people didn't think of themselves as literary people. They were simply reporting.

DAVIS: The people who were putting it down weren't, but the people who were speaking were pretty self-conscious.

DOLMETSCH: It was an oral literary tradition, in a sense the tradition of forensic discourse.

DAVIS: But it got into written form. Julian Boyd has edited a volume of treaties that was printed by Benjamin Franklin, in which you find the forensic quality included. He uses Franklin's version rather than William Parks's version. And the treaty prose gets into the gazettes. Sometimes parts of these treaties are included in the gazettes, particularly if a governor makes a speech at one of these treaty assemblies. That complete speech is given even if the rest of the treaty isn't. I found this Indian material the most fascinating thing that I've done so far, and the longest.

LEARY: That's probably one thing that we're interested in in almost every area of American literature. Even Leslie Fiedler is prodding us on that. We must pay more attention to the Indian relationship.

DAVIS: Of course I'm principally concerned with how the white man, the southern white colonist, looked at the Indian. What did he see and how did it affect him?

BAIN: And you say there are two general views? That the Indian is a noble savage, and also that the dead Indian is the good Indian?

DAVIS: Yes. Of course it's a concept of primitivism that goes much behind Indian-white relations, but they do appear there, and sometimes in the same individual you get an ambivalence in attitudes towards them. Captain Smith, for example, has both attitudes.

SIMPSON: Have you read Leslie Fiedler's book on the Indians, *The Return of the Vanishing American*? He makes a great deal out of the mystique of Pocahontas. I think he has something to say that you'd be interested in.

BAIN: William Arrowsmith has been collecting Indian poetry and Indian rhetoric, but I don't think he has published it yet. Most of his work seems to deal with trans-Mississippi Indians, however. He has been giving a paper called "Indian Poetry: The Poetry of Earth" and sees close relationships between the poetry of primitive cultures of ancient civilizations, especially Greece, and the literature of the American Indians.

DAVIS: I wonder if we have to jump from this period to William Faulkner and "The Bear," and his discussion of the Indian and other things, too, or whether there is a sub rosa tradition, or a subliterary-level tradition, which continued all the way through?

LEARY: What is fascinating to me in what you're saying is that you're pushing back two hundred years the controversy which we had with Cooper about the noble savage versus the bloodthirsty Indian. Does that go back, in your judgment, right to the beginning of colonization?

DAVIS: I have the documents for it. Susan Myra Kingsbury's *Records of the Virginia Company of London* show it right there—those four big volumes which the Library of Congress published. It goes straight on through the period to the very end of it, to 1763, with the Treaty of Augusta, and the speeches when the governors of the four southern colonies got together with the Indian chiefs and took everything away from them.

LEARY: What we're getting to, then, is that there is a continuity in American literature on the Indian right from the seventeenth century on through.

DAVIS: Tomo Cheeki, the Indian chief Philip Freneau writes

about, for example, is found all through Georgia literature: that's where Freneau got him from, because Tomo Cheeki had been to London and become sort of raised there, and this is true of several other Indians before him. Richmond Bond of The University of North Carolina at Chapel Hill did a book on Indians, *Queen Anne's American Kings*. You've got all sorts of examples of the problems that Cooper presents, as far as the white man and the Indian are concerned—not just isolated ones but a steady stream.

LEARY: It's a little complicated, though, because Freneau got his Tomo Cheeki directly from American sources, but he also got it from Tomo Cheeki in England, and Steele in *The Tatler* reported Tomo Cheeki's appearances there.

DOLMETSCH: Could I return to what you were saying earlier about these Indian treaties? In reading these speeches of the chiefs in the treaties—and, as you all know, an Indian wouldn't regard these treaties as treaties unless the speech of the chief was printed, put in there in toto—and in reading the addresses made by the governors and the commissioners and so on, is there any discernible difference between the language that one encounters in the northern treaties and the southern treaties?

DAVIS: That's a good question. I would say there is no difference, except in the attitude of the viewer. The southern viewer sees it a little differently from the Pennsylvania viewer or the New York State viewer or the New England viewer—the New Englanders were out of this thing mostly. I was saying that the secretary to the head of the Maryland commission at one of these treaties, Witham Marshe, left us his diary. It's a fascinating thing. He said that he went to all the sideshows as well as the main tent at this treaty—that is, to the powwows that the Indians had among themselves, which were really pantomimes or musical spectacles, and he gives the songs they sang, the kind of dances they did, and so forth. But my point is that this is a southern point of view that he is relating all this from. Of course I'm not trying to make the point in this book that all these things are in any sense regionally southern.

LEARY: Can you expand on that? Why is that a southern point of view?

DAVIS: For one thing, he compares some of these songs and dances to those of the slaves in Maryland, for example, and there we get into our slave society, and the South. But I think the important thing here is that this is copied into the only printed matter the South had, really, its gazettes, and therefore came to the attention of any literate southerner.

LEARY: But the gazettes didn't come until the middle of the eighteenth century though, did they?

DAVIS: Well, the *Maryland Gazette* was 1727.

LEARY: And yet they are reporting things which happened?

DAVIS: No, they're not reporting any of the early treaties. Now there is one of them that Governor Effingham of Virginia attended in the 1680s at Albany, of which we have a record in the legislative records of Virginia. But all that does is to show there is a continuity here. And of course Governor Spotswood's treaty of 1722. One of the proofs of the fact that there actually were golden horseshoes given for the western expedition is the record of the assembly he attended, just as he was being fired as governor of Virginia. As a gesture of the fullness of generosity that everybody felt at the end on each side, he took the horseshoe from his lapel and gave it to the principal Indian chief and said, "Now when you come through our territory here is the symbol of safe conduct through the mountains." The gazettes weren't in existence when that particular incident happened, but just as soon as they get started they begin to record these things.

LEARY: This may be a provocative question, but is it your opinion that the history of literature in the seventeenth-century South is something which is probably better handled by the historian than by the literary scholar?

DAVIS: There is far less literature in the seventeenth century surviving, but I would not say that that's true for all of it. The approach may be more that of the historian. For example, John Grave's Quaker *A Song of Sion*, which is an awfully poor poem, one of the few surviving southern poems of the seventeenth century, would be approached from a historical point of view; there's no point in approaching it from much else. You could point out the two kinds of couplets or whatever rhyme schmes he uses, but it's pretty mechanical and pretty dull stuff. But when you come to Captain John Smith or those records of Bacon's Rebellion, you've got something that is genuine literature. The best dissertation I've ever had is a recent one on Bacon's Rebellion in American literature. Especially the chapters on those records that were written in the seventeenth century, either right at the time or soon after, if you can include the one that Thomas Mathew wrote in 1705. They are good by any standards of literature and should be weighed, I think, by critical standards rather than simply the historical. As the literature matures, as the colonies mature, you approach it more critically than historically.

LEARY: One problem that any of us as students of colonial literature faces in relation to our peers in other areas of American literature, it seems to me, is to define what we mean by "literature," and I think until we do that we're going to have a very difficult time explaining to a person who is interested in Hawthorne or Melville or Whitman that this thing we're talking about is important because it is literature. Why do we justify these materials on the Indians, the reporting of the Indians, as literature?

DAVIS: I'm not trying to do that yet. My topic is "Intellectual Life in the Colonial South." All of this is part of the southern mind and incidentally it may be literature, and I may defend it or discuss it as literature at times, but that's not the only thing I'm interested in, by any means.

LEARY: Lewis Simpson, could you help us on this?

SIMPSON: I've worked on this a good deal, but I never have solved the problem. The basic use or meaning of the word is simply "letters . . . the use of letters." In the civilized tradition, according to my theory, you come to that point after the decline of the Middle Ages or with the rise of the medieval universities, at which the use of letters begins to become a kind of spiritual criterion. Arnold J. Toynbee somewhere makes the flat statement that the Republic of Christ becomes the republic of letters. I've never been able to trace down the phrase "the republic of letters" with any exactness. I've found it in word lists and dictionaries back pretty far; by the sixteenth century it's a conventional term. It appears on the tombstone of Julius Caesar Scaliger: he was a citizen of the republic of letters. I haven't been able to find the term in classical literature, but I've studied to some extent the whole question of the polity of literature, and the idea of such a polity obviously has its origins in classical civilization, since it's renewed at the time of the Renaissance. In other words, you do get a republic of letters, so much so that it's still defined in Webster's dictionary today and it means "literature," in one sense, and it means "the body of men of letters" in another. So this is a community, a cosmopolitan community, a polity of letters. The term, "literature," in that broadest sense, means the use of letters, and it seems to me that the primary element in Western civilization has not been art or music, but the use of letters.

LEARY: What do you mean by "the use of letters"? Do you mean the use of language to communicate?

SIMPSON: I mean the use of the written word, but also of oratory. I mean the disciplined use of letters. The spoken word—well, take American literature, for example—the spoken word was really as important as the written or printed word, perhaps more important, even into the nineteenth century. I am thinking of oratory; we've lost the feeling for oratory today. But it's a disciplined use of letters. In other words, in the rhetorical devices, in the use of rhetoric, we have a discipline that was the assimilative force in Western civilization, though it no longer is. Literature in that sense becomes a very basic term and yet a very elusive term.

LEARY: It seems to me there are two things involved here. What I judge Richard Davis has been talking about is the expression of a people in a given area, what they're doing, what they're about. Now, Carl Dolmetsch, I think when we get further into the eighteenth century we get a tradition which is self-consciously belletristic.

DOLMETSCH: Yes, I think there's another side to it—that is, the historical context in America of the meaning of the word "literature" or "letters." Wouldn't you say that our seventeenth- and eighteenth-century ancestors would not have recognized the distinction that we make between belles lettres and literature in general?

SIMPSON: They would not: there's plenty of evidence to show that. Even mathematics was a term oftentimes synonymous with literature in the eighteenth century.

DOLMETSCH: So we have perfect justification as literary historians to be concerned with what many of our colleagues contemptuously call "documents," and nonliterary phenomena, and so on, because their definition is too narrow. They have accepted the nineteenth-century, or later perhaps, definition of belles lettres as meaning literature.

BAIN: And they've forgotten that the various forms practiced in seventeenth-century English literature are precisely the forms which seventeenth- and eighteenth-century Americans practiced: the personal narrative, the promotional tract, and tales of travel and adventure. English literature is filled with accounts of this sort from places other than the American colonies. And, of course, the sermons, too.

LEARY: Yes, that's true, but the travel literature at some point, even in England, becomes transformed into something which Ben Jonson or Shakespeare or somebody takes up, and Marvell makes into something else.

DAVIS: You could say the use and intent of the same material would make a difference in a narrow definition of literature and a broad definition.

SIMPSON: We use the word "creative writing" for imaginative literature. We say imaginative literature, creative literature, trying to make a distinction that I don't think troubled Shakespeare at all.

LEARY: I think that's true, but it seems to me that after his first book, the *True Relation*, John Smith becomes, in addition to being a promoter, something also of an imaginative person who is creating.

SIMPSON: Yes, you could say that the *True Relation*, like Bradford's *History of Plymouth Plantation*, for example, is a beautiful prose poem. Smith has certainly that kind of language at times. There does seem to grow up a kind of literary journalism that begins to appear as printing becomes more common, and of course by the nineteenth century you see the distinction between journalism and what Poe called "literature proper" beginning to emerge. Poe insisted that he was interested in literature proper. He was going to found a magazine—first he called it *The Penn*, and then later *The Stylus*. The stylus is a deeply symbolic name: the idea carries us back to classical times. Of course he never got his magazine off the ground, but he dreamed of it all his life. It was going to be a journal which would set the tone. In fact, Poe thought he would become a kind of literary dictator in America. He was actually engaging in that kind of high form of literary journalism, which at the same time was being conducted in England by Carlyle and many others. The great age of the man of letters in England, of course, was in the mid-nineteenth century and on down to the First World War.

LEARY: Well enough, and true, but I'm afraid I've drawn us a little off our topic.

DOLMETSCH: May I amplify a little bit on something you said? You mentioned that English writers in the seventeenth century and at the beginning of the eighteenth century were utilizing travel literature and other things of that sort for what we recognize today as being chiefly belletristic ends. Toward the end of the eighteenth and the beginning of the nineteenth century, our own writers were doing the same sort of thing that the Elizabethan writers and the Restoration writers had done with similar material, if you look at it in that way. And what we're really comparing, it seems to me, if we compare the literature of America in the seventeenth century with that of London, is unfair in a way. This has been said before, and it's not in any sense original, but it's something we have to keep repeating. It would be fairer to make a comparison between the literature of Yorkshire or Wales and the literature of America in the seventeenth and eighteenth centuries, because the American colonies were overseas provinces of England. And it is not fair to compare the literature of Virginia in the seventeenth century with the literature of a metropolis of 500,000 people, the seat of empire, London, which was a magnet and drew people from all over the place.

LEARY: Yes, but I wonder whether we're not saying that what the early South produced, up to, say, 1720 or 1730, were the raw materials which later someone else made into what we now would call literature.

DAVIS: I don't think there was a cultural lag, and neither does Carl Dolmetsch. I do agree with him about the comparison not only with Yorkshire but with Ireland, which was made over and over again. And some of those who came to Maryland were developing a real literature, as Leo Lemay's recent book points out.

SIMPSON: When you get into the eighteenth century, you come to that point where the idea of a commonwealth or republic of letters reaches its height. Consider a southerner like Thomas Jefferson—he was certainly a major citizen of the republic of letters, just as in the middle states Benjamin Franklin was.

DOLMETSCH: And William Byrd of Westover.

SIMPSON: So you begin to get in the colonies by that time a sense of relationship to a cosmopolitan order of letters that is stronger, of course, than it had been in the seventeenth century. I think you see it even in the Puritans. In the southern colonies it probably wasn't as strong, because they didn't have perhaps as coherent a literary and intellectual life as they had in New England.

DOLMETSCH: What I was simply trying to maintain was that if you compare the literature of Virginia in the seventeenth and eighteenth centuries with the literature of any province of England during the same period, it comes off well indeed, but if you compare it with the literature of London, it doesn't.

SIMPSON: The colonies, in other words, were not as provincial as some of the home provinces were.

LEARY: That's a very good point. But I wonder whether we're not a little off our subject. Perhaps the question I should have asked should have been this: In getting together the materials for your studies of literature in the colonial South, what did you feel you needed in scholarship which you didn't have? What, in short, did you need that wasn't there?

DAVIS: Everything. I had to be the spadework man, and the cultivator, and the fertilizer, and so on. That's the reason I'm very pessimistic about my result, but I hope the future will understand what I've done.

LEARY: What you will come up with is something which somebody twenty years younger than you will talk about along the lines of what you said this morning about Howard Jones's work on the seventeenth century.

DAVIS: Right. That's what I want them to say. We've been picking Perry Miller to pieces ever since his books came out and I think we will continue to do so. But I want to get this said. The chapter I'm working on right now, on "Books, Libraries, and Reading," and the chapter I've just done on education, have to do with southern literacy. I find every indication, including old Philip Alexander Bruce's years ago in the *Institutional History of Virginia in the 17th Century*—and he went to county records— that there was a higher literacy rate in the Chesapeake colonies than there was in New England.

LEARY: I'm going to ask this question of each of you. If you had a dozen good, bright graduate students, in what directions would you send them to do the kind of work which would make your work possible?

DAVIS: I would put them to editing primary documents first of all.

LEARY: Then one of the things that we decide about colonial southern literature is what was decided about American literature in general in the 1920s, that we need to do very much?

DAVIS: Yes.

LEARY: Carl Dolmetsch, I'd like to move into the eighteenth century and give the same kind of question to you.

DOLMETSCH: Well, I think first of all we need to know more than we do now about the state of literary knowledge. What could a writer, for example, in the eighteenth century depend upon as knowledge that a potential audience would bring to anything that he wrote? Last year one of my graduate students was editing for his M.A. thesis the St. George Tucker essay on patriotism, one of the better of the Old Bachelor essays, and he came across a quotation in the essay which he had to gloss. The context suggested that it might have come from George Washington or from Thomas Jefferson, or from someone else who was a contemporary or a near contemporary of Tucker's. So he went all through all the papers of George Washington, the speeches and writings of Thomas Jefferson and so on, without any avail, and then suddenly in the correspondence between William Wirt and Tucker he ran across Wirt telling Tucker a very cryptic remark, "Bolingbroke is more read in Virginia than you realize." This was the clue that sent him to Bolingbroke, and he found not only the quotation, but three-fourths of Tucker's essay, almost word for word. Now how much was he read, how much was Bolingbroke known in Virginia? Does this indicate why Wirt didn't publish the essay? Did this indicate something about the literary climate and atmosphere in Virginia at that particular moment, at the end of the eighteenth and beginning of the nineteenth century?

LEARY: In other words, we need to know more about what people were prepared to accept as literature?

DOLMETSCH: What was the literary climate, what were the tastes? We need to inventory, for example, as Richard Davis suggested this morning, every colonial southern library, to make a kind of census to find out whether there's truth in the assertion that such and such a writer was influential in the South.

LEARY: A good deal of what was written was predicated on what the writer recognized would be known, or recognized, by his readers.

DOLMETSCH: Well, if you believe, as I think we must pretty much do in this profession, that the greatest source of literature is literature, that follows.

DAVIS: The point that both Caroline Robbins and H. Trevor Colbourn make is that the source of the literature of ideas is history. I think that we have a parallel situation.

LEARY: What do you mean by "the literature of ideas is history"?

DAVIS: Both of them are talking about political matters, and Caroline Robbins, in *The Eighteenth-Century Commonwealthman*, deals with a group she called the "real Whigs,"—as opposed to just anyone who might have called himself a Whig in late seventeenth-century and early eighteenth-century England—or "Commonwealthmen," and what they read—Algernon Sidney and Molesworth, and Locke's "Two Treatises on Government," and so on. Colbourn picks this up. The title of his book is *The Lamp of Experience*, and you recognize the source there. The trouble with his book, as some of the reviews have shown, is he comes no farther south than Virginia, except for one little inventory of a South Carolina library. I wrote him that he could have found ten times as much proof of his thesis in the South as he found in the middle and northern colonies.

LEARY: We need something, then, like Thomas Goddard Wright's work on the New England libraries. Robert Bain, I wonder what you would contribute to what we're saying?

BAIN: I agree with Mr. Davis that we need to make available primary materials in easily accessible, well-edited editions. But I'd like to add a project that has interested me, and that is the collection of letters, many of them still in manuscript, that record the colonial experience in the South. As a number of people have pointed out, the letter was one of the primary means by which colonials made people in England familiar with and aware of their circumstances and their lives. That is perhaps why George Alsop printed those letters at the end of his *Character of the Province of Mary-Land*. The letter was a means of making others know. I suspect that there are hundreds of unpublished letters in all kinds of libraries up and down the eastern seaboard and in libraries in England. These letters could tell us a great deal about what the colonial experience was, what it meant to the men and women who lived it. With this kind of primary material available—and easily accessible—we should make better judgments about life and letters in the South. I also think that the letter is an important literary form; in the works of such men as Franklin and Byrd, for example, letter writing became an art. They are not the only practitioners, either. The letter is a literary form, it can have grace and style, it can possess all those qualities associated with literature.

LEARY: Am I wrong, however, in thinking that literature is something which is self-consciously produced? When a person is writing literature he is consciously writing literature. We have two different things here: there might be the natural expression of my letter to my mother, or to my wife, or something, which is filled with much experience. But isn't there a distinction between that, and something which I am writing because it is literature?

BAIN: I think you are defining the term "literature" too narrowly. Some letters deal with the kind of cheese I ate this morning, or may thank a sender for the package of cheese sent from England. But if a letter writer tells his friends in England about his experiences, he too has an audience in mind. Then letter writing becomes something more than information transmitted; it can be a consciously shaped world of words to give readers in England or elsewhere the writer's feelings and ideas about his experience. And such writing is as consciously done as that in Captain John Smith's *General History*, or at least parts of the *General History*.

DOLMETSCH: I think we again have to go back to the historical context. Just as Robert Bain suggested at the beginning of his statement, the letter could be a quite self-conscious literary production. Whether you were writing for an audience of one or an audience of a thousand, you took pains and care to make a literary composition of it in a way that you don't today, and that people haven't done now for I don't know how many generations.

If you look, for example, at the letters of William Byrd of West-over, you get a perfect illustration of this. In many instances—they're turning up now—there are several copies of a letter, from the rough draft in the letter book to the finished product which was sent and received. I've looked at some letters of Byrd's in the British Museum, and also at Harvard in the Orrery Papers. More recently some of the rough drafts have turned up in a new letter book that the Virginia Historical Society has just acquired. Byrd will write the same letter, in effect, to a half-a-dozen different English correspondents, varying it slightly for the particular person who is going to read it. He'll add a paragraph, put something else on here and there, but it's a literary composition, a literary production. Now granted that not all letters that Byrd writes, or that anybody else writes, are in that category. Some that he wrote were just business letters, very mundane things, but there are a good many letters of other kinds, and incidentally, to come back to the statement that libraries are full of this material, they're turning up all the time, in great numbers. The Byrd letters, for example—the Virginia Historical Society has gotten a huge batch of these.

DAVIS: I wrote an article for the 350th anniversary of James-town which I called "The Gentlest Art in 17th Century Virginia," which was about the letters. The earliest Virginia libraries had "secretaries," guides, in other words, the little manuals of letter books, and they used them. The letters were conscious art. Some were for business purposes, but most of them were not; they were rhetorical devices, or studies of rhetoric.

BAIN: Isn't that how Richardson began writing *Pamela*; he started to write a book about letter writing?

LEARY: I'm haunted, though, by the letters that I'm going to receive in the next month from Aunt Susannah and so on—the Christmas letters, which are completely worthless. What's the distinction? This letter writing in the seventeenth century and the early eighteenth century was a conscious literary art, but you say it came from guidebooks.

BAIN: No, that isn't what Carl Dolmetsch was saying. He was saying that there are letters from Aunt Mary and Aunt Sally about the cheese they sent last week. But other letters have purposes much different from that. Another purpose is to give the letter writer's sense of place, of time, of milieu, to someone who has never seen the new country and may never see it. The author of this kind of letter shapes his words and attitudes consciously so that he can convey his sense of life in the New World to that unknowing person. One purpose of such letters is to give the writer a chance to shape for himself in words the meaning of that experience.

SIMPSON: In the eighteenth century, letter writing was a primary means of communication. Consider the letters of Thomas Jefferson, in which he corresponds with the philosophes all over Europe. Letters were their major means of communication. They wrote letters and letters and letters, and of course many of those are simply to convey information about experiments or what not—they don't have anything particularly personal about them.

LEARY: That's right. I once made a statement in print that there were three kinds of literature which came from colonial America: literature *of* America, that is the professional tracts; literature *from* America, that is the letters and so on that you describe; and finally literature *in* America, literature which was written for the consumption of people in this country. It seems to me that comes very late.

DAVIS: What do you mean by "very late"?

LEARY: I would say about the 1720s and 1730s.

BAIN: There's evidence even earlier than that. At the beginning of the century when Beverley wrote his *History* (1705), both he and Cotton Mather, who published his *Magnalia* in 1702, were conscious of those English critics. Beverley and Mather were conscious of two audiences, one in America and one in England. This awareness, I think, creates some curious tensions for colonial American authors.

DAVIS: And as far as the southerner is concerned, since he

had no printing press, he was passing these things around by hand, in longhand.

DOLMETSCH: Let me give you one of the most cogent examples I know of. In the winter of 1728-29, after he came back from the Dividing Line expedition, Byrd wrote to John Percival, the Earl of Egmont, and Charles Boyle, the Earl of Orrery, and Sir Charles Wager, almost the same letter, an identical letter. He was full of this experience, and he writes about it glowingly, and he gets a letter back from the Earl of Egmont, saying (I can't remember the exact phrasing), "What a marvelous experience you've had, what a great benefactor you are to your country, and so on. . . . You should imitate Caesar and be your own historian." This I take to be the germ from which the *History of the Dividing Line* sprang. This was what I think gave Byrd the idea of putting flesh on the bones of his rude journal, which was an expense account book to begin with. The letter, in other words, was really very much at the heart of the literary world of the colonial South.

LEARY: I think we can all agree on that. We have the letters, we have Richard Davis's suggestion of the study of the relation of the Indian, we have the accounts of exploration. What else do we have?

DAVIS: Religious writing. There are two chapters on religion in my book. One was on organized religion in the South, which has really nothing directly to do with literature. The other was on the sermon and theological tract in the South, of which there were a great many more than are usually realized. As I said this morning, there are only two seventeenth-century sermons known from the South, but there are hundreds and hundreds of eighteenth-century ones, printed and in manuscript, which show us a great deal about the southern mind. Most of them are Anglican, but not all of them by any means.

LEARY: Are we going to indicate, as Babette Levy did and as Perry Miller did with the New England sermon, that there is a definite formula for the southern sermon—that it is an art form?

DAVIS: I have already indicated that. Perry Miller was absolutely wrong when he says, in the two articles that he did for the *William and Mary Quarterly* (included in *Errand into the Wilderness*), that the southern sermon followed a Donnesque style, or intimates something of that kind—that they didn't use the plain style. I found *one* ornate sermon from the eighteenth century extant in the South out of the hundreds I've read, which was not in the same plain style which Perry Miller outlines exactly in the first volume of *The New England Mind*.

LEARY: I'm glad to hear you say that, because I think one of the things that students of colonial literature must do is to rescue it from Harvard. Can we think of another form of literature that we should consider? Do we have many diaries?

SIMPSON: The study of diaries is certainly important. I think one great general need has to do with the whole question of the colonial origins of a self-conscious South. It's certainly no new question, but it's one that we need to keep coming back to. I've become more or less convinced that we never have understood slavery in the South, and that slavery in the colonial South in relation to the southern mind, or to the possible development of the southern mind, is a very important subject. In the diaries, perhaps, you can get, as in letters, possible primary sources. I'm not sure now how much the primacy of this theme will come to you directly. It may come through implications, possibly, but I think light is thrown on this to some extent by keeping in mind always that we can compare New England and the South. I've come to think more and more of New England as a kind of nation, and of the South as a kind of nation, and that both of these nations had certain redemptive qualities, or missions, in mind, not necessarily always directly. Of course, New England's origins as a spiritual nation are very definite—a people who were given or felt they had a mission given to them by God. I was in Boston last summer, and I was struck once again by what little is left of the tremendous coherence there once was in this group of people. It was apparent just from walking around the Boston Common, for example, and going over to the Park Street Church, where I embarrassed my wife by giving a lecture to a little girl who was a guide. The little girl was interested, and cute, but she didn't know much about what she was talking about. Here I was, from the South, telling her about the church, where I believe the first abolitionist sermon was preached. I was struck by the loss of coherence that had gone on. In the South, you see, you didn't really have that kind of coherence, but I've been intrigued with the idea that maybe there was more than we've recognized, and that out of the colonial South there did come the origins of the South that was to be finally defeated at Appomattox. That's one reason why I've been putting so much emphasis on slavery and the southern mind. The South really was a slave society, and it started being one very early in the game. William Byrd was not a bourgeois. He helped to found what was really not an old traditional order but a new kind of order, and this was a slave society. If you go along with Eugene Genovese in trying to distinguish between a slave society in what became the United States, and slave societies in the islands and in South America, you do come to the conclusion that there were important differences. The colonial South was developing into a more coherent world than we sometimes understand. Genovese goes so far as to say that the Revolution in the South liberated a slave empire, or slave kingdom.

LEARY: I very much like your point about the cohesion of New England as opposed to something that you think is perhaps more cohesive than it would seem, but in the South we had four or five pockets of cultural activity, and the interchange, the communication between them was very, very little.

DAVIS: This is one place where I agree with Carl Bridenbaugh, which I usually never do. The Chesapeake society is there, and the Charleston society, to which Georgia attaches itself more or less up to the end of my period at any rate. Then Bridenbaugh identifies a Piedmont society—I would just make it North Carolina, which is different from the two farther South states and from the two Chesapeake states. I think you've got those three.

LEARY: And was there the same kind of communication

among those pockets of culture as there was between, say, Hartford and Boston?

DAVIS: Yes.

BAIN: And by the middle of the eighteenth century, you have the history of the theater in the South, a history that shows common cultural bonds. And when the Southwest (Alabama and Mississippi) began to be settled, theatrical companies toured such places as Columbus, Georgia, and Mobile and Montgomery, Alabama.

DAVIS: This takes place from Savannah right on up into the Chesapeake Bay to Upper Marlboro, Maryland.

BAIN: In addition, colonial newspapers copied from one another as well as from English journals and papers, so that in those towns with newspapers, information about events in other colonies was fairly common knowledge. This was true before the American Revolution.

LEARY: It's always seemed to me that we need to do more of the kind of thing that William Charvat did for the later period. What about the publication of books in the South? How many books were published, and where were they distributed? I've done a little work on it, and my results seem to suggest that a book would usually be published in about five hundred copies.

DAVIS: Even in the 1780s, there would still be five hundred copies published, probably. That's what was usual, apparently in all the five major colony presses up and down the coast, when they did publish a book.

DOLMETSCH: We were talking earlier about the Indian treaties and their place in the development of southern rhetoric and of American style. It's been asserted, in a very provocative speech that Edwin Wolf gave about a year ago, that the real origins of what we think of as distinctive in American literary style, as opposed to English style, in the colonial period and thereafter, can be traced to these Indian treaties. This is why I was asking about the language in them, and whether there were any differences between northern and southern speeches in the beginning, or whether that comes later on.

DAVIS: I don't think we're ready to answer that question as yet. For example, as I asked this morning, does the Indian style change from the conversation between Powhatan and Captain John Smith, to those last dialogues of 1763? It does, and it shows Ossian-like qualities even before Macpherson's poem. It gets more Biblical as it goes on. The King James Bible, or the Geneva Bible, or the Bishops' Bible, might have been used as a basis for some of the indirect discourses in Captain John Smith—if they are indirect. The style becomes more and more Biblical in imagery as time goes on, and yet there is the constant presence of the animal and nature images all the way through this period.

LEARY: And yet you want to look at the intention of the translator.

DAVIS: I would want to look at the intention of the translator, his degree of education, and a number of other things. I'm sure that James Adair is a remarkable example. His book, which he calls *The History of the American Indians*, but is actually on the southern Indians, particularly the Choctaws and that group, gives some very different selections from some of the earlier books. This may not be the time to introduce this, but no one has said anything about legislative oratory, and only incidentally, the executive oratory. It was an important enough thing in its time for Benjamin Franklin to parody Governor Gooch's Speech to the House of Burgesses in the Capitol.

LEARY: Do we have records of that, available for study?

DAVIS: Yes. There are lots of those in every colony.

LEARY: Lewis Simpson, you were going to say something about the Indian business?

SIMPSON: One of the topics suggested for research was "The Image of the Indian in Early Southern Writing." It occurred to me we should also have "The Image of the Slave, or of the Negro, in Early Southern Writing" as a possible topic. I feel more and more that slavery is probably the real *key* to the South, and that in spite of what you say is true—that the South had a great diversity of people and cultures even—the real coherence that the South eventually attained was as a slave society. I think that, in spite of the fact that the South in colonial times was diverse and that it continued to be diverse, the plantation myth and the plantation image became the prestige symbol of the South, and also the operative symbol of the South. Thus the image of the slave, if we can discover it in the early colonial writings, directly or by implication, is I think a very important subject. The image of the Indian is also important. Did any Indians own slaves in colonial times?

DAVIS: Yes. Especially in South Carolina and North Carolina.

SIMPSON: I know they did in Mississippi later on. In connection with my remark about there having been a New England coherence, and about searching for some principle of coherence which could account for the development of the South into the nation which fought the Civil War, I haven't found any real coherence like that which you can trace in New England, but insofar as I can find it existing, it seems to relate primarily to slavery, and the conception the South came to have of itself as a redemptive slave society. You come down to the point where Henry Timrod writes his poem "Ethnogenesis": here is the South, a slave society that is going to redeem the world. This is the kind of glowing vision that Timrod had at the beginning of the Civil War. I think that it may go back to colonial times. It's not just something you begin to pick up in the 1820s.

DAVIS: I might say that the whole point that Colbourn and Robbins are making would fit in with that beautifully. What they're suggesting is that the southerner read so many of these English liberals, and that he read Bolingbroke. The southern libraries had the works of ten liberals and two or three conservatives—later they had Hume and Bolingbroke, and they had Hobbes from the beginning. But then there was a middle group of thinkers who could be interpreted either way, and the southerner tried to interpret them as representing a constitutional government, a representative government. Then we have this whole group of genuine liberals, as both Caroline Robbins and Colbourn point out. Now that could have been combined with their belief in slavery into your idea of a redemptive vision.

SIMPSON: I don't think it's at all a matter of logic in a strict sense, but of implication and association. How did Thomas Jefferson, who was in some ways opposed to slavery, actually justify it, since he owned slaves all his life? Maybe he freed one or two, I don't remember.

DAVIS: He just couldn't afford to free his slaves.

SIMPSON: But there were southerners who were opposed to slavery and in favor of colonization, like Jefferson, perhaps, but who certainly were not really abolitionists at all—they didn't conceive of the possibility of abolition. However you look at it, slavery was central in those portions of the South in which it appeared in strongest form. But also, I think, it tended to be central even in portions of the South in which there was little slavery.

LEARY: Carl Dolmetsch, isn't it true that St. George Tucker wrote one of the first essays against slavery?

DOLMETSCH: Yes. I think the first in the South. I'm not absolutely sure of that, but I believe in 1796.

LEARY: It was very different from the New England attitude, I suspect.

DOLMETSCH: Yes. He appended to his codification of the statutes of Virginia a dissertation advocating the abolition of chattel slavery in Virginia. He didn't say throughout the South, or in America, or any place else but in Virginia.

LEARY: Was it on humanitarian or economic grounds?

DOLMETSCH: It was on humanitarian grounds. He wrote another essay on slavery, which is now being edited by one of my students, for the Old Bachelor papers, advocating its abolition, and indicating that although it is true that mistreatment of slaves under slavery is an abuse of the institution, rather than endemic to the institution itself, the institution itself, because it lends itself to abuse, should be abolished. This is a very interesting argument, and as far as I know it was the first time anybody in the South put forth that argument. That was in 1811.

SIMPSON: He was an out-and-out abolitionist, not a colonizationist.

DOLMETSCH: What has always intrigued me is what happened in the generation between St. George and Beverley Tucker, father and son. In 1835 Beverley Tucker was already taking the defensive redemptive view.

SIMPSON: That was the combination you had in Virginia in the last debates on slavery, in 1830-31, right before the nullification crisis. These were the last open debates on slavery. I don't know the answers to any of these questions. But I think that in the study of southern literature—not by the historians so much, but by the literary historians—we have tended to neglect slavery, and have tended to follow the view expressed by Allen Tate, that the South was a traditionalist culture on the European model. I don't think that's really true. The South was not a feudal culture, but was more nearly something different from anything else: it was historically unique, and in trying to understand the southern mind, and southern literature, we need to understand more about slavery in relationship to the South in order to understand more about southern literature.

LEARY: In the few minutes we have left, we might address ourselves to the question of who are the colonial American writers who most need investigation now.

DAVIS: Number One is Dr. Alexander Hamilton of Annapolis. I've read every word of that material myself, in all three places: part of it in the Maryland Historical Society, part of it at Johns Hopkins, part in the Library of Congress—and he is *good*. He will rival William Byrd.

LEARY: Who's your candidate, Carl Dolmetsch?

DOLMETSCH: There are several: all Virginians, as you might expect: John Mercer, Benjamin Waller, Robert Bolling of Chellowe, and of course St. George Tucker. I hope before too many years pass we will be able to get everything of Tucker's work before the public. But after that there's got to be work done on him.

LEARY: Somebody suggested that we need a good book on the Virginia Wits—the Mumfords and the Tuckers, William Wirt, and so forth, something comparable to the Connecticut Wits.

DAVIS: There was an Annapolis group, the Tuesday Club, of which Dr. Hamilton was the principal one. Leo Lemay has the feeling, and I do too, that there was a comparable group in Williamsburg. There was one in Charleston—the Meddlers Club.

LEARY: It seems to me what we're coming to is the recognition that literature in the colonial South, literature as it's recognized by most people today, begins about in the 1730s. I mean a belletristic, conscious literature, written deliberately to be read for enjoyment.

DAVIS: If we say that, we say it because we know it was printed then. There may have been a lot written before that which was simply passed about in manuscript.

DOLMETSCH: It was only because the first presses were in Annapolis and Williamsburg and so on that we can say this. One of the suggestions is that we try to get a collection of southern colonial newspaper verse. We have the impression that there was so much more verse written in the South in the eighteenth century than there might have been in the seventeenth century because it got printed in the newspapers, and most of it is still there in those newspapers. It's awfully difficult for the student to get at, because it's scattered through these periodicals and newspapers. If somebody could bring that together in a comprehensive collection, how good it would be to have. Leo Lemay has given us a census, up to 1765, and he plans to continue it up to 1800, but what a blessing it is just to have the census. Now if somebody will put a graduate student to work to go in and collect it, assemble it.

BAIN: There are other belletristic pieces, too. The Meddler and Monitor essays and others need to be collected.

LEARY: Dick, I was rather surprised this morning by what you said about Kenneth Silverman's collection of colonial verse.

DAVIS: He makes two important mistakes. He says, in the first place, that there was no elegiac tradition in the South, and there definitely was one. I've got a dissertation to prove the quantitative size of it. But it is an entirely different kind of elegy from what New England was producing. It's a secular elegy. Even when a good Presbyterian like Samuel Davies, who was as close as we came to a New Englander in the South, was asked to write an epitaph for a lady's tombstone, he wrote three, and he mentions God—and just God, no Trinity, no Christ—in only one of the three. You can go through a hundred of these elegies and not find any mention of Christianity in any of them, but you'll find Apollo and Damoetas or Theocritus and so on, the pastoral tradition. The Renaissance pastoral tradition is what the southern elegy produces.

LEARY: There are two people that concern me; one is William Byrd and the other is William Wirt. How are we going to get a good study of either of those men?

DAVIS: Carl Dolmetsch and I have discussed the Byrd situation, and of course Joseph Robert has been working with Wirt for years.

DOLMETSCH: In the case of William Byrd of Westover, it's like describing an iceberg, because every time you think you've got enough of his work to go ahead, more is discovered. I've been working on Byrd for the Twayne series for about ten years, off and on. I'm embarrassed that I haven't finished, and part of the reason that I haven't is that every time I get ready to sit down and write the final chapters of the thing, something else of Byrd's turns up. There is the *Commonplace Book*, which we now have. In the last three months the Virginia Historical Society has acquired a whole section that was omitted from the Westover Manuscripts, including apparently a fascicle of that folio of the Westover Manuscripts that was just wrenched out at some point along the way, with a fair copy in it of the "Female Creed," the satire on women, and a thirty-three-page essay on religion which Byrd wrote, which nobody ever knew about before, and which changed the whole picture of William Byrd. Plus 39 manuscript holograph letters of Byrd's. Thirty-three of them are the originals of letters that were in the Huntington Library in Miss Nicholas's bowdlerized nineteenth-century transcripts, which proves that Louis Wright was exactly correct in holding up his edition of letters which he had ready to go years ago, and in saying, "I'm not going to do it because the originals of these bowdlerized things will turn up and I'll be embarrassed." And he would have been. Then there are six letters, in addition to that, which haven't been seen before. And there's more to come. What we have, I am convinced, of Byrd's writing is only a fraction. You know what James Kirke Paulding wrote in the early nineteenth century about his visit to Westover, and the large trunk of manuscripts he saw there? They were scattered, obviously, and maybe at last they're going to come home.

LEARY: Am I correct, then, in thinking that three major desiderata would be a definitive study of Hamilton, of Byrd, and of Wirt, as three colonial writers?

DOLMETSCH: May I add St. George Tucker to that list?

LEARY: I would be happy to have St. George Tucker added. He's in a somewhat different tradition. It seems to me he's in the Francis Hopkinson, Washington Irving, or Oliver Wendell Holmes tradition, on the outskirts of literature. William Wirt bothers me more than any of the rest, because he's so very important and he's been handled so badly, right from Simms on down. Robert Bain, is there anything you want to give us in peroration?

BAIN: I'd like to return to Richard Davis's point about style. There is much work to be done on style, and not just sermon styles, but style generally. Our assumptions about a southern prose style or styles need to be reexamined once we have sufficient primary material available. Maybe we also need some better criteria for looking at style. Something happens to southern prose style. I don't know when it happens, but something happens at the end of the eighteenth century or the beginning of the nineteenth to change the shape of what seems to me to have been the principal literary style of earlier southern authors.

DAVIS: That is, it emerges then, it's become obvious then. I think one of the men you mentioned, Carl, John Mercer, is one of the people who leads to this, and he has barely come above the surface. We're just beginning to know who he is.

LEARY: Do you feel, Dick, that we
well in hand, that Philip L. Barbour has

DAVIS: Yes. You know he's editing th

LEARY: I'm looking forward to it. How
that be?

DOLMETSCH: Five or six, easily.

DAVIS: And he's just been back to Hungary,
and has cleaned up the last of the things he was
Smith describes in the *True Travels*.

BAIN: Will the *Sea Grammar* be part of that ε

DOLMETSCH: Everything, the complete works, eι
Institute of Early American History and Culture.

LEARY: Our time is almost up. Lewis Simpson, can
us a final word, as benediction?

SIMPSON: I don't know whether it's a benediction or nc
would suggest to students of southern literature, in spite
desirability of studying much more intensely the people ν
been mentioning, that we not fail to continue to study intensiν
Thomas Jefferson. I suspect he's one of the really great litera
figures of the Western world, and a profoundly literary mind.
think as students of literature we ought to study Jefferson from the
literary point of view.

LEARY: Would it be possible to write a literary life of Thomas
Jefferson?

SIMPSON: I think probably it would be. Somebody might well
present him in something like his full dimension as a literary
figure.

LEARY: Jefferson and Franklin are so difficult, aren't they?

SIMPSON: Very difficult, and very, very important. The
whole question of Jefferson as the slaveowner and master, as one
of the really great philosophes of the eighteenth century, the
drama of Jefferson's life, is fascinating. I got on to the idea in an
essay I contributed recently to a book on cultural nationalism
edited by H. Ernest Lewald, called *The Cry of Home*. The essay
was called "Southern Spiritual Nationalism." I was comparing

of the queries in *Notes on the State of Virginia*. There is one which Jefferson gives a terribly pessimistic view of slavery. But after that comes a beautiful vision of the yeoman American. There's a drama there that's very intriguing. Jefferson had a very dramatic imagination.

LEARY: I have a strong feeling that we need to know more than we do know about literary Charleston. There have been two or three books on it, but none of them seems to satisfy, and my small knowledge reveals things that are not in the books.

SIMPSON: We don't really know much about the various places that were something like literary centers.

LEARY: What were the literary centers in the colonial South?

DAVIS: Charleston, first of all; Wilmington, North Carolina—I'm finding that so many libraries existed in and around Wilmington. And of course the others—Annapolis, Williamsburg, and so on.

LEARY: There was a little literary club in Wilmington that corresponded with Laurence Sterne.

SIMPSON: The South was far more literate than we presume it to have been. We think of New England as being about 100 percent literate, but there was far more literacy in the South, so that the kind of culture in which Thomas Jefferson becomes one of the peaks was really a culture which had a good deal of literacy in it.

LEARY: It depends on what is meant by literacy. According to the 1790 census there were four million people in the United States. We can assume that so many percent of them were black, and so many were illiterate, and in the 1790s we had an eight-year interference of education during the Revolution. So you can't make an absolute judgment, but there couldn't have been more than two million people in the United States in 1790 who were willing to write or read literature. I should think that with the proportion of the slave population in the South larger than in the North, there may have been more, numerically more, literate readers in New England than in the South.

SIMPSON: New England was a highly literate world, and of

course I don't mean to say that the South had that kind of literacy. In fact, I would argue just the reverse, in a sense, and say that illiteracy was a very important literary factor in the South, and that's been true all the way along.

LEARY: That's something we can't get, isn't it? It's very hard to get the folk tradition, what stories the illiterate people were telling.

DAVIS: The chapter I've finished on education will show that we had the schools in the South. We had far more schools than anybody has ever known, all through the colonial period.

BAIN: I have been looking at indenture records, which indicate that many indentured servants who came to the colonies in the seventeenth century could read and write.

DOLMETSCH: Many of them served as schoolmasters. If you take the publication of poetry as an index of literacy and culture, then I think this would bear out, Lewis Simpson, your feeling about the literacy in the South. If you look at Leo Lemay's calendar of verse in colonial newspapers, after the establishment of the southern newspapers—the *South Carolina Gazette*, the *Virginia Gazette*, and so on—you find there was far more verse published in the South than in the North. New England and the northern colonies, of course, had the edge earlier on, but they had printing, which we didn't in the South. But after you get a kind of parity in printing, then there's far more Augustan verse in the South than there is in the North.

DAVIS: Philip Alexander Bruce compares southern literacy with rural England's literacy, and discovers that the South compares very well.

LEARY: I think it is perhaps appropriate that, with that note on literacy, we close.

6. Nineteenth-Century Southern Literature

MODERATOR:

Hugh Holman

PANELISTS:

*Philip Butcher, Richard Calhoun,
Charles Davis, Jack Guilds, Thomas Inge,
Robert Jacobs, Rayburn Moore, Charles Ray,
George Tindall, Arlin Turner*

HOLMAN: As far as southern writing is concerned, we can define the nineteenth century as beginning about 1820 and lasting through the first decade of the twentieth century. Although there are a number of literary figures in the background all during this time, relatively few prominent figures are in the foreground, and most of the attention that has been devoted to nineteenth-century southern writing has been to this relatively small group. Would it be proper for us here, considering the large amount of work that's been done on him, to decide not to discuss Poe? Is that agreeable with everybody?

DAVIS: I would object to the exclusion of Poe, because I think he is terribly important in understanding one of the basic problems that we have in southern literature of the nineteenth century, an imagined distance between that literature and the rest of the literature in America. Poe exemplifies a form of alienation, a deep sense of rejection, that provides a classic pattern for other writers whom we have later on in the nineteenth century. Actually, the tradition which has developed in southern writing does not become really integrated into the general American tradition until the end of the nineteenth century in America. I wish to yield to

Robert Jacobs for an opinion on this subject, which he knows a great deal more about than I do.

JACOBS: I agree with your comment, and disagree at the same time, which establishes a paradox that I'll try to explain. I agree that Poe sets up the pattern of the alienated artist, and one perhaps peculiar to southern literature, although by no means confined to southern literature. But this pattern of alienation exists both in Poe's personality and in his work. I'm interested in further study of Poe's taste, because in many ways his taste—the things he liked in art, in music, in landscape architecture, and so forth—is quite representative of the taste of his times, and so a good bit could be done about Poe's taste as representative of the taste of not merely the southern culture, but of American culture of his time.

DAVIS: I have one comment on that point. The adjective I used was "imagined," and I could not agree with Robert Jacobs more when he says that Poe shares much with the other intellectuals and artists in America, and I've been enormously impressed by how much he does possess of the common culture of America. At the same time, he felt his alienation more deeply than did other writers of the time. His neuroticism contributed a good deal perhaps, but I think the alienation itself is in part a southern phenomenon.

CALHOUN: Poe has to be included, at least for the purposes of comparison and contrast. If we're going to talk about criticism, Poe has to be there. If we're going to talk about poetry, Poe has to be there. If we talk about periodicals and editing magazines, Poe has to be there. And finally Poe has to be there as a major writer for comparison and contrast with minor writers. We have to see what the differences are in these cases.

MOORE: Poe's influence on other writers, especially minor writers like Hayne, for example, surely oughtn't to be overlooked here.

GUILDS: Arlin Turner commented this morning about the importance of letter writers of the South as a means of understanding the Old South, and made a point of the value of the Simms letters in this connection. I would wholeheartedly agree that I don't know of a better way to come to understand the whole social environment of the South than to read those letters. But the Poe letters are also very important in this regard. If a southern writer is a writer whose formative years were spent in the South, this fits Poe, and his letters reveal that he is a southerner better than his essays, poems, and tales do. As a matter of fact, I've often wondered why we don't make more ado about the literary letters of America. We don't have any writer who is known primarily for his letter writing. But I think this is one of Simms's major contributions to our literature. If someone made a study of the literary letters of the Old South, including Poe's, we would have a very significant document that would open all sorts of doors.

RAY: Speaking of the Americanism and regionalism of Poe, I think that some of the students of recent Baudelaire criticism may feel that the parallels between Poe and Baudelaire are so significant that Poe may be viewed much more as a force in his time rather than simply in the American scene.

BUTCHER: It's been mentioned that he has a sense of alienation, and it occurs to me that the alienation may be related to the "minority mentality"—a sense of representing a tradition or a set of values contrary to those held by a dominant group. I think Poe's feeling in regard to the publishing weight of New England might be one sort of expression of this minority mentality. He has a sense of obligation to defend a set of values which are not quite those prevailing in the more dominant literary culture.

DAVIS: Nothing demonstrates the sense of that minority mentality better than the example that Charles Ray has presented. It's perfectly true that Poe had a tremendous impact upon the dominant French poetic tradition of the nineteenth century; not only Baudelaire, but Mallarmé and Valéry as well, responded very deeply and centrally to Poe's achievement as a poet and a critic. But the fact is that when we look at the response of a major modern poet, that is to say T. S. Eliot in that remarkable little document called *From Poe to Valéry*, he is at a loss to explain the reason for the respect for Poe. He cannot really understand how a poet of Poe's limitations could have an impact upon Baudelaire, perhaps the most important poet of the nineteenth century. Once again it's a matter not simply of an estimate which is accurate or valuable—it's a matter, I suspect, of inherited prejudices serving to warp the approach to a writer like Poe. Eliot does not understand the cultural situation of the nineteenth century.

HOLMAN : The relation of Poe to Baudelaire underscores Poe's fundamental sense of alienation, because it is this that fascinates Baudelaire when he begins writing about Poe : the extent to which Poe is outside his culture and rejected by his culture. Perhaps in the case of Mr. Eliot the reverse had happened; instead of being excluded by his culture he had rejected it, and hence he didn't quite understand the feeling which was present in Poe. I would like to ask Jack Guilds if he feels that we really need to do the letters of Poe over.

GUILDS: Oh, no. I think John Ward Ostrom did a good job, and I'm not prepared to say how many letters may have since turned up. What I'm saying is that I don't believe that the letter writers of the South have ever been put into the context of the literary history of the South, and I think that this is a major topic that someone should be encouraged to undertake.

JACOBS: One thing we can find from Poe's letters, in contrast, say, to those of Philip Pendleton Cooke, is that Poe felt alienated partly because he was one of the very few writers in the South who felt himself to be a professional, and in his letters this role is apparent. When you read Philip Pendleton Cooke's statement that he sat down and wrote with the reluctance of a turkey-hunter being kept from his sport, you see the difference between the amateur spirit which prevailed in southern writing and Poe's professional spirit. Poe knew he was a professional; Philip Pendleton Cooke did not think of himself so.

MOORE: I'd like to support the view with another reference to Hayne. Like Poe, Hayne strove to be a professional man of letters despite the difficulties in his way, but, unlike Poe's, his letters have never been completely published. The edition that came out in 1944, though still useful, has never been really adequate because it could not include the letters at Duke University. Those letters have not been edited but when they are published, they'll give us a much better idea of Hayne than we have now.

INGE: I think that Poe's importance as a world writer, or as an American writer, is not open to question, but perhaps his importance as a southern writer is. I'm not sure to what degree we've ever fully defined his southernness or the southern qualities in his work. Perhaps what we need is more work on Poe's milieu, and it might be that in examining more thoroughly the environment in which he lived in the South as well as in other parts of the country, we might learn more about him. If we're going to talk about his taste, we need to know what there was in his environment to respond to. Perhaps this would be a fruitful line for Poe research—not on him directly but on the milieu in which he lived. Just as we have plenty of studies of Faulkner, I think, but we don't have enough good studies of Faulkner which depend on the total context in which he lived.

TINDALL: I'm reminded of a story that James Patton, a former director of the Southern Historical Collection here, told. He said it used to be at the University of Virginia in the English Department that when you wanted to inquire what research a graduate student was engaged in you asked him, "What phase of Poe are *you* working on?"

GUILDS: I think what we've concluded is that maybe Poe as an individual doesn't need to be studied in greater detail, but that Poe as a part of this whole culture of southern literature does. I feel he is a part, and I think he does throw very significant light on it, and it would be difficult to study if he were excluded.

CALHOUN: May I bring up a question about the other major figures of this period? During this conference do we need to consider Mark Twain as a southern writer, or can we exclude him? Certainly there are southern elements and if the most significant book on Mark Twain in the last two or three years is on Mark Twain and John Bull, certainly something could be said for Mark Twain as a southern writer and Mark Twain in the South. There is a sense of the southern community in Mark Twain; there's an influence of southern Calvinism on Mark Twain, and, of course, the influence of humor, southwestern and southern humor. But do we need to consider him during this conference, or has enough been said?

HOLMAN: Louis Rubin and I debated the question of whether Mark Twain was a southerner or not last Christmas at the MLA meeting—I was maintaining that Mark Twain was not, and he was maintaining that he was. For the purposes of this conference, however, I will say that Mark Twain is in bounds and, if you want to play that ball, it's there to be played.

DAVIS: I think that Mark Twain has to be in bounds. Richard Calhoun has presented some very cogent arguments there and he's just touched on them; there are more. You find in Mark Twain an obviously complicated reaction to the racial situation, to the presence of the blacks in our society. We learn much about the position of blacks in the southern system, and this is a strong reason to consider him as a southerner. What we know in terms of Mark Twain's reading and his background seems in some ways typically southern. I have in mind the kind of eighteenth-century reading that he presumably came in contact with, if we can believe some of the critics who write about Mark Twain. The difficulty we have with a writer like Mark Twain—and we have it with Poe, too—is that he is not *only* a southern writer—he is something else, as well. He has a universal dimension which makes it difficult for us to define him in any smaller way, but southern I think he originally is, as Mr. Eliot, for example, is decidedly American, not simply because he was born in St. Louis, but because he received his early conditioning in America.

TURNER: I'd like to endorse what Charles Davis has just said very strongly, especially with reference to the matter of race in Mark Twain. We have testimony from many sources that Mark

Twain was complex, a real puzzle, but interestingly we've dealt with him as if he were very simple and straightforward and direct all of his life on the question of slavery and race, when actually he was far from that.

MOORE: A good starting place would be Arlin Turner's *Southern Review* article on Mark Twain in this regard—"Mark Twain and the South: An Affair of Love and Anger."

RAY: Of course Mark Twain and Poe, both products of the South originally, had opportunities to live in other parts of the country, and it seems to me that one should take into account some of their literary relationships, for example, that of Mark Twain and Joel Chandler Harris. The popular view of Harris is that he was probably very often a propagandist for the New South and simply spouted what may be called the "southern line." I think, however, that if one goes both into the Uncle Remus stories deeply and into some of Harris's short stories one will find that Harris was a very complex man. That point is that these writers all, at different times in their careers, display racial points of view that aren't always consistent. This ties in to what I understood Arlin Turner to be saying earlier about not only the diversity of the South but also the diversity of the attitudes of the representatives of the South, to such an extent that often we have to ask "what *is* a southern attitude?" And certainly that isn't a simple question to answer in the 1970s.

DAVIS: If we want to determine the southern quality in Twain we should perhaps compare him with another major writer who is not southern on problems having to do with race. I think that there are significant differences if we compare him, say, with Melville. Melville made very shrewd use of black characters, largely, however, for symbolic significance. We have black characters ranging all the way from Pip in *Moby-Dick* to Babo in *Benito Cereno*, and somewhere in between Black Guinea in *The Confidence Man*. Melville has symbolic reasons; he has thought in terms of the structure of his novel. But in Mark Twain we have something a little different. We have the attempt, at least, in

Pudd'nhead Wilson and other works of that kind to deal with problems of consciousness. And Mark Twain can do so because he has come from the kind of experience that has exposed him to the questions of consciousness, involving relationships with blacks and, indeed, in blacks themselves. I suppose there is a possible problem of consciousness in some ways for any white southerner who was born and brought up in the early nineteenth century, and it's one which Mark Twain faced and tried to resolve. I think that he has characteristics and qualities of a southern writer in this regard.

HOLMAN: I wonder, since we have moved from Mark Twain into the issue of race, if those of you who were present last evening and heard Lewis Simpson discussing the nature of the antebellum southern experience, essentially in the terms of the Marxist historian Genovese, found anything in that which set your mind working in different directions from the directions in which we have been traditionally thinking about the plantation system and things of that kind.

DAVIS: One of the problems, of course, that intrigued me about Lewis Simpson's paper, and one that has to do with much scholarship on the plantation system, and on slavery in general, is the discovery of the fact that the plantation system was a good deal more complicated than U. B. Phillips presented it as being. It's the whole notion of there being a black community functioning in the South. Genovese does suggest that this possibility exists, that there was a network of communication, an acceptance of general symbols, of the sort that existed in these communities, that we don't find presented to us earlier by representations of the southern plantation system. One of the reasons, of course, that we have been denied knowledge of this kind is that we have rejected as historical evidence—and both Lewis Simpson and Louis Rubin talked about this—certain materials that we do now accept as being evidence. I'm thinking of the antislavery narratives, which Mr. Phillips did not accept.

HOLMAN: I wonder if we are not reasonably well agreed that

the very useful concept of the plantation tradition as it was defined in the early 1920s by Francis Pendleton Gaines is now an important tradition for serious reexamination on a larger scale in terms of the implication it has for the literary works that appear in it. Certainly almost everything, it seems to me, that we see about this tradition in literary history represents an extremely simplified view of what the whole structure of antebellum southern life was.

JACOBS: I am engaged right now in compiling materials for a magazine issue that will deal with the subject of the sources of terror for the American imagination. Now when one thinks of the terror tale in one form or another, existing, say, in Poe—it exists in Faulkner—it seems to be not an exclusive thing for the South, yet to be more present in southern fiction than in fiction from elsewhere. And the suggestion, of course, is that this terror was always present, that with the plantation life you have what we call superstitions. The other thing is you always had the danger of the slave revolt. And so terror becomes a part of the southern experience that I don't think has been adequately explored.

DAVIS: That is a topic that deeply interests me. I suppose one person who's talked a little bit about it is Leslie Fiedler in that extraordinary work of his, *Love and Death in the American Novel*. The point I remember especially from Fiedler is the comment he makes on *The Narrative of Arthur Gordon Pym*, having to do with the natives of the island of Tsalal—you recall that they were all black, down (or up) to the teeth. What Fiedler is saying there is that that terror was not simply the terror that emanated from Poe's soul, though Poe maintained that it did, but that this is a terror, as Robert Jacobs has suggested, that comes out of the social system in which Poe functioned. The natives of Tsalal were also the black slaves in Virginia who periodically threatened to revolt.

BUTCHER: To go back to Hugh Holman's comment, there is a need for revising our judgments about some of the monuments that have developed for the study of southern literature. The Gaines volume on the southern plantation, for example, makes judgments that were extremely useful for its time but that may now require a second look. From that volume one gets the sense that in *Swallow Barn* J. P. Kennedy offered only one kind of representation of the southern plantation. On looking at Kennedy's volume, however, it is clear that he has criticisms of that social institution as well as very flowery praise for it, and if we're not careful we resort to easy generalizations and conceive of Gaines as meaning exactly one thing, and Kennedy one thing, and we now might well go back and look at these works again.

RAY: One of the things I presume this conference is trying to accomplish is the correction of some views, and I would suggest that one of the reasons for a great deal of the misunderstanding on both sides of the color line and perhaps more on the white side is that too many whites have read too few black volumes, and I refer specifically to the *Autobiography* of Frederick Douglass. If we want to get a picture of the plantation, in the perspective of one of the most representative black men of the nineteenth century, I suggest that we read carefully the *Autobiography* of Frederick Douglass.

BUTCHER: In that same connection, I think what might well be done too is to extend the study of Douglass into his full career. We've given a good deal of attention, in reprints and in reading lists, to the two early Douglass autobiographies, without sometimes looking at the torments of the later years and the complications of his political and public career in his last years. The full story might be an even more rewarding one than simply the account of his earlier years, as useful as that is.

GUILDS: Somewhat in the same vein, I believe I mentioned earlier Mary Chesnutt's *A Diary from Dixie*. If you read this in its entirety, you do find many comments from the point of view of a genteel white which are highly critical of the slave system of the South. This is one of the reasons why we need to look at these diaries and letters.

HOLMAN: Before we leave Frederick Douglass, I might mention that Patsy Perry completed here last year a dissertation on

Frederick Douglass as an editor and publisher, which, I believe, contributes a dimension to the view of Douglass that I'm sure people deeply involved in the study of Douglass are fully aware of, but that the average person has not been. The dissertation examined what he did in the various journals that he published, not only what he wrote but what he published, how he managed to finance them, and various things of this sort. It is fascinating material.

DAVIS: I wish I knew rather more about that than I do, but it seems to me that it is very interesting to make a comparison of the reaction of Douglass to the Gilded Age, of a black man who was well equipped to be a sensitive and responsible leader, with that of a man like Henry Adams, who stood poised at the beginning of the Grant administration for some post having the significance appropriate for an Adams. Douglass, in a sense, had that kind of experience, and the frustration of his expectation should make for a very interesting story indeed.

CALHOUN: To come back to a point made about Poe and Mark Twain as major writers, were we implying that a nineteenth-century southern American writer would have to be something other than just a southern writer to be a major writer? Are we suggesting that perhaps there are tensions, a dichotomy, in their view of the South, a kind of dialectics, in these two writers, which make them major writers, and is this evident in other southern writers in the nineteenth century? Louis Rubin said last night we should go to the edges of southern literature in order to find out about the South, and we did have a few suggestions here of something other than a plantation mythology in nineteenth-century southern literature. Can we explore that further?—these tensions or dichotomies in the South as revealed in nineteenth-century southern literature.

HOLMAN: We would probably all agree that a great writer always transcends his region and is more than a voice of his region, and probably that a great writer is always in some way or other in an antagonistic posture toward the world around him.

We don't find great writers who are comfortable and at home in their environment, and one of the things that happened to the antebellum southern writers, the men of talent—some of them men of almost startling talent, when you look at individual things they did—was that they were at home and had at least ostensibly accepted, or thought that they had accepted, the terms of life in the region that they lived in. Therefore the kind of healthy and natural tension and antagonism which should have released that talent and challenged it simply didn't take place. A writer I'm thinking about particularly is William Gilmore Simms. The longer Simms lived the more he became a part of his region and the less willing he was to exert a truly critical faculty upon it, at least in his public utterances and I suspect in his private feelings. But, Jack Guilds, you probably don't agree with me.

GUILDS: No, I believe I do agree with you there, because you do find Simms uttering some criticisms of the South in some of his earlier work. I'm thinking of—I don't know if you would interpret it in the same way I would—*Caloya: or, The Loves of the Driver*, which I think can be read as perhaps one of the pioneering works in race relations in American literature. In this story he's dealing with the black, the Indian, and the white, and he certainly wouldn't have thought of raising such an issue any time after 1850. So I think he learned what he could do. Maybe a few of you here, who have been associated in one way with the Simms edition, may have read the manuscript story, "The Humours of the Manager," which for whatever reason was never published during Simms's lifetime. In that story, he raised some racial questions. This fact is the only contradiction I can think of to what you're saying. But it may be significant that he didn't publish "Humours" and didn't even seem to make a real effort to get it published. He dealt with the safe subjects; he didn't want to alienate the South. His loyalty was to the South more than it was to his own work, I think.

HOLMAN: I wonder if "Caloya" and the history of its reception might not prove to be a fruitful study for someone. "Caloya" was the story, you will recall, which was published in the *Mag-*

nolia in 1842, and was severely attacked by some readers on the grounds of vulgarity and immorality. But I wonder if underneath that attack there may not have been some sense of the racial issues operating in the story. This story has been ignored in a large measure, aside from quoting Simms about it. Almost all of us, I suspect, have quoted at some time or other Simm's defense of it as being realism, telling the truth, but the nature of the attacks on it generally has been assumed. This is a way, I think, of getting back into what was really going on in this region, and it's quite different from what we've done in the past— the sort of thing that Louis Rubin was urging upon us last evening.

CALHOUN: Certainly in the southern magazines, when the southern editors of antebellum magazines were trying to find an audience, there are implicit criticisms of the South and even the agrarian society which you can read there when they had difficulty finding writers or an audience. There's almost an element of pathos which creeps into some of the editorials at times.

TURNER: Not to change the subject, but perhaps to take another hitch on it, we are thinking here of ways to encourage more research, more undertakings that we might carry out or might pass on to our students. I think we all agree pretty well that individuals take hold wherever they find a handle; this is obvious. A student writes a dissertation or a thesis because material is handy, and we're going to do the same thing in our own research. But while we're talking around the table here, I think we are right to suggest areas that might be overlooked otherwise. One thing I think of as being perhaps important if there were going to be joint effort (and there may not be, though it might be appropriate) would be getting at the foundations: the lesser writers, the out-of-the-way pieces, that may be about as typical or as representative or as useful in studying a particular topic at a particular time as some of the major ones which we've been looking at. I've not liked the American studies approach, when it sometimes tends to say that you can't use the major writers, you have to use only the minor writers. I don't mean, of course, that we give any less attention to major works. But I mean that we do learn a great deal from drawing in more foundation material, as it were. So to make available primary materials, for example, to make some of these out-of-the-way stories of Simms's available, is what I'm talking about.

GUILDS: I totally agree with what Arlin Turner has said. He was urging that we encourage our students at least to make deeper studies of second- and third-rate writers to deepen our understanding of the whole southern literary culture. Another thing that I don't believe we've mentioned thus far, but I'm sure we're all aware of, is the value of the southern literary magazines as the things that really open up many doors. From my own experience I say this, for you do read the second- and third-rate and fourth- and fifth-rate writers when you read a southern literary magazine. Just to take any one of them and to go through it is a tremendously rewarding experience, not in the sense of literary satisfaction but in simply finding out what the lesser lights were thinking. So the kind of series the *Southern Literary Journal* has been sponsoring, studies of individual southern magazines, is particularly rewarding. Maybe we need a new look at the forest again, as well as the trees—someone to take a look at *all* southern magazines—at what the composite picture is. That's a tremendous job, but it's begging for someone to try to do it.

INGE: I would suggest that the student might well go a step below even the southern literary magazines and give serious long looks at the major newspapers. When I was going through Tennessee newspapers in the Carnegie Library in Nashville and in other places looking for Sut Lovingood stories I don't know how many other interesting pieces of poetry and fiction and humor I came across, but because I was dead set on one purpose I simply didn't have time to pay much attention or make many notes. The newspapers in all the major southern cities are loaded with all sorts of literary riches, it is to be hoped with more Sut Lovingood stories and pieces by other humorists and serious writers as well.

DAVIS: I hope that Tom would find more Sut Lovingood stories; I'd be delighted if he could. But actually the more serious problem involved in what we're talking about is the relationship between evidence of low culture—not much of it had the quality of the Sut Lovingood stories—to what we sometimes call higher art, and this seems to me a fascinating connection. The point has been made about the southern correspondence and the material we find in southern periodicals. I think that point should be made again about southern rhetoric. Perhaps we've heard too much of it recently, but I'm thinking in terms of another context—the relationship between rhetoric and fine art. The thing that occurs to me now in trying to document my point a bit is how art was produced from the antislavery narratives. A form came into being, essentially to serve a rhetorical purpose. An art form emerged, related to but different from the rhetoric—a distinctive type of prose fiction. I'm thinking especially of William Wells Brown's *Clotel*, which, like *Uncle Tom's Cabin*, was built upon the slave narratives. A successful rhetorical instrument becomes the basis for an artistic structure. Relationships of this kind have been really little explored.

RAY: I read the Atlanta *Constitution* once from around 1850 to about 1908 and my reason for it was a young man who started on the *Constitution* as a paragrapher and later became the famous Uncle Remus. He learned to write these brief humorous paragraphs from a series of southwestern humorists, and this leads me to the point I'd like to suggest for possible investigation, namely, a work that I would call an anatomy of southern humor. Now we're all aware of the work of people like Walter Blair, Franklin Meine, and many others, but I don't believe there has been undertaken a rather scientific analysis of the kinds of humor that appeared first on the southwestern frontier and later in the works of Joel Chandler Harris and Mark Twain particularly. The interrelationships are clear and they've often been pointed out, but I don't think the analyses have been made.

HOLMAN: I think that some of us have been almost frightened

away from that particular approach by the experience we had in reading Walter Blair when he did it. I had a colleague once a number of years ago who spent a fair amount of his life trying to analyze American humor in the broadest possible sense to 1750, which was back in the time when it should have been controllable. He finally emerged with the conclusion that as far as the basic devices and the basic thrust of humorous materials were concerned, it was impossible to give them national, much less regional, characteristics, that you find essentially the same devices, the same attitudes, showing up in Europe, in New England, in the South, and wherever you turned. I'd like to put this example in the context of some of the remarks we heard last evening and this morning. The southern humorist established, for example, a peculiar sort of distance from his subject matter. There seems to have been a kind of class and caste system operating for the southern humorist that doesn't always operate in the rest of the country, that is worth looking at, worth doing a little bit more with. Judge Longstreet is amused but quite remote from the people he's describing; Joseph Glover Baldwin is writing as "our far-flung correspondent" for the *New Yorker* magazine does today rather than reporting actively on the people, but here again the characteristics are in a mode or manner rather than in the literal subject matter of the humor itself.

BUTCHER: We've had several suggestions that students should be encouraged to go back to early publications—the magazines, the newspapers—and I'm reminded that we do a disservice in having students read textbooks where they come upon stories and essays and poems out of context. I suspect nothing is more rewarding than for the student to find these in the original publications where, by flipping the pages, he gets some sense of how excellent they are in transcending the limitations of their time, in being mountains where there are plains and valleys. This matter of relating the work to the other things that are part of the period can be shown in this sort of thing: the centerfold in a particular magazine featured an illustration of black troops at San Juan Hill, and on the back of this centerfold was Henry James's novel *The Awkward Age*. How better can we see how removed that novel was from the full range of American experience than by seeing it in those pages? When it's taken out and put in book form we get a different impression altogether. So it does appear that there is a great reward for students and for all scholars in having available these early publications where we may get the full range, and where we can study some of the second- or third-rate people and also perhaps come upon new Sut Lovingood stories.

JACOBS: I'd like to hark back to the question of humor. It strikes me that much southern humor from the time of Poe on down has been concerned with wordplay, word-coinages, and so forth. Poe coins words like *Goosetherumfoodle* and *Thingum Bob* and apparently the people of his time found that funny. There are letters to the *Southern Literary Messenger* praising Poe's vein of "delicate, tasteful humor." Now we're not likely to think that Poe is very funny today, but when we look at the southwestern humor of his time and later we will find coinages like "slantindicular"—"I looks up at him slantindicular and he looks down at me slanchwise." Then if we examine the dialect stories of the time of Joel Chandler Harris and Mark Twain, stories in which mispronunciations often seem to supply much of the fun, perhaps we can tie in the penchant for verbal humor with the rhetorical tradition of the South. Only in a region where eloquence wins unqualified admiration would people consider vulgate attempts at lofty language laughable. I do not mean to say that this mode of humor is exclusively southern. It just seems to me that we find more of it in southern writing, from Augustus Baldwin Longstreet to Faulkner, than we do, say, in the literature of New England.

DAVIS: I want to second the point that Robert Jacobs has just made. I was interested in Hugh Holman's earlier comment that the colleague who devoted himself to the early stages of American humor came up with the notion that there weren't distinctive characteristics, at least prior to 1750. It may be possible indeed that these distinguishing characteristics that we're talking about didn't emerge until the early nineteenth century. I would suspect so. I remember with some affection a very good course I had with Walter Blair at the University of Chicago on native American humor. There does seem to be a distinction to be made in American humor which is very important, a distinction between the humor that developed here in the South at some time after the beginning of the nineteenth century and the humor that we find Down East, in New England. You remember Jack Downing, the creation of Seba Smith, and work of that sort—we have a sense that the humor there is often terribly committed, terribly political, and that it was not really humor for humor's sake; it's not the feeling that we have really in much of the work of the Southwest humor tradition.

TURNER: Turning back to what Hugh Holman said a while ago, I rather agree with the thought that perhaps we don't need philosophical or psychological disquisitions on humor to deal with the southern humor, but the matter of ancestry may be more useful, and that's in part what's been said by one or two around the table here. Most of the humorous writing appears to come directly from something oral and seems to have no connection with anything that has ancestors. Such often seems to be the case when Mark Twain makes a phrase. Surely some of the writers were acquainted with European rogue stories and other literature of that kind; it's apparent that the people who were sending in sketches and narratives to the newspapers were acquainted with Addison and Steele. Walter Blair alludes to that background, and, in fact, develops it somewhat in an essay he wrote once on tradition in American humor. But some further exploring might be done very usefully there. When I teach a seminar on American humor, the students, many of them, are prepared to encounter a strange growth that comes from nowhere and has no connections.

CALHOUN: Let me raise one other big question here which might be explored. If we had an American literary renascence from the 1850s, why was there no southern renascence, say from

1850 to 1855, other than for economic and political reasons, and why was the American renascence either denounced in the South or little known in the South? I am aware that it was little known in some areas of the North, too.

HOLMAN: Would you agree that the first southern literary renascence occurred in 1835 and ended that year too? It is very interesting to ask why it was that at the time when the fresh intellectual currents of the American mind were creating a new, fresh, natural, and indigenous literature, the South was really going ahead writing traditional poetry that often sounded almost like doggerel, that placed a much higher emphasis on sound in a simple sense than it did on significant content, and continuing to write novels that were in imitation of Sir Walter Scott. If you parallel 1850-55 in the Middle Atlantic states and in New England with those five years in the South, the results are shocking. And yet if we look at it in terms of fundamental abilities, there were people whose careers were active at this time, who should have been producing certainly a different kind of writing, a more serious kind of writing. I wonder though if part of it isn't what Ellen Glasgow called a "confederacy of hedonism," a kind of refusal to use literature seriously, or to view it as a serious vocation. Literature was almost an avocation to the southern writer before the Civil War, something that he did for ladies' books.

DAVIS: I think Hugh Holman's point is dramatized when you look at the epic impulse in American literature. The epic is one of the important art forms in that great intellectual ferment which was the American renascence, when used by Whitman or suggested by Melville in *Moby-Dick*. An old form becomes something new in "Song of Myself." In the South the epic impulse was much less experimental, much less intellectual; it tended to be a form of domestic romanticism. Think of Henry Timrod, who aspired to write an epic. His conception lacks boldness, both in ideas and in form; you have the sense that everything is given, that the world has somehow closed in on him. It is not simply a matter of the acceptance of the foundation of his society which must be the slave culture, but that's part of it. A part of this acceptance is the unwillingness, which Longfellow felt, too, for reasons which were very different, to experiment in verbal forms and to entertain radical ideas. I'm suggesting that perhaps the problem is a bit more complicated, because the North in a different way is also involved in this failure to face the problems of literature with high seriousness.

GUILDS: I'd like to make a point at least half facetiously, but not completely so, because I think it is something that we should be concerned about in our efforts to promote or to talk about things southern, and that is the very question that Richard Calhoun raised when he talked about what happened in the 1850s as an "American renascence." I mean, it normally is not called a "New England renascence," which actually it was. But yet when something happened in the South it was called a "southern renascence"; it was not called "another American renascence." I wonder if by having conferences such as we're having right here we're not in a sense playing into the hands of those who say that the things that are southern are not American, and things that happened in other regions, particularly the Northeast, are American. I raise this somewhat facetiously, but I've always been concerned about this very thing. Why was the renascence in the 1850s an "American" renascence, and then the one in the 1920s a "southern" renascence?

BUTCHER: I think this is another indication of what I call the American minority mentality idea, that here is a kind of defensiveness, a sort of posture, which we often associate with minority positions, and I would agree that this might just as well have been termed an "American" renascence as the other. The assumption of an authority or an identity for the New England writer of the period wasn't used in the same way for the southern writer.

MOORE: It seems to me that there are several things involved in regard to this question. One thing we need to know is who characterized the southern renascence as "southern," and who

characterized the New England renascence as "American." Did
the New Englanders think of themselves as Americans, and leave
everybody else out? It would seem to me that this is a very interesting question and one that ought to be fully explored. For example, Jay B. Hubbell's book is called *The South in American
Literature* so maybe that might provide us with some help on this
question. In regard to Hugh Holman's point a while ago, about
Ellen Glasgow's characterization of southern "hedonism," there
may be something to that in regard to professional men of letters.
We certainly haven't had many, and even for those who wanted
to regard themselves as professional men of letters there was always a problem, of course, of relating themselves to the community and trying to separate themselves from the community.
That's not a peculiar southern problem; that's really an American
problem, too. The American artist has always had some difficulty
in relating himself to the community, and he has not always been
very successful in doing it. Melville, for example, cut himself off
from his audience finally, and Thoreau never did have much of an
audience. You can go over the American renascence and find
many of the writers who were contributing to it, who didn't really
have a very large audience, especially with regard to their best
books.

DAVIS: I have a moderately simple, or simpleminded, comment on what you have said. It seems to me one of the reasons
why the term "American renascence" was used was to distinguish
it very simply from Europe, and it was an impulse that came out
of Emerson, obviously, to make that distinction. One of the reasons that the southern writers did not use the term is that important in their thinking at the time was to reject America, to reject
what America had become, and I think that's very essential in the
sense that they used the term. Obviously their essential stance
was one which in general disapproved of technological and urban
America.

RAY: I'd like to move the discussion to just a minor tributary
off the main subject for a moment, to talk about the whole ques-

tion of literary nationalism. Now in the 1870s and later the Atlanta *Constitution* was very much concerned about sectionalism in the literature. Harris, as one of the new southern editorialists, commented on one occasion, "What does it matter if I'm northern or southern. The important thing is if I'm true to my own true self," which suggests that although the controversy was raging, the respectable southern men of letters had a pretty healthy notion of self, although they felt that self, at least the literary aspects of it, was on the defensive.

JACOBS: I'd like to take Charles Ray's comment, throw it back a number of years, and pose two questions. The first is, in the antebellum days, what did the southerners regard as literature? It was not simply what we call belles lettres. The *Southern Literary Messenger* in the late 1830s and the 1840s—I believe Benjamin Blake Minor was the editor at that time—issued a call for a southern history. Minor wanted to rewrite history because all the history had been written by the Yankees, and the southerners responded by writing history. I think one of the historians was a man named C. C. Campbell, from Petersburg, Virginia. And I was amused to find in the pages of the *Southern Literary Messenger* an account of the Pocahontas story with an attempt to make her into one of the first ladies of Virginia, endowed with all of the qualities of the southern belle of the myth. At least one issue of the *Southern Literary Messenger* during that period was, I would estimate, about 85-90 percent history, and this tendency continued for a few years. They called it "literature"; we would call it "history." They called scientific publications "literature"; they did not restrict the term "literature" merely to belles lettres. So it may be the lack of what we could call a southern renascence, or it may have been that belles lettres weren't very important, and that the people who could write were writing history.

HOLMAN: We've been going now for a little over an hour, and I wonder if we need again to see if there are specific recommendations which we would like to make. We have certainly suggested very strongly that we need more work on the letters and the diaries of southern writers, that this is a neglected aspect of southern literature as well as southern culture. We've suggested that we need to look into newspapers and magazines as a source for a measure of the mind of the South; and we have suggested that humor might be explored again in terms of what is distinctively southern about it. Are there other specific concerns that we would want to transmit to the future?

RAY: I think there's been a neglect of writing about blacks or by blacks who originated in the South. One of the topics suggested here is that black writers, probably like other writers, often don't remain in the South, but a considerably large number of black writers did originate in the South. Take a man like James Weldon Johnson, who was a very big figure in the black literary spectrum, who originated down here; so did Albert Hunter, David Walker, George Moses Horton, Charles Chesnutt, and many others. One of the real needs is a more complete bibliography than we have. Individuals and organizations have contributed some bibliography, but certainly one of the great needs of the South is for a black bibliography of the kinds of things that have been produced in the last century, not a bibliography of writings about the South, but a bibliography of southern writing.

TINDALL: In listening to all this, it seems that much of it is in the direction of fragmentation, of investigating in further detail, studying more obscure authors. I wonder what the feeling of the people here is about the desirability of getting some kind of synthesis. Isn't it time for a good overall literary historian who could pull it together? I would think, for instance, of the Southern Renascence of the twentieth century. Nobody has yet done that, has as yet written a "Flowering of the Southern Renascence" that pulls it together. In some other ways historians may have something to contribute; there is an area where our fields intersect, the area of social and intellectual history. When you speak of exploring the milieu in which Poe operated, it brought to mind those sociological studies of communities that have been done, which tend just to cut a slice through the community at some point in time which has no depth to it. There are community studies like the one that Thernstrom did on Newburyport, Massachusetts, but I can't think of any such study that's been done for the South.

GUILDS: How about George C. Rogers's study of Charleston?

TINDALL: Well, it's not the same type of thing as Thernstrom's study, which was a much closer and more detailed study of the community during a period of time. Actually he was exploring one simple question, that of the myth of upward mobility in American society, and he came out with some serious doubts about that myth, at least as applied to that one town. On a larger scale Hugh Holman suggested the question of the plantation myth; maybe that's due for exploration in somewhat broader terms than Gaines dealt with it. But there are lots of other areas. I've got a student now interested in and beginning to explore, for example, the question of the whole myth of Reconstruction as it developed, beginning with the image of Santo Domingo before Reconstruction and bringing down the development both in historiography and literature rather than mythology.

DAVIS: I think of three other things that might be done. To return to Poe—there seems to be something of an obsession with him today—the whole problem of relating a major writer like Poe or Twain to the intellectual and social currents of the time is something that needs to be fully explored, though something has been done with both Poe and Mark Twain in this respect, but obviously, I think, not enough. It has to be done with a certain amount of imagination and a certain kind of documentation which is now possible. The second thing, suggested by Louis Rubin last night, is the reexamination of certain movements of the sort that we're not really proud to remember today. He alluded, of course, to the prose romance, the Thomas Nelson Page tradition, the *In Ole Virginia* tradition, which most of us would be happy to forget forever, especially some of us who were, as I was, born in Virginia. There are obviously elements in it that need to be explored more fully, reservations that are present that we never examined before. I would add that a third kind of development needs exploration, and that is the examination of forms that have gone out of favor. I'm thinking especially of dialect verse, in which there is a great deal of variety and a great deal of unevenness of quality. I'm thinking not of Paul Laurence Dunbar now but of a writer named James Edwin Campbell, who was writing also at the end of the nineteenth century. We discover a development in dialect poems of certain folk elements, of a tendency to look with an amount of tough-mindedness and reality at the situation of blacks at the turn of the century.

BUTCHER: I noticed that our discussion groups are divided in a chronological fashion—eighteenth, nineteenth, twentieth century. We may have to find the means to deal with our students in terms of the degree of distance for them between our own time and the nineteenth century. We probably have to recognize that these students did not grow up with any sort of family or personal familiarity with what the nineteenth century was like, even in their family recollections. They would get this only as an intellectual experience or a formal educational experience. One has to read Poe with a sense not of how stereotyped some of the images are now but of how fresh they were in the original, and the student doesn't get this without some emphasis being placed on it. Some of the things that we speak of as stereotypes have to be seen in terms of an original presentation rather than in the constant replication of them. What distresses me is not only how remote the nineteenth century is for students, but how remote much of the twentieth century is.

GUILDS: I've been thinking ahead to the discussions tomorrow morning. "The Continuity of Southern Literary History" is one which I'm going to find very interesting, but it poses a problem that Philip Butcher was touching upon earlier. There's a tendency, particularly in the study of southern literature, to think that southern literature of the nineteenth century is one thing and southern literature of the twentieth century is another. Although I know that Hugh Holman and others have tried to show, I think convincingly, that there is a continuous tradition, most scholars just don't teach it that way. It is assumed that the southern renascence started something new and unrelated to nineteenth-century southern literature. It may be relevant to this group to be aware of the fact that we do precede the twentieth century, and it may be of concern to us in the nineteenth-century group to recognize this problem. It's been pointed out many times, of course, that there is no real difficulty in showing the roots of twentieth-century New England literature, let us say, in nineteenth-century New England literature. But we haven't to the same degree been successful in convincing ourselves or others that there is a continuity, say, from Simms to Faulkner. It's almost as if Simms were one tradition and then Faulkner were another.

HOLMAN: I wonder if at least part of this problem is not one that we've almost always gotten around rather carefully for understandable reasons, the problem that there were in the South few writers who combined both talent and the will to make art out of what could have been a situation for very fine literary expression— the tensions of the South. The South in the nineteenth century, with perhaps a couple of exceptions, did not produce any literary people of the first order in America, judged by purely American nineteenth-century standards. That's a part of the answer to why we didn't have a southern renascence in the nineteenth century. The circumstances, in actual fact, for the production of a substantial body of literary material were not much more favorable in 1922 than they were in 1850 for southern writers, if you put everything together. But there was a quality of the critical mind operating in 1922 which wasn't operating very forcefully in the South in the entire nineteenth-century. The question, I think, might very well be "why was it that the entire culture was so inhibiting to the South's men of talent?" By and large New England and the Middle Atlantic States gave their men of talent the opportunity to utilize that talent in ways which we still regard as distinctive, even if they're not great. The South, by and large, did not give its writers in the nineteenth century an adequate way of utilizing talent, and so it gets dribbled off, a little here and a little there, and we turn to speeches, letters, diaries, and poetry written as an avocation rather than as a commitment, and novels which are "cast in worn-out molds," to use Hawthorne's phrase, and that are supporting a status quo which is grievously under attack, and should be under attack. I'm not now asking that a nineteenth-century writer view his world with twentieth-century eyes, but certainly the easy acceptance which we find in so much of antebellum writing seems to me to be a partial failure of the environment, or something, together with an absence of genius. We just didn't produce any literary geniuses in the nineteenth century, unless we count Poe and Mark Twain.

CALHOUN: I'd like to comment on that. In addition to *will*, doesn't it take some *courage* on the part of the writer to separate himself from the community, to get a perspective, and then rejoin the community but maintain a literary perspective, whether this is Hawthorne and the seventeenth-century Puritans, or it's Melville, or the writers in the 1920s in the South? Southern writers in the antebellum period did not have that kind of courage.

DAVIS: Let me confirm the points made by Hugh Holman and by Richard Calhoun. It seems to me that we have in the great writers of the 1850s in the North a willingness to face total reality. We have the desire most dramatically put by Thoreau who went to Walden to "face life," he tells us, and by that, of course, he meant life as a whole. Similarly with Whitman—he wishes to bring into verse the whole of reality. I fail to find anywhere that willingness expressed by any southern writer, and I suspect that this is not a matter of talent; it's a matter of a disposition that comes from the sense that parts of the culture have been declared off limits.

TURNER: I have used the word "self-conscious" before today, and I'm not sure how useful it is, but two of the aspects that have just been mentioned are involved in what I have in mind. It's in part the community, of course, which forces the author to be self-conscious, to adhere to accepted beliefs and assumptions; it's also

I think certainly the author himself. We use such phrases as "if an author of sufficient independence of mind" or "sufficient genius which lets him go above and beyond. . . ." I think both elements are normally present; the author himself, we rather feel, who hopes to produce a work of real worth must not ask his neighbors what it ought to be—must not feel that he has to ask his neighbors or the local press, what materials, what subjects, he is at liberty to use and what attitudes he can take toward them. I would say that during much of the nineteenth century in the South this was just asking too much of an author. Conditions were asking too much. As a matter of fact, you can ask this: if an author had written such a book, where would it have been published? This question would be especially appropriate late in the century, when the northern publishers likewise were vetoing books that southern authors with very firm wills wanted to write. Some potential authors backed out of writing altogether.

JACOBS: It's striking that some of the journals were run by groups of friends. There was a kind of community feeling in that they had very much the same ideas and attitudes about things. When Thomas Willis White, for example, was running the *Southern Literary Messenger*, he could call on his good friend Beverley Tucker, who was teaching law down at William and Mary, to write a review that would agree with White's preconceptions. When Tucker writes a review of a play by Bulwer-Lytton and damns it up and down for immorality, White writes him an appreciative letter and says, "My only objection is that you didn't give Bulwer half the drubbing he deserved." White and Tucker thought alike most of the time, but there was poor old Poe, who thought differently. He was not a member of the inner group, and he would attack people they didn't want attacked. For instance, he attacked William Gilmore Simms in a book review, whereas the others would have considered Simms "one of ours," a southern author to be encouraged instead of "tomahawked."

HOLMAN: I'll commit absolute treason and suggest that what you have described is not quite as different from what happens in the twentieth century in the southern renascence as we sometimes think. Much of the best of twentieth-century southern writing has been done by a mutual admiration society. Southern writers and critics review each other and praise each other and form a coterie and talk to each other. I think that what happened in Nashville in the 1920s and 1930s would indicate that that cliqueishness in itself does not necessarily prevent the operation of a high kind of intelligence and a good critical mind. It can whet the cutting edge as well as dull it. I agree with you that by and large in the nineteenth century it seems to have dulled it, but the tendency of southern writers to congregate in groups, to form clubs, to stand together, has been a part also of their strength. Perhaps it is because there are so few, and they are separated from the rest of their world. They publish little magazines which are their own, which they put together because they want to publish things, like the *Cosmopolitan* in Charleston in the 1830s, but that does not necessarily prevent some of those magazines from being *The Fugitive*. There still has to be that critical quality of mind operating within that context, but if it's operating the context is not necessarily a deterrent to high literary art.

GUILDS: Is it the consensus of this group that there is not a continuity between nineteenth-century southern literature and the twentieth century? Is that what we're saying? If it is, it's going to be interesting tomorrow trying to establish that there is a continuity.

HOLMAN: I think I'm the one who introduced that notion a few moments ago, or was one of those who did. I think there is, and that what we've been saying in no way attacks the concept of continuity of theme or attitude or subject matter or problems or anything of this sort. The big difference is that a group of writers appeared in the twentieth century in the South who dealt with these things with a kind of directness and honesty that by and large the nineteenth-century writers, confronted with essentially the same themes, did not display. The great theme of southern experience, unquestionably, is the theme of race. The nineteenth century either took stereotyped attitudes toward it or took highly defensive attitudes toward it. In the twentieth century, though many of the literary figures who dealt with race have not been exactly flaming liberals, they have still looked at the issues that were present in it with a kind of honesty that did not show up in the nineteenth century very often. I think the continuity is in the issues, the subject matter, the themes which have interested southern writers, and the change is a matter of talent, or perhaps of courage and the will to work.

TURNER: If I should try to apply my word "self-conscious" to the Nashville group—in my own mind I thought I could—in their poetry and in their criticism and in their writing of poetry and fiction and the like, it seems to me they were largely, and in their own minds were, part of the world of letters, the community of letters, and they were firmly devoted to a universal, nonlocal, nonregional image. I have a feeling that when they turned to political, economic, social, and religious topics (such as appear in the essays of *I'll Take My Stand*), then it seems to me they became self-consciously members of a group and a region, and became subject to the kind of limiting compulsions, whether positive or negative, we have been talking about.

DAVIS: I wish to comment on what Hugh Holman has said. True, we had an overwhelming preoccupation with race in the early nineteenth century, but along with it there was a vision of a happy, beautifully ordered life. That vision had the support of romantic aesthetics and seemed very real, if not attainable, to the writers of the early nineteenth century. The late nineteenth century brought a very different set of conditions. The dream of the earthly paradise became more remote and progressively less viable. The claim to reality, no matter how tenuous, which serious art always requires, was denied completely by the agonies of racial conflict. This involves directly the history of the South after *the* War. I open this Pandora's box with some reluctance, since at the end of a long session, we may say many things which we'll regret tomorrow.

HOLMAN: We have been going now for a period of time substantially longer than we were assigned, and I wonder if there are compelling desires on the part of any of us here to introduce other subjects or to say further things. If not, then I thank you very much for having put up with my attempts to goad you.

7. Twentieth-Century Southern Literature

MODERATOR:
Louis D. Rubin, Jr.

PANELISTS:
Cleanth Brooks, Norman Brown, George Core,
Blyden Jackson, Lewis Lawson, Paschal Reeves,
Walter Sullivan, Floyd Watkins, Dan Young

RUBIN: Our task today is to discuss some of the problems that we face in understanding and interpreting our very complex field of twentieth-century southern literature. To start things off, it seems to me that the central theme that runs through so much of this literature involves the reentry of the region into the mainstream of American, international, industrial, and urban society. At every stage along the way, we come up against the whole problem of change and continuity. And not only that, but in the study of southern literature of the twentieth century, what we have in one sense is the breaking down of certain established southern modes, and also their continuance, as occasioned by the change in the South. Indeed, we might even say that the work of Faulkner, Ransom, Wolfe, Tate, Warren, Welty, and the other great southern writers of the 1920s, 1930s, and early 1940s almost seems to be at a kind of midway point, where, as Allen Tate pointed out in his essay "A Southern Mode of the Literary Imagination," the old southern rhetoric becomes dialectic. So that we face the question of what is "southern" about southern literature not simply as a matter of information and identification, but as something having to do with the very nature of the literary strength of these writers.

[133]

BROOKS: I quite agree. This is certainly a way to get into it. This is not said in opposition to Allen's fine essay, which, I think, is so fruitful, but to test the further dimensions of it: if we mean by "rhetoric" something like a presentation of the surface of the world, outward show, a celebration of a way of life, then the older southern literature was "rhetorical" and so less profound than the southern literature that succeeded it; and we describe the superiority of this later literature properly in calling it "dialectic" if we mean by dialectic that it involves a wrestling with moral problems and a quarrel within the self. The finest literature always embodies a tension of this sort.

But suppose the dialectic goes on and the quarrel becomes an argument for its own sake—problems considered simply as problems to be dealt with intellectually and "logically." Such is, as we all know, one of the basic meanings of dialectic. In such case, won't the life-giving tension have been lost? Won't we have moved out of literature altogether?

If I may invoke the name of Marshall McLuhan—not precisely my sage in these matters, but a man who has made some very acute observations in his time—McLuhan has remarked that the dialectic mind, the purely dialectic mind, moves out of literature altogether and into the world of strict logic and technology.

Though in this conference we are interested in what is happening at the present and only incidentally interested in the past, nevertheless, an examination of the past may tell us something about where we may be going. It may offer tests of Tate's thesis and illustrations of what he means in proposing it. Tate has accounted for the New England Renaissance of over a century ago as a movement into "dialectic" conceived of as the New Englander's questioning of the older culture and as a quarrel with himself. But wouldn't Tate say that in time the fruitful "dialectic" became sterile—that is, insofar as literature is concerned—and the great literature of New England faded away.

RUBIN: I also think there is another problem which comes into this. Walter Sullivan has written an essay called "Southern

Literature and the Joycean Aesthetic." This is also the period when the literature written by southerners becomes much more involved with the main currents of European literature. It becomes more international—not only as involving the example of Joyce, but of Eliot and so many others. Faulkner is a perfect instance of this. You find in his fiction the fruits of the most advanced, most complex psychological developments in the way of literary form and language, being applied to much the same life experience that the writers of the nineteenth century were dealing with. So once again we have this two-way vision. The impact of the literature of Western Europe—of Joyce and Eliot, of, directly or indirectly, Freud, Marx, all the great seminal Western ideas—is brought to bear upon what is still pretty much a kind of traditional experience. One thing that strikes me, for example, is how tremendously influential a book like *A Portrait of the Artist as a Young Man* has been for so many southern writers. Take, for example, Wolfe's *Look Homeward, Angel*, or Jean Toomer's *Cane*. Those books wouldn't have existed as they are without *Portrait of the Artist*.

BROOKS: I think your instancing of Joyce is a very important matter—and of Eliot, too. Joyce came out of an old-fashioned, traditional civilization, pretty well ingrown, perhaps stagnant, well behind the times. He had to abandon backward Ireland in order to write: he got away to the Continent; he became a great experimenter; he read the French symbolists; he read Ibsen—but what did he write about? Nothing but Ireland. So you get the fruitful tension going on within Joyce. The interesting question is: what could Joyce write, at the end, besides *Finnegans Wake*? In that wonderful esoteric ragbag of a book you find yourself enveloped in "rhetoric" once more, a rhetoric so involved that it is simply a series of arabesques. The *Wake* seems to me almost completely without tension—as tensionless as pure "dialectic."

SULLIVAN: You know, in that famous interview in the *Paris Review* Faulkner said, "Well, I never read Freud," but then he had sense enough to add, "I know I was influenced by Freud." It seems to me that's rather more significant than even Faulkner realized. The next generation, for example Bill Styron, *has* read Freud, and perhaps this is the next move forward toward the dialectic. I want to throw in one more bit of dialectic, which is based on my tremendously good response to everything that's gone on in this conference so far. You've noticed—you couldn't help but notice— that every one of the papers gets back sooner or later, and usually sooner, to the relationship of black and white, the black experience, the white experience, and the interlocking black and white experience. I was deeply impressed by Lewis Simpson's paper, and I was thinking as he went along—you will recognize my own peculiar bias in this—that here in the South up to World War II we had, side by side, the sense of guilt on the part of the white man in his relationship to the black man, together with, in the predominant Christian religion, a vehicle for dealing with that guilt, and even an explanation for it: we are guilty because all men are sinners: we know all men are sinners and we confess our sins every Sunday. Sometimes in between, we go back and sin again. This didn't get us out of our situation, but in a way it made the situation less intolerable for everybody concerned. But now, when the metaphysical framework is gone, all the terms of the dialectic are changed. The guilt becomes a secular guilt, with only a secular way to deal with it, and the only way a secular society can deal with guilt is to deny the nature of man, to say that man is ultimately perfectible. And since that really isn't true, when this idea permeates society the possibilities for literature are considerably reduced.

BROOKS: Isn't this what Allen Tate meant when he wrote in his essay on Emily Dickinson that Emerson had destroyed the possibilities for tragedy in New England?

RUBIN: This strikes me as being another tie-in between the situation of the black writer and the central problem of southern literature. In this case the religious identity has all sorts of direct, specific, political overtones. After all, for the slave, and even more for the freedman, his religion—the Protestant church—was the one thing that he had all to his own. As he has entered more into the mainstream of modern American society, he has had to give this up too. You get the problem in an almost exaggerated form in Jean Toomer's *Cane*, which I think of as a book about just this matter.

JACKSON: You've got me straining at the leash now. Two things which have been said in this dialogue seem to me to be highly fruitful. In reference to the matter of a dichotomy between dialectic and rhetoric, one of the real problems of the black militant writer of today is that he stays on what I would call the wrong side, that of the rhetoric. But there's an interesting problem here. I think that probably the two best novels written by Negro writers in the relatively current world—I use that word rather than "contemporary"—are one done by John Oliver Killens, his first, called *Young Blood*, which is set in Georgia—Killens himself was a native of Macon, Georgia—and one which is much more recent, *The Autobiography of Miss Jane Pittman*, by a writer with whom I hope you will become acquainted if you aren't already, Ernest Gaines. Gaines's novel seems to me to be one which has more dialectic than rhetoric. Although I like *Young Blood* very much, what is wrong with it is that it leans more toward the rhetoric. In other words, you've got more sociology in Killens's novel, and more art, if you want to put it that way, in Gaines's.

I've also been listening to what Walter Sullivan was saying about the metaphysical frame of reference, the sense of guilt. I am thinking of a novel which has been underestimated, and about which there's some very confused reviewing and criticism—a novel by James Baldwin, called *Another Country*. It is shot through and through with many things, including by the way all sorts of sex, and many people have been fascinated primarily with the sex. It's a much more important novel than it's often given credit for being, and I think I see why now. The novel has a chap in it named Rufus Scott. He's a Negro who disappears early in the novel; he jumps off the George Washington Bridge, commits suicide. I hold that the novel is his novel, that everything else in it is related to him and has significance because it explains why he jumped off the bridge, as one review that I read pointed out. This particular review, by Terry Southern in *The Nation*, says that in this novel Baldwin seems to be saying something which can point to two conclusions. Color caste in America has left such a tremendous impact on Americans, whether they are white or black, that there's no immediate redress for either one—it will take a little while to get over it. In the case of the Negro you have a chap like Rufus Scott who cannot make it with a white girl from Georgia, Leona, because he has too many caste-induced frustrations in him that he can't work out. On the other hand, the white characters, who are leaning over backwards to be tolerant, can't make it either, because of their own conditioned reflexes. I suppose that what Baldwin wasn't able to add overtly was this metaphysical dimension, which would have integrated the whole novel—in more than one sense. I think we could also take the dialectic-rhetoric distinction and look for it in *Another Country*, and get some resonance that would be helpful.

RUBIN: This matter of the movement from a Christian to a secular framework is important, provided that we understand what we mean by it. We are talking about religious attitudes, essentially, not the dogmas of a particular church. If we remember that, then I think this is one very good way of realizing how much the South has changed, and how its writers are confronted with a different foundation on which they can ground their values, so to speak. It certainly is true, with almost every writer I can think of. If we approach the matter from the standpoint of urbanization, or politically, or in terms of race, each approach seems to imply the others, and each one is contained in the others.

LAWSON: There are those who would disagree that the South ever was Christian, and that there is any sort of change that results from a Christian decline.

RUBIN: Probably we've been using the wrong word; we don't mean "Christian," we mean "Protestant."

LAWSON: All right. Walker Percy says at one point that the

southerner prefers to be buried in the church, but he would like to live as the stoic, and that any decline which results in a malaise these days is caused by the decline of the stoic attitude. What we've lost more than anything else is a sense of oblige, of responsibility, and he seems to see that as the significant change between these times and other times in the South.

YOUNG: There's another point which might be made. There are those southern writers who insist that in the South, at least for a time in the twentieth century, the writer continued to believe in ritual, long after his belief in the dogma had passed. Perhaps one thing which might be missing now is the continued belief in the ritual—in manners, customs, what have you.

BROWN: I'd like to make two points about Walker Percy. First, he was asked on one occasion why the South had produced such a great literature in the Renascence of the 1920s and 1930s, and he said simply, "because we got beat," which seems to suggest that he saw the origins of the Renascence in the historical experience of the Civil War rather than in a religious past. The second point is that it seems to me that his novel *The Last Gentleman* is a kind of epitaph for the Southern Renascence, because he is saying in it that the traditional values of an agrarian society, which have been celebrated by writers like Faulkner and Warren in their fiction, not only cannot be accepted by young southerners today, but cannot even be perceived by them. These traditional values and the agrarian way of life in which they were rooted have receded so far now into the past as to be beyond recovery. In a sense the last gentleman of the novel is not Bibb Barrett, it's his father, because his father tried, however imperfectly, to live by the code. But Barrett can't understand the code. He can't even begin to live it, because he doesn't understand it.

RUBIN: To frame what you've said in terms of southern literary study—I think this is what Lewis Lawson said, too—a potentiality might exist for looking at Walker Percy's work as a new stage in the southern literary imagination, different from anything that has gone before. I don't mean by that that the South is seen as changed overnight, and that nothing remains. But I spot this way of thinking about Percy's fiction in the way that many people have been writing about him.

BROOKS: May I break in? I want to make a distinction, not a separation, but a distinction for the purposes of argument, between Walker Percy, the novelist, whom I much admire, and Walker Percy the apocalyptic and social critic with whom I share some ideas and opinions. It may be that it's over and done for with southern literature; it may be that its great period has come to an end, though I don't see Percy's novels as constituting its epitaph. Moreover, I applaud Percy's insistence as a social critic on a return to first principles. As a Roman Catholic convert, he takes seriously the metaphysical underpinnings of a society. He thinks dogma is important—and so do I. He is not a mere regionalist or a local colorist, and yet I know of no contemporary author who has given better testimony to the indelible character of southern culture as it still exists. He is one of the few people who can take an Alabama coed and distinguish her manner precisely from a girl from Dallas, or one from Winchester, Virginia. Look at his last novel: he's infallible in such matters. His account of the southern manner and southern ethos—in all its local variations—rings true every time. Of course this complex of character traits may, I grant for the sake of the argument, be on the wane. Maybe all the parts of the United States will quickly become interchangeable; but when that happens—if it ever does—American literature will be done for, sure enough. On the other hand, the fact that a distinctive southern character has lasted sufficiently far into our time so that Percy can still discern these delicate nuances indicates that perhaps as a prophet of change in the South Percy is more gloomy than he need be.

REEVES: What we're suggesting, as I understand it, is that the South is changing so much that it can no longer produce the same type of writer as it did. I know Walter Sullivan has an essay on this in his book *Death by Melancholy*, and Dan Young has strong opinions about it, but what I'd like to say is that it has not changed yet, and there are people who have a response to a value system built on a culture that had its religious roots. I think Percy is an excellent example of that. His mother was from Athens, Georgia, and then he had the Mississippi Percy background, and though he himself has become a Roman Catholic convert, nevertheless he has in his background all of the potential that these other writers have. And let's remember that he's an artist. We don't want to confuse art and polemics. In other words, the southern situation may be changing, so that our young people growing up now may not become southern writers in the sense that we have known them, but there's still enough of the South remaining so that it is able to produce a Walker Percy.

RUBIN: What you are reminding us of is that though much is taken, much abides; I mean that, whatever the occasions that brought forth the older southern attitudes, whatever the institutions and so forth which helped form them, the attitudes are still very much a part of it, even though the institutions and occasions may disappear. And the interplay of these attitudes, the change *and* the continuity, makes a writer like Walker Percy still very much an inheritor of a great deal of the southern literary tradition.

SULLIVAN: Let me bring up something else here. We're talking about Walker Percy's last book. Add to that Madison Jones's last book, *A Cry of Absence*. These are two of the best books that have been written by southern novelists recently. But notice that one of them goes back to the 1950s, while the other is set well beyond the present day. Why aren't they writing about the present time?

JACKSON: We're skirting the issue which is in all of our minds— whether or not there is a South left, whether or not American culture has become so homogenized that the South itself has succumbed to it. You step off an airplane in Minneapolis or Dallas, and you're in the same airport. You look at a subdivision in New Orleans and a subdivision in Rochester, and it's virtually the same subdivision. You can extend this. And what has just been said, it seems to me, emphasizes this development—the fact that the writers who are writing now have to return to the past in order to stay southern. I know this is true in Negro literature. Of the two novels I mentioned, *The Autobiography of Miss Jane Pittman* goes back into the nineteenth century and is thoroughly southern. But if you consider a poet with whom we are all well acquainted, Melvin Tolson, you discover that he can't quite do this, because Tolson is not involved in recovering the same kind of a past. In *Harlem Gallery*, he's intensely interested in some things which can apply to this very moment and you get an altogether different situation. How homogenized is our culture in America now, and have we all succumbed to it?

YOUNG: This is exactly the point I would make. When we think of Allen Tate or Robert Penn Warren and some of the essays they wrote, Tate in particular back in the 1930s was saying that he thought there was something very definite that differentiated the southern writer of the 1920s from writers in other sections of the country: the looking both ways of the southern writer, as opposed to the new provincialism of some other moderns. But the point that Blyden Jackson is making, or at least the one I would make, is that I don't really know what the young southern writer sees about his culture now that would make him believe that the South is any different from Rochester or West Texas. There are, it seems to me, some superficial differences, but not the kind of fundamental difference that Tate and Ransom and others were talking about in the 1920s.

REEVES: The great theme of the era that we've been going through is the civil rights movement. The way that the young writers who have not yet written will respond to this movement, I think, might indicate whether the South has remained distinct.

YOUNG: That's exactly my point, though. The civil rights movement, and how people are going to respond to it, is not a southern issue any more. Reaction to that issue would not differentiate the South from the North or West or East.

RUBIN: It is no longer a southern issue, but that doesn't mean that in the past it wasn't primarily a southern issue. And it is still very much a southern issue. It continues to be very much a part of southern experience, and the fact that as an issue it's spread to Detroit and Los Angeles and so forth really doesn't change that. This is a central theme of southern literature and I don't think you can get very far by suggesting that the response to this issue is going to be less southern because it is more like the response of the rest of America. If anything, I would turn it around.

SULLIVAN: You can remember, and I can remember in my own southern experience, as a young man that all our attitudes were bad, and paternalistic, and so forth, but also that there was always what we can call a sense of guilt. Nobody was moved, I suppose, to do anything about the situation; you didn't know what to do about the situation. But it was always there, you know, and, damn it, you couldn't live your life without the gnawing, perhaps even subconscious, sense that the world was not really all right. What this meant was that you were forever seeing a concrete example of your own flawed humanity. So there was never a day when you could get up and say, "I'm a good fellow." There was never a day that you could get up and say, "Everything's all right with the world." Things are a lot better now—not as good as they ought to be, but they're a lot better—and the better they get, the more possible it is for us to say, "Well, we *are* all right; we're doing all right, and after all we're better off than they are out in Los Angeles." So your essentially southern sense of southern doom dissipates.

WATKINS: What we're talking about, in part, is what Robert Penn Warren in *The Legacy of the Civil War* calls "the great alibi." You can alibi, and still be guilty as hell. But we never have subscribed to the treasury of virtue, which he also mentions.

RUBIN: We have that, too, though. I think that in a different way there's plenty of that available in the southern writers.

WATKINS: That's probably so, but never as much as in the Damyankees!

LAWSON: I would say, on the contrary, that with the decline of the sense of guilt that Walter Sullivan is talking about, we're not better off, but in fact worse, because the sense of guilt was replaced by the sense of anxiety, which wasn't in the past a southern trait, but which we can feel and see, for example, when getting off an airplane in Atlanta. We are beginning to suffer from the same kind of nameless feeling of anomie which used to characterize the eastern seaboard. It seems to me now that the southerners that I read have this same sense of enfeebling dislocation, which they can't get rid of.

SULLIVAN: We're losing the sense of guilt that we had, and I think it hurts us.

RUBIN: Walter, are you and Lewis Lawson both suggesting, then, that perhaps one of the items on the agenda of southern literary studies in the future should be a look into a possible change from guilt to anxiety over race in the southern mind?

CORE: The essential texture of southern life, it seems to me, is more continuous than the other factor that we are talking about, the metaphysical foundation of that life. In other words, the manners are perhaps more continuous than the theology or the metaphysic behind the life. In this sense, the contemporary southern writer has been deprived of his presumed metaphysic. I don't think he ever really had a definite one; Richard Weaver, for instance, has pointed that out; but he had a much more definite set of values out of which to write. So in this sense he faces the same problem that the writer faces elsewhere in the country: what has been described as "postmodernism." He is writing from a metaphysical standpoint in a postmodern world, searching for new values. If you talk in terms of anxiety and guilt, and if you don't have the metaphysical foundation for the anxiety and guilt, then you cannot have the redemptive moment in literature—or at least that redemptive moment won't mean anything. Lionel Trilling, for instance, has argued very ably in *The Modern Element* that the whole matter of redemption is an essential element in modern literature. The lack of such a redemptive dimension in present-day literature strongly indicates that it is postmodern.

BROWN: I'd like to disagree with Lewis Lawson's comment

that anxiety has not been a trait of the southern mind. I believe it has been. Before the Civil War, for example, there was a great deal of anxiety in the South over the threat of black rebellion. We can find the origins of this in the Haitian revolt in the 1790s or with slave insurrections such as Gabriel Prosser's, and especially Nat Turner's in 1831. Portions of the South were periodically swept by rumors of slave insurrection, which would throw the white population into near hysteria. After the War, when the threat of black rebellion was lessened because slavery had been abolished, there was still the anxiety over the black rapist violating the white woman. Wasn't that a continuing anxiety in the southern mind? How can you explain the phenomenon of lynching? I don't think you can separate the anxiety from the guilt.

WATKINS: Aren't we talking about two different kinds of anxieties, though, one about the self and one about the society, which can be two very different things?

JACKSON: I'm still thinking about this matter of what is distinctly southern in southern literature. All of this hangs together, it seems to me. The phrase that Lewis Simpson used last night is highly appropriate—"a sense of community." What I'm about to say now may seem farfetched. I believe that in the South itself there is a greater sense of community than there is elsewhere in America, and even when there is color caste in its most virulent form, we still find this strong sense of community. I used to go driving through the South back in the days when if I pulled up to a gas station, there'd be a white waiting room and either one or two colored waiting rooms. And yet I noticed something. No matter where I was in the South, when I stopped to get gas this white fellow who was waiting on me had to visit with me. Even though he knew that we had this problem of color caste, I was human to him to that extent. So he couldn't put his gas in my car without visiting. And the anxiety comes in, I think, in this way: the sense of community made both whites and Negroes even more aware of the hierarchical nature of their culture, and it was the hierarchy that bothered them. It wasn't the lack of a sense of community, but that they knew there was a flaw in the way it operated. I think one of the liberating factors in southern literature now is that this particular flaw in the golden bowl is not as glaring as it used to be.

YOUNG: The closest I've come recently to the kind of southern hospitality you are talking about, this concept of humanity, was in Denver, Colorado—in the department stores and the gas stations and the taxi driver who took me from the airport. Not in Nashville, Tennessee, and not in Atlanta, Georgia. I realize what Cleanth Brooks has written about the sense of community and its importance in Faulkner, and I think it is important in all the people of that generation. That's what I think is missing now. This is what the writers who now try to find what Warren calls the past that lies behind the personal past discover is not there.

BROOKS: Let me break in just to give a factual comment, one drawn from my own personal experience. I am a southerner who for the last twenty-five years has lived in the Northeast. To use an analogy from the British Isles: I feel very much like a Scot who always thinks of himself as a Scot even though he teaches at the University of London and enjoys it, finding there great library facilities and excellent students and congenial colleagues whom he likes very much, and who has a pleasant little place out in Surrey only twenty minutes or so from Waterloo station. Now he's come back to Scotland, and he gets there only to find that all his Scottish friends at home are saying, "Old Scotland's gone; you can't find it anymore; it's just like England." I'm bewildered. I can immediately find that I'm in the South. I can find it in a dozen ways, though many of them are intangible ways. You're talking about what seems to me a completely different experience from the one I know. But go ahead, and I'll listen with attention. Yet for me you here today are the best justification that the southern attitudes and virtues remain, and I think that the very fact that you're worried about the change that you say has occurred proves that the "southern" attitudes do remain.

RUBIN: I think what Blyden Jackson said is a very important point to consider in the study of southern literature. The notion of "community" tends to be bandied about, and the trouble with it is that automatically we think of community as something good. Therefore whenever we talk about the community, anything that is bad is a violation of community. The Old South and the twentieth-century South could both be communities, and have in those communities a tremendous amount of injustice. Yet the injustice was perpetrated on a community basis. A community is not necessarily good, in that sense—it's simply a community. Now the other day I was teaching Faulkner's *The Hamlet,* and I was thinking about the difference between Will and Jody Varner, on the one hand, and Flem Snopes on the other. Cleanth Brooks goes into this in his chapter in *William Faulkner: The Yoknapatawpha Country.* Nobody can say that Will Varner's attitude toward the community was one of entire or even primary benevolence. Will Varner was a usurer, an extortioner, and he had many, many despicable traits, and the people of Frenchmen's Bend suffered a great deal from Will Varner's selfishness. But the difference between what Will Varner and Flem Snopes did is that Varner could do such things within the community, whereas with Flem Snopes there was no sense of community whatever; it was entirely economics. What Flem did, frequently, were the same sorts of things that Will Varner did, but what Flem was violating was what was always present with Will Varner, the sense of the community. It seems to me that in *The Hamlet* Faulkner was chronicling one very important aspect of what we're talking about.

BROOKS: I agree with you completely, and let's put it this way—I think community is a good thing, just as I think union is a good thing. (Lincoln justified the bloodshed of the Civil War because the Union had to be saved.) "Union" is a quasi-sacred term. Yet, considered absolutely, some "unions" are not good. Much depends on what's being united to what. Thus, *in general* community is, I think, a desirable thing, just as coherence and harmony are desirable things, but this doesn't mean for a moment that there are not faulty communities, communities that incorporate what most of us see as some of the wrong values. Thus it has been from the beginning of time. It's only the utopian millennial expectation of the American that insists upon a community without flaw. Partly because of this millennial delusion—but also because of other reasons—in America we are in danger of losing the idea of community altogether. We are moving in fact toward atomization, everybody a number in an IBM machine. What results is inhuman: an all-too-human genuine community may be wicked, cruel, and wrongheaded, but it's not inhuman. Complete atomization, however, is inhuman; the faceless anomie of our great cities is terrifying. To recur to Louis Rubin's example from *The Hamlet*: Old Will Varner was a real son of a bitch, granted. But he was a man of appetites and affections, meannesses but also humane concerns—even on occasion of a kind of folk poetry. But Flem Snopes is a monster—scarcely flesh and blood at all.

YOUNG: I agree with you. All I'm saying is that the sense of community you're talking about, as we see it in Frenchmen's Bend, is the last vestige of this kind of unity; the writers of Faulkner's generation were the last in the South to have this concept of community. I think the ones born a generation this side of Faulkner, Walker Percy, for example, can't rely upon the community in the same way the older generation could.

BROOKS: I have to stop talking here; I'm outvoted. You say—and you've had far more recent experience in the South than I have—you say the old sense of community is gone. I'm sorry to hear it, for that's not my impression.

SULLIVAN: I think what we're saying is that it has dissipated to the extent that the possibilities for southern literature have been seriously damaged. Not that it's gone; not that the South is not different—it still is—but there's been some modification.

WATKINS: It depends a good deal on where you live. Walter Sullivan and Dan Young live in Nashville. I live in Atlanta.

JACKSON: May I speak on this point, in terms of what seems to have happened? Let's think of the Southeast—down through Florida and as far west as the western boundary of Louisiana, and perhaps part of Texas—as the homeland, the American homeland of the Negro. This is where he was brought in numbers, in bulk. Now think of this homeland as an amoeba. It seems to me that what happened, through the phenomenon of Negro migration, was that this homeland excluded pseudopods. These pseudopods show up as the ghettos in northern cities. The two that we all know best would be Harlem in New York, and the South Side in Chicago. Two more that we remember very well now are Watts in Los Angeles and Hough in Cleveland. Those pseudopods were really southern. Langston Hughes catches this beautifully at the end of *Not Without Laughter*, when he has a southern boy and his mother walking down a street in the South Side of Chicago hearing a congregation in a storefront church singing an old southern spiritual. Well, it's a southern congregation that has picked itself up bodily and brought itself North. I hope this illustrates in a concrete way my biological metaphor. What I would argue is that the pseudopods then became amoeba, and they excluded pseudopods in their turn, and those pseudopods came back South. So that in Nashville now, and in Atlanta, you've got pseudopods of the southern Negro who went North, and then either came South himself or else his forms of life, his life-styles, were adopted by people in the South. This has been a process that we can demonstrate. The sociologists could provide us with data that would substantiate it. Now whether or not all this has affected the sense of community is an interesting thing, and that's why I've brought it up.

RUBIN: Where do we look, in twentieth-century southern literature, for the image of what we've been talking about?

CORE: Well, obviously we don't look in the apartment building or the hotel or the suburb or the airport: in *The American Scene* Henry James used the great city hotel as a symbol of the faceless modern world. What I'd like to do is get at the distinction, what Floyd Watkins suggested a moment ago, that the quality of urban life is one thing and the quality of life outside these great urban areas an entirely different matter. If there is homogenization, it seems to me, it is largely in these urban areas. Atlanta and

Denver do have a great deal in common: Atlanta is distinctively different from a great deal of the South as the South historically remains.

BROWN: If we are looking for a distinctive southern literature, we have to look to the remaining rural areas of the South. To me the symbol of southern community is the family. In reading Peter Taylor's works, especially his play *Tennessee Day in St. Louis*, which treats of a pseudopod Tennessee family in St. Louis, it seems to me he reveals the death of community in the disintegration of southern families.

RUBIN: This is a good point, but just the same, let's remember that Thomas Wolfe came from a city of forty thousand, not too big by northeastern standards but pretty big by southern standards. Eudora Welty came from Jackson, Mississippi, a city of fifty thousand. Walker Percy lived a great deal of his life in New Orleans and that area. Certainly most of the younger southern writers do not come from rural backgrounds, and do not write primarily about rural backgrounds. Yet a great deal of this traditional material is still there in their work, isn't it?

BROWN: I think in the case of Eudora Welty that Mississippi was overwhelmingly rural and I don't believe the fact that she lives in Jackson invalidates the argument.

JACKSON: I want to cite two novels which illustrate in their content my metaphor about the forming of pseudopods, and so on. Both of these novels were written by southerners, although people tend to forget that they are southerners. One is a southerner named Ralph Ellison, and the other is a southerner named Richard Wright. Even though he died in Paris, Richard Wright was born in Mississippi, and the homeland of his imagination was the Delta South. If one reads *Native Son* and *Invisible Man*—and these are the two best-known Negro novels—what he gets in both is the South that's been extrapolated. *Invisible Man* is a book that perhaps most people would think does not do this as much as *Native Son*, and yet it happens there, too. You remember the anonymous invisible man in New York. It's when he gets to Mary's house—a woman who has come up from the South—that the novel really begins to move the reader. The Harlem that riots is a Harlem which is composed of migrants who are rioting, and the witches' sabbath that you have in the riot is really the South in the North.

WATKINS: The most crucial statement that I can make on this point is very derivative, but if I could teach my students one thing, this is what I would teach them. There are so many critics who say that Faulkner is not writing about the South. What they really mean to say is that he has universal meanings. They don't know what they're saying. A parallel is Cleanth Brooks saying that *The Sound and the Fury* is not about the decay or decline of the South, but it is about the fall of the family, and that the family declined in Connecticut and California before it did in the South, although it's more accelerated in the South. People outside the South, as far as I can tell, don't know what he's talking about.

BROOKS: You're quite right about that.

WATKINS: The point is that it has a southern vehicle, and meanings that will apply to anywhere, but other people don't know the difference between the vehicle and the meaning. If I could teach a student that, I'd be willing to quit after the first day.

RUBIN: When you read the *Oedipus Rex* you don't automatically assume that everybody in Thebes spent most of his time trying to murder his father and sleep with his mother.

LAWSON: Cleanth Brooks was saying earlier that he had seen so much evidence of the South since he came down here, and he lamented the fact that we ourselves couldn't see it. The point could be made, however, that he's dealing with a group of very self-conscious southerners here. We are self-aware, we're conscious of being a part of a unique situation; and I think that the younger writers who have followed in the wake of the southern literary renascence have all been self-conscious writers, and maybe they have responded more to the image of the South postulated by the generation of the Renascence than they have to the changing reality of the South itself. In a way, we've been using up the capital which was deposited in the bank by Mr. Faulkner and by the others, and what the succeeding generation of writers, such as Styron, has produced is not so much a response to the changing South as it has been a parody in many cases, of Wolfe and Faulkner and their contemporaries. If we are going to continue to look for a southern literature, then, what we'll probably start seeing is a shift westward. We'll be searching for a reality which is somewhat more like the image of the South presented by Faulkner and people like that, so the scene of southern literature will jump across the Mississippi, and we'll begin looking to Oklahoma, Texas, and places like that—writers such as Larry McMurtry and others who still are able to present the kind of small-town or rural presentation of class structure and manners such as we used to know.

RUBIN: One of Norman Brown's suggestions for this conference was a study of the southern writer in Texas.

JACKSON: Are you saying, for example, about Styron, that conceivably one of the reasons he wrote *The Confessions of Nat Turner* might be that if he had chosen Norfolk or Southampton County today as the setting for a novel, he wouldn't have been able to get a southern consciousness as readily as he got it in choosing the historical image of the *Confessions*, which took him back?

CORE: I think that's a very shrewd question. It may be that the South, the old material of the southern novel, can better be recovered historically in the deep past. I think of a very fine first novel, *The Coming of Rain*, by Richard Marius, for example, which is about life in East Tennessee after the Civil War. It may be easier to go back and write about something which occurred in southern history in the past—as Styron did in *Nat Turner*—than it is for a writer to cope with his experience today and the world around him.

SULLIVAN: I want to point out something. I think *Nat Turner* is a bad book. Maybe that's too much to say . . .

RUBIN: It's not too much, Walter, it's just wrong.

SULLIVAN: . . . but I'll tell you why. If you look at the last part of *The Sound and the Fury*, at Jason dropping those tickets into the fire, or Dilsey on her way to church, this tells you more about the South, more about black and about white, and more about all the history of them and all the relationships and all the injustices and all the love and all the hate, than all of the rhetoric that Bill Styron gives us in *Nat Turner*. Why is this true? Well, we've discussed the community. I think also it goes right back to what Cleanth Brooks started with. We couldn't find a better example of the move into the dialectic, the move into the intellectualized performance, than *Nat Turner*. And Faulkner did the same thing; if you examine his work you get up to *Go Down, Moses*, and the place where Isaac McCaslin says, "We're just not going to play; it's a nasty game and if we play at all we'll be tainted by it." How could you violate community more than that? And that was the end of the community in Faulkner. After that he wrote an outline for *A Fable*, intellectualized it, and wrote a very bad book. Now I think this is central to our study of southern literature, and it's the central problem that we have to grapple with no matter whether we decide simply to put the emphasis in our study of southern literature on Faulkner and not on Styron, or whether we intend to try to deal with the reasons behind Styron's failure, if you'll pardon the expression.

REEVES: We've said a lot about Faulkner, and a lot about Styron; the point is that Styron is not Faulkner. Part of the problem is if he lives another thirty years, I don't think he will become one. But he's a good writer. The South is changing and he's writing about the changing South. There are other young men who are writing about the South, the sense of community, the result of the fragmentation of the family, and we have one right here ten miles away in Durham, Reynolds Price, who is treating some of these same themes in a very modern way; it reflects the modern South, but it reflects, more than that, modern life. If he were a young Faulkner, I think we'd pay more attention to him, but even so I think that we are getting, from writers who were shaped in their formative years by the same value system, the same kind of response. They responded to what was historically southern, and they are producing it in works of art.

RUBIN: I think you're quite right. If I may make a personal reference, I wrote an essay, or gave a talk and published it as an essay in *The Journal of Southern History*, about ten years ago and I called it "The Difficulties of Being a Southern Writer Today; or, Getting Out from Under William Faulkner." I think that is a very real problem for any southern writer. It's what Flannery O'Connor meant when she said that nobody wants to be caught on the tracks when the Dixie Special comes through. We have this massive literary example, this great genius who towers above all the others, and he can't help but have his impact on the imaginations of all the others. But there's another thing we ought to remember too, in terms of the study of southern literature. Perhaps one of the problems of the southern literary scholar, the literary critic, is how to get out from under William Faulkner, and not use Faulkner and what Faulkner did so well, as a yardstick against which to measure what dozens of other writers, good and bad, have done, since it may not be the right kind of measure at all. In literature all books don't measure exactly the same, and the scale may be completely wrong. I think one of the problems of southern literary criticism is the habit of going back and measuring everybody against Faulkner. Sometimes it doesn't work. I don't think it works with Eudora Welty, who I think is a marvelous writer. But she's not the same *kind* of writer as Faulkner.

REEVES: Nor is Flannery O'Connor.

RUBIN: I think she's closer to Faulkner in terms of her notions of what the dynamics of fiction are. But there's another modern southern literary tradition that I sense, for example, though I've never quite been able to articulate what I think it is. It seems to involve a completely different kind of approach to the dynamics of fiction, and to the notions of time and community and so forth. You find it in Thomas Wolfe and in James Agee and in Eudora Welty. I don't think that it's in the Faulknerian mode at all, and if you try to measure what they do and use Faulkner as a standard for measurement, you aren't going to be able to measure what you're trying to measure.

BROOKS: I think this observation is so good that I'd like to add a little note to it. This is, as a matter of fact, the perennial problem of literary scholarship. We're always going to have to avoid mechanization, stereotyping, the third-rate, the fourth-rate, the lazy person who takes the obviously big figure and measures everything by him. It's very difficult to teach southern literature today for the reason you've given. Everybody measures so completely by Faulkner that they won't see what this other writer or that writer has. But I think that is something we're stuck with, as long as human beings remain human, as long as reviewers are frequently lazy in doing their work and depend on stereotypes.

CORE: Just as people have used Shakespeare as a yardstick for a long time.

BROOKS: Exactly, and to the great detriment of some very fine Elizabethan dramatists . . .

WATKINS: I'm revising my opinion of Eudora Welty. I thought she was just beneath Faulkner, Warren, and Wolfe, but with her last two novels she is, in my judgment, pushing the very best of them all.

RUBIN: *Losing Battles* is a magnificent book, but I think that *The Golden Apples* is even better, and I was very interested to see in a recent interview in the *Southern Review* that she thinks so, too. I think she has tended to be overshadowed, as many people have said. She's not just another good southern woman writer; she's a major writer.

WATKINS: *The Robber Bridegroom*, which was her very first novel, is one of the most delightful pieces I've ever read.

BROOKS: A thought about Katherine Anne Porter: I think that at her best she's a very fine writer, and not in the least like Faulkner. Now I find her completely southern, in my definition of "southern," just as I find Faulkner, but nobody would ever mix up that pair; there's no reason why they should. But both of them seem thoroughly southern.

JACKSON: What we're saying now is not only a reminder to us that writers are individuals, but also it returns us to another point we've already made earlier—that there are many Souths. For example, you mentioned Wolfe and Faulkner in almost the same breath; one can't help but remember that Faulkner's South is not Wolfe's South. There are overlappings, but they are two different Souths, and there are many Souths.

BROWN: I want to ask the meeting if you feel that the younger southern writers are going to continue to produce fiction which is distinctively southern. I think this is a key question. I must say that (I'm a historian and not a professor of English) I'm pessimistic about the prospect. Jonathan Yardley's review of Eudora Welty's *Losing Battles* in the *New Republic* referred to it as perhaps the last good "southern novel." This seems to suggest that we think of the southern novel as being rooted in the agrarian order, even though Miss Welty lives in Jackson and Wolfe lived in Asheville. The writers weren't themselves farmers, they weren't living on the land, but with the South becoming increasingly urbanized and industrialized, in other words with the agrarian order disappearing, are young writers, whose experience is an urban, industrial experience, going to be able to write anything that is recognizably southern?

BROOKS: Are they going to be able to write anything at all?

RUBIN: I do think—now maybe if I lived in Atlanta, I might not say this, but I'm still not sure—that although it is quite true that the South is rapidly becoming industrialized, it is also true in some ways that industrialization is being southernized in the same process. Even if we leave out Atlanta and a couple of other cities, there is a tremendous amount of the traditional southern experience left that is still very valid and still very viable and creative. I don't think that it's gone yet, or anything like it.

BROWN: But is the rural South isolated from the Atlanta phenomenon? Haven't TV and radio and the automobile brought the rural country into the urban environment?

RUBIN: That's true, Norman, but the point is that the best

literature of the South did not come out of the South when that was the case; it came out of the older agrarian South when that was breaking down, and that process is still very much going on all the time.

BROWN: But it was by authors who had had an actual historical experience with an older, traditional agrarian South, and that's not the historical experience of the younger southern writers, because the process of change has gone on too long for that.

RUBIN: It comes back to the matter of the tension between the two, and I think it's still very much present. Lewis Lawson, you have done some good work on Walker Percy. It seems to me that what you said about Walker Percy earlier was that you really think that he represents the emergence, as it were, of a different way of looking at the whole problem.

LAWSON: I don't know whether or not he's representative of a group. I know that he's different from others. Whether he's just a sport, or the beginning of a new trend, I don't know.

RUBIN: And would you maintain that in that difference, there is still something to be encompassed within the body of recognizably southern literature?

LAWSON: Yes, indeed. I was wondering: we've been talking all this time about southern literature, but we haven't once mentioned any genre except the novel. We haven't talked about short stories, or poetry, or anything like that. It used to be that you could almost be geographical about it, and say that Jews and southerners wrote novels and middle westerners wrote poetry. If there is going to be any great change in the southern imagination, maybe we might begin to look for it by looking for the rise of more poetry in the South, and the decline, in quantitative terms, of the novel. I wonder if anyone can see the beginnings of a more important school of poetry in the South, which would indicate a framework of literature which is not reflective of the decline of the family so much as it is reflective of the decline of the individual. It seems to me that poetry recently has been written more about the disintegration of the individual, whereas the novel has customarily talked about the decline of the family, or even before that, the decline of a class. Is poetry coming to the fore as the distinctive southern genre, or are we still in a novelistic period?

CORE: John Crowe Ransom said, forty years ago or close to it in the *Virginia Quarterly Review*, that modern southern poetry was not greatly different from the poetry of the rest of the country. It seems to me that's becoming a stronger and stronger tendency all the time.

WATKINS: The question is both bigger and smaller than the question of the South and the poetry. Yesterday I taught James Dickey's poem "The String," which is fascinating to me because I can't make any string figure with my hands, and so I always ask whether a student can make a string figure for me. I had a student in class yesterday make every imaginable design by string—Jacob's Ladder, a cup of coffee in the air, or whatever it is—and it fascinated the class because they hadn't even known that Dickey's poem was about string figures. This is southern, and its nontelevision, and it's cultural, and it's something to do besides watch television or even read poetry, and it goes back to what even the South ultimately gets back to.

JACKSON: May I respond, on this question of poetry, from my particular vantage points? Insofar as Negro writers are concerned, there are virtually no southern poets who are writing now. Nikki Giovanni was born in Tennessee, but her voice tends largely to be the voice of the urban North as much as of anything else. You could almost give a categorical answer to the question so far as Negro writers are concerned.

SULLIVAN: Is "The Mediterranean" a southern poem?

BROOKS: Yes, absolutely.

SULLIVAN: I think so, too, but in the sense that *Absalom, Absalom!* is a southern novel.

BROOKS: Well, maybe so. The point is that poetry, as has already been pointed out, tends to be less limited in range; the lyric in particular is not talking about social relationships nearly as primarily as any short story or piece of fiction will. In the case of Ransom, Tate, and Warren, you had three poets who were writing a great deal of their poetry, particularly when they were all writing, the earlier Warren and the other two, about what Warren calls, and I would call, the "crisis in culture." It was what was happening to America; what is happening to the South is the very theme of most of Allen Tate's poetry. So this is intensely southern, perhaps because it is universal. They are talking about a collapse. Allen Tate is writing about the same theme that Eliot was writing about in "The Waste Land." He comes at it in his own way; he uses his own perspective. My own experience with poetry is that we are not getting a great deal of terribly good or striking poetry from the South now, and what we're getting is basically vaguely international, or Anglo-American. A. R. Ammons, I think, is probably regarded by a good many people as the most distinguished of the younger group of modern southern poets—he and Dickey. Ammons is a kind of Wordsworth-cum-Wallace Stevens; I'm not intending any denigration of him, but it's that kind of thing and much of it is written about his personal life at Cornell University and the landscape there as well as the southern landscape of his boyhood. I think this is in the cards, granted, that our day has not been a day of epic poetry, or dramatic poetry, primarily, but lyric poetry, and lyric poetry always has less to do with the social issues and the family.

RUBIN : It comes without what Red Warren referred to as "the documentation."

BROOKS : That's right, without the documentation.

RUBIN : It's in the documentation that the writer automatically moves into the images which he knows around him.

YOUNG : I think this is the point we've made. Only two or three of John Crowe Ransom's poems are obviously southern poems, in the sense that they have southern backgrounds, landscapes, that sort of thing, so you could say "this occurred in the South." If you contrast Ransom's poetry with the poetry of James Dickey, obviously more of Dickey's poems are set in the South, they include southern landscapes. But Ransom's poetry is southern in a way that James Dickey's poetry is not southern. There are certain attitudes, customs, which we were talking about earlier, that are involved, and this is the difference. I think that for scholars and critics one thing we need to do is to see if we can determine if there is anything distinctive, if there is anything unique, about these contemporary southern writers. Ransom, Tate, Warren, and Faulkner were, I think, distinctive and unique in their time. As someone has said, few characters in Hemingway have grandfathers. All of Faulkner's characters have grandfathers and great-grandfathers, and everything else. You know this. You can pick a novel up and read one paragraph, and if you didn't know it was Faulkner you'd know it came out of the South between 1920 and 1950.

RUBIN: I've been trying to jot down a few of the ideas we've been playing around with, in terms of what they might mean for the student of southern literature dealing with the literature of the twentieth-century South. I think we all seem to be fascinated with the idea that Allen Tate introduced, about this change from rhetoric to dialectic, and what that means. Lewis Simpson said something last night that particularly interested me. It was that the terms on which we're dealing with this whole business of the Southern Renascence and the changing South and the cultural crossover, in a sense, come out of Allen Tate's essay "The Profession of Letters in the South," written in 1935. I have found again and again, and I've heard Hugh Holman say this too, that it is almost impossible to come across an important idea about southern literature—twentieth-century southern literature or any other kind of southern literature—that at one time or another Allen Tate hasn't suggested. One of the important jobs of the scholar or critic (I think the one is the other if he's any good) has got to be the study of Allen Tate's work in terms of the South. He never set out to be a scholar of southern literature, in the way that we would consider, say, Jay B. Hubbell as a scholar of southern literature, and he never set out to be a systematic, conceptual critic, though he has probably the best conceptual mind of anybody of his generation. Yet what he has said about southern literature is of absolutely first importance, and somebody ought to really pay attention to this. I blame myself most of all because I have written about him in these terms and I haven't even begun to touch the surface. Obviously another point which has come out today is what Walter brought up: the existence of traditional Christianity or Protestantism as a kind of external moral referent and a measurement of human failure in southern society. It's had a lot of failure to measure, but it's always been there to measure the failure, though maybe it hasn't been used nearly as much as it should. It seems to me that it would be well worth the student's time to consider twentieth-century southern literature and what's happened to it in those terms. Another point we kept coming back to is the whole business of community. This is what Lewis Simpson talked about last night. I gather that you all think that this lies at the center of the southern literary experience, that somehow the experience of the individual writers grows out of that kind of community relationship, for good and for bad. This is a theme which really ought to be developed, and the southern novel provides an excellent example of it. We've also talked about poetry, and here we noted immediately that the southern poets of today, as Cleanth Brooks said, tend to write out of an international or Anglo-American attitude rather than what we would call a distinctly southern sensibility, though as he pointed out, this is part of the nature of poetry. Perhaps there ought to be a great deal more looking at more recent southern poets to see how they do differ from the earlier poets.

REEVES: Their problem is getting out from under the shadow of Dickey right now, the young ones.

WATKINS: Wouldn't you agree with me that the influence of the Protestant tradition also should not be considered wholly derogatory, as it has been by so many people?

RUBIN: Of course, and I don't think it always has been handled that way. I think, for example, of Cleanth Brooks's handling of *Light in August*, where the matter is beautifully stated.

WATKINS: But consider William Van O'Connor on Faulkner.

RUBIN: I want to say something about another book, which, as Blyden Jackson will quickly tell you, has been written about almost to exhaustion: Jean Toomer's *Cane*. I would like to suggest that *Cane* has a tremendous amount to say about the South and the southern experience, but this aspect is what has not been dealt with to any extent. Would you agree with that, Blyden?

JACKSON: Yes, it's a southern book. It's an interesting problem. W. E. B. DuBois once said something about it that was very true; he said that most people who read *Cane* forgot how little time Jean Toomer spent in Georgia. He brought some perspectives to it that were not Georgian, really. It's a very fine book. It illustrates, it seems to me, something that we've been talking about today—the sense of community. I won't go into this at great length, but the book does make you feel that here are some people who share some attitudes, some values, and a sense of their own past, white and black, which has made them into a coherent body of people.

RUBIN: In the five minutes we have left, I'd like to ask any of you to mention quickly anything you think we have left out.

REEVES: We haven't discussed the terminal date of the southern literary renascence.

RUBIN: We *have* talked about that, Paschal, really, haven't we?

REEVES: We've talked around it, and the conclusion I draw is the one I had when I came, that it is still continuing, perhaps not on the same level but certainly with as much vigor, though perhaps with not as much genius.

JACKSON: I've been wondering whether or not a second southern literary renascence would be possible now.

REEVES: It seems to me the point we've made is that one is still possible, but all of us are apprehensive about when the material for it will be too much exhausted for future writers to continue using it. Fifty years is a long time for a literary movement.

RUBIN: I think the development that lies ahead in southern

literature, which has only begun to be touched, is comedy. We've had some good comic writers already. After the period when something looks tragic, it begins to look comic. I think of Barth's *Sot-Weed Factor*, for example. That's just a start, and we'll see a lot more of that.

BROOKS: There is one idea that gathers up a number of things that you've all very properly put down that I'm not going to talk about now at any length, but I'm more and more convinced that this is the big American theme, and the South has its part in it, as a contrast basically—it's millennialism. The chronic intellectual disease of Americans from the time that they landed on Plymouth Rock has been millennialism, and the South has had its own infection, but in general it has stood against it, and this is where the tension of which we have spoken earlier has been coming from. I think the future of any southern literature will depend upon whether we become utopians and millennialists too. This issue is powerfully related to Christianity, the community, and, I would venture, the human dimension itself. Will the human dimension remain? Will there still be a possibility of tension between what I want to be or ought to be and what I am? Or will we decide that if we will just brainwash everybody and get more IBM machines, everything can be made perfect? If so, that's the end of literature.

CORE: The ultimate question here might be: is literature possible for postmodern man, in or out of the South?

SULLIVAN: I've been trying to deal with this question of community in a different way. We talk about community, and we talk about place, and I was intrigued by what Blyden Jackson said a minute ago—he spoke of attitudes, values, and a sense of the past. I was thinking that one of the best examples of community that I know is the Children of Israel on their way out of Egypt, going, they hoped, to the Promised Land. They don't have much of a sense of place while they're moving, and they raise hell from the time they leave until the time they get there—it's a magnificent story if you haven't read it recently—and every day somebody rises up and says, "Yes, but what's God done for us lately?"

What's so marvelous about this, however, is that they've got this built-in corrective. They've got the Ten Commandments—they've got the book of Leviticus before they're through with it, you see—and so there's no question about what is right and wrong. They're sinful in terms of what is right and wrong, all right, but there's no argument, there's no situation ethics. There's no question of what is right and wrong, and there is built in to their situation the corrective for the wrong. Sometimes the corrective was harsh, but the corrective was there. Now it seems to me that this is really what we mean by "community," this sort of thing. Maybe we ought not to pay so much attention any more to these very fine southern literary traits of being great raconteurs and loving the old home place and so forth, but get back to the importance of this basic delineation of what community really means.

8. The Continuity of Southern Literary History

MODERATOR:
Hugh Holman

PANELISTS:

*Robert Bain, Norman Brown, Richard Calhoun,
Charles Davis, Richard Beale Davis,
Jack Guilds, Carl Dolmetsch, Thomas Inge,
Lewis Leary, Rayburn Moore, Paschal Reeves,
Arlin Turner, Floyd Watkins, Dan Young*

HOLMAN: We are here to discuss the continuity of southern literary history. Someone has raised the question of what particular word among these four we are going to emphasize, "continuity" or "southern" or "literary" or "history." It's not a bad question. I suggest that one of the first things we might think about is the question of whether or not the three relatively distinct periods in southern literary experience do really constitute a continuity. For those of us who were together yesterday afternoon, this discussion represents a continuation, in a sense, of one of the questions that we were discussing then—that is, whether or not there are common characteristics that moved beyond the earlier period into the nineteenth-century issues of southern writing and that still continue as significantly into twentieth-century southern writing. I propose that we begin with that question. Do we or do we not think that there is a continuity of interest, of subject matter, of theme, however different the mode of expression may be, or even the attitude toward the subjects may be, among the three major periods? Or do you agree with me—I'm not sure you will—that there are the three major periods? Maybe there are four.

LEARY: Would you name the periods?

HOLMAN: The first is the period of colonial literature, what has been called the "era of good feeling," approximately down to the election of Jackson; then the period from the middle or late 1820s until the 1920s; and from that period on into the present. Do you agree that these constitute the periods?

C. DAVIS: Don't you have to indicate what the continuity is rather more substantially? For example, it seems to me very clear that there is the question of matter, which is what you have raised before; then there is the question of style; and there is a question—this is a more complicated one, perhaps—of consciousness or of sensibility. These are three quite different variables, and there may be a continuity in one and not a continuity, obviously, in the others. There may be, for example, between the nineteenth century and the twentieth century, as Roy Harvey Pearce has indicated, a kind of disjunction in sensibility and in consciousness. And so when we look at the problem we ought to look at it in terms of, perhaps not these variables, but some specific variables of some kind.

WATKINS: I believe in continuity, but I'm not sure but what we have so much continuity that we don't have periods in literary history. That is to say, for example, you have omitted as a mark of change the Civil War, which may be the most drastic shift in southern history. Or, if you want to look at it another way, take 1940. Some areas of the yeoman South actually entered the twentieth century only in 1940 because of poverty up until World War II.

HOLMAN: I take it that there are two issues that my question has raised for us. One is whether or not in trying to discuss continuity we do need, as Charles Davis has suggested, to break it down and discuss continuities—continuities of subject matter, continuities of style or language, continuities of sensibility. The other is whether or not the periods which I suggested do constitute adequate divisions of history. I take it that there are some of us who feel that the Civil War not only had an impact upon southern culture that I'm sure none of us would ignore, but that this impact also represented a serious break in subject matter and sensibility for the writers. That, I think, is the real issue here as to whether or not the pre-Civil War and post-Civil War writers represented a major break as forms of literary expression, not as forms of national or dreamed-of-national experience.

GUILDS: If you were asked the same question about American literary history, I don't think you'd break it the way you did, and it becomes a very interesting question as to why, if we follow your divisions, it would be different for the South in American literature than for "the main body of American literature," where we would talk about periods like "the rise of realism," and this kind of thing. Are we not going to pay attention to that in southern literature, for instance?

CALHOUN: One reason, of course, is the fact that the South in the 1850s did not participate in the American literary renascence of that period, and most of us who teach American literature in two semesters tend to divide at that point. It doesn't work as well with southern literature, so certainly there is something missing right at the dead center of the history of American literature as far as southern literature is concerned.

INGE: Aren't these chronological divisions mainly a matter of convenience, after all, to enable us to discuss these things within some limits, and therefore to press them much beyond that might not be worthwhile? Right now, I think, 1970 has been some kind of a major division in American literature in general, probably in southern literature too, but we're not all sitting around evaluating this, and one hundred years hence 1970 may be considered an important breaking point. To push beyond this into philosophical considerations may not be fruitful.

C. DAVIS: I should like to add one footnote to this and the whole reference to the War. What reminded me of it is that in terms of intellectual continuity, in terms of continuity in culture, the thing that seems to me very clear is that the historical event is not beautifully coordinated with what happens in the culture—that there is often a kind of lag. I would propose that the impact of the Civil War is not really felt completely until a generation after the War itself. In some ways one could make the case that the impact of the war in 1776 was not fully felt until the emergence of Emerson in the 1830s.

YOUNG: Hugh Holman made a point in another connection that's important here. We talk about "the South"; there are many Souths. If we want to talk about a division in what we in other connections have called "the Southwest," or Mississippi—the Faulkner country—between 1815, roughly, and 1860, a great deal was happening there different from what was going on in Virginia. This was the time in which there was not only the War itself, but the end of a philosophic attitude that had developed very rapidly—a social, political situation—the whole business. You cannot disregard the fact that the most important date in the literature of that section of the South, the Deep South, is 1861. Before that was the old, and since then there's been something else. I really think rather than the three dates you need four: the first ending somewhere around 1815, the second at the Civil War, the third coming up to 1920, and the fourth from 1920 to the present.

CALHOUN: When we talk of past literary histories of the South we all mention, of course, Jay B. Hubbell's book, *The South in American Literature, 1607-1900* and we always mention Edd W. Parks's *Southern Poets,* and we mention Gregory L. Paine's *Southern Prose Writers*—these are solid scholarly works—but if we're in any sense revisionists here we might also consider, by stressing that word "history," what their limitations are in stressing continuity and dividing southern literature into periods. One obvious ingredient missing in these books is the twentieth century, but these are our past histories and the studies we always mention.

WATKINS: We can't consider continuity of history without also considering place. For example, Lafayette County in Mississippi was in the frontier about 1830 and you moved thirty miles or so west past Batesville and get down into the Delta—when was that settled, Dan?

YOUNG: In the 1820s.

MOORE: Helena, Arkansas, is thirty-five miles due west of Batesville and was surveyed and founded in 1820.

WATKINS: So you've got the frontier in southern history from 1830, and earlier in other places, till well into the twentieth century. Faulkner was writing about the frontier in many different periods.

YOUNG: Many people thinking about the South, about the South generally, and Faulkner's South particularly, are really talking about Mississippi between 1830 and 1860. That's what the South is for them.

CALHOUN: A footnote to what Floyd said is that the Census Bureau lists the demographic center of America by decades; in other words you can look back—this is of interest to the literary historian—and see where the center of America was, as far as population is concerned. No one has done this for the South and southern regions for 1830, 1840, 1850, 1860. Where was the demographic center of the South?

C. DAVIS: I'm still not absolutely sure that this kind of equation which you are making actually between historical development and cultural development is an adequate or a profitable one. You can speak of a demographic center—and obviously there's some significance involved in its moving westward gradually—but at the same time the cultural development is not really governed in very much the same way. It depends on circumstances of publication and on the presence of universities and on where the genius develops, and things of that kind as well.

BROWN: I think we all agree, and it's been said several times during the conference, that geographically there are many Souths, but yet we speak of one South. C. Vann Woodward in *The Burden of Southern History*, a very influential book in both history and English, defined the history of the South as the collective experience of the southern people, black and white, and said that it was history and not geography that made the self-conscious South; perhaps we could try to identify in the South's history these continuing themes which have given the South a sense of identity, and which have provided materials for its writers.

CALHOUN: I would like to suggest one theme of interest to me, the traditional southern theme of agrarianism, at least through the 1930s, and the distrust of technology and industrialization. And then if we turn to forms, thinking of Richard Chase and *The American Novel and Its Tradition*, I would be interested in pursuing the romance and the continuity of the romance as a form in southern literature.

INGE: You need not stop at 1930. Just a couple of weeks ago I was invited to write a defense of agrarianism in the 1970s; because I had done an anthology on agrarianism, the writer assumed I was an agrarian, but I wrote and told him I was not. His particular publication has a program not unlike the twelve principles in *I'll Take My Stand*, and the implication of the man's letter was that this is the only viable alternative to modern industrial progress. I would think it is even more difficult to take a stand on those principles in the 1970s than in the 1930s, but agrarianism is in Western thought one of the most persistent themes. It's not particularly southern, either, but because of the plantation system and because of southern history, agrarianism takes a different turn in the South.

CALHOUN: Of course in the colonial period it was *the* view of America. I'm interested in the 1850s; I've worked with *Russell's Magazine*. In the South agrarianism became then a theme to use against industrialism as a method and against positivism as a philosophy in the North. Allen Tate was mentioned night before last. Certainly the enemy, to Tate in his essays written in the 1930s, is logical positivism, and his hope is the possibility of the South surviving if it maintains an opposition to technology and positivism; so there is a continuity. Recently we've had a counterculture against technology on the part of young people, looking for alternatives to our technotronic society, as I believe Erich Fromm has called it, or the megamachine, as Lewis Mumford has called it.

REEVES: There's a possibility we will have a return to agrarianism by the amoeba-like process of developing communes in rural areas, the complete reaction to the technological and urbanized society, but whether these people will ever get down to producing anything of a literary nature there's no way to tell. As we look at it from our own point we could say that agrarianism in the South is not through yet; it may not spawn another group like the one at Vanderbilt, but England only had one set of Lake Poets in the nineteenth century, and I guess we should be glad that we had one set of agrarians.

C. DAVIS: What is exciting about the ideas presented by Richard Calhoun is the fact that reality has somehow become pastoral. Obviously at the end of the eighteenth century the notion of the agrarian paradise—and that, of course, is overstated—was very immediate, but once we move to the end of the nineteenth century it is not. What we have here is a form of pastoral, which, I don't need to remind you, is always written by people in the city who are rejecting city values in terms of an ideal of some sort which does not in fact exist for them. That, it seems to me, is what happened in the 1920s and indeed what is happening in the pastoral revolution that Tom Inge was asked to participate in.

BROWN: I think that the pastoral literature of the South has been characterized by a certain sadness and melancholy, and that you can find this even before the Civil War in William Gilmore Simms and in John Pendleton Kennedy—they're already celebrating a golden agrarian age that is in the past and is receding further all the time. It continues, for example, in Thomas Nelson Page's *In Ole Virginia*—a sadness and melancholy, and even a recognition that flaws were developing in the plantation order which would doom it to extinction, even without the War.

GUILDS: That's a particularly good point. There has been, even back before the 1860s, a difference in tone, you might say, in southern writers. Hugh Holman has pointed out that in *The*

Yemassee there is this sense of tragedy not unlike what you find in Faulkner, a sense of the inevitability of defeat. And this may be a characteristic of southern writers that we find in both the nineteenth and twentieth centuries.

WATKINS: There is much less opportunity to be agrarian even in the country now; for example, I know of a sharecropper, a peanut farmer, in South Georgia who drives an air-conditioned tractor, and he cultivates his peanuts from the time when he turns the land over in the spring until the time after he's gathered them— he cultivates them, he uses insecticides, and he fertilizes them— without ever stepping on the land. So even he is less agrarian than his father was.

R. B. DAVIS: We might want to take this theme of agrarianism back to the colonial period; I would prefer the word "pastoralism," which would suit much better there, and I was thinking particularly of the southern colonial elegy which Kenneth Silverman denies existed. It existed very strongly; it was almost, if not purely, a pastoral elegy, and curiously, in opposition to the nineteenth century, it is as joyous as an elegy can become. Even beginning with "Bacon's Epitaph, made by his Man," which is not very joyous but still has a somber stoic joyful quality. I had a student make a collection of eighteenth-century southern elegies, in which God and the Trinity are mentioned only once, but Apollo and Theocritus and the rest of them occur in almost every elegy. They're not at all like the New England nor the tombstone epitaphs, nor like any of the other elegies, but they are pastoral essentially, and sometimes even in terms not just of eighteenth-century or seventeenth-century English pastoral, but of the southern landscape. But I'd still call it "pastoral" rather than "agrarian"; there's no sowing or reaping.

CALHOUN: I prefer the term "pastoralism" myself, although I mentioned "agrarianism." If we pursue pastoralism as a theme in southern literature, when is the pastoral, as you're suggesting in the eighteenth century, idealization per se for the sake of idealization, and when in the Emersonian sense does it become social criticism? I think later in the South, as opposed to Northern Industrialism, it did. So there are two aspects of the pastoral. In *I'll Take My Stand* it's social criticism, obviously.

INGE: I'm a little bothered by combining pastoralism and agrarianism in that fashion because of the things that pastoralism suggests. The tradition emphasizes lament, sadness, and melancholy. I get images of the poet lying under the tree and watching the sheep as he laments things. But much of the agrarianism of the South has not been a lament; it has pursued something, a positive ideal. The title itself, *I'll Take My Stand*, is not a retreat, but it's an assertive, positive position, and because of the pastoral tradition and its relation to the agrarian tradition the agrarians were misunderstood. Davidson was cast as an arch-Romantic, which I don't think is accurate. So combining the two traditions presents problems, and the associations which come with one are not the associations which come with the other. But then you try to define agrarianism and you're up another tree with another kind of problem.

YOUNG: It seems to me, too, that even back to John Taylor of Caroline and Thomas Jefferson there's something besides pastoralism in the usual agrarian attitudes; it becomes social philosophy, particularly in John Taylor.

C. DAVIS: Don't we have a difference in forms of pastoral now? It would be in some ways natural for a cultivated man in the eighteenth century to write in a form which he inherits from England, or inherits from the general European tradition. On the other hand, the kind of pastoral which develops out of the nineteenth century uses unconventional forms, that don't fit the pattern that comes from Theocritus really, but the mode which is expressed in it seems to be close to that and we call it pastoral.

REEVES: Aren't we going in cycles anyway, a cyclic approach to the continuity of southern literary history? If Hugh Holman omitted the War a hundred years ago as a great trauma of the South, we a hundred years later are going through our great trauma of this century, and we don't know what literature will be produced. It may be a continuity of theme, it may be a continuity of subject matter, but I think that as we get more crowded, "environmentalism" is simply a synonym or euphemism for the pastoral. We're going to have this pastoral longing with us and we're going to find literary expression of it. Even as it disappears perhaps as a way of life, as it becomes more difficult to find a place to pitch a pup tent just to get away from it all, there's still going to be in some cyclic way a recurrence of the pastoral in American literature, and certainly in southern literature.

BROWN: Paschal, don't you think that pastoral literature has had a definite therapeutic value for the country, not just for the South but for the North? William R. Taylor in *Cavalier and Yankee: The Old South and American National Character* says the South didn't really believe in the Cavalier but only in the need for him, but he also suggests that for a North that was experiencing rapid change the southern plantation as a symbol of order and stability had a great attraction. And someone said yesterday in one of the papers that in the post-Civil War period northern editors were demanding romantic stories of the Old South from their southern authors, a fact which again suggests that the northern people undergoing rapid change also found this kind of literature comforting and satisfying. What you're suggesting is that in another period of accelerated change people will turn to the South and to the pastoral tradition for solace.

REEVES: Yes, that was my implication. People are always attracted by nostalgia. I had my own cultural shock when one of my students just a few weeks ago discovered the 1950s, and she felt all of this wonderful nostalgia and wanted to write on somebody who wrote way back then, and who hadn't been worked to death. I haven't quite recovered from that. I put her to work on Elizabeth Spencer.

MOORE: Elizabeth Spencer, I'm sure, would be delighted to know that she belongs to the good old days. She, by the way, is a writer whose work we ought to be studying.

BROWN: I might mention something Cleanth Brooks said in a

conversation the other day—that in his Faulkner class at Yale he finds that his students crave the kind of values that Faulkner offers, they find them attractive because they're in search of values, and Faulkner is a symbol of stability and order and values. He offers them the old verities.

REEVES: This is one of the appeals of southern literature to a number of people. They may respond to it kindly or adversely, but they respond because it has a value system, and the writers make judgments, and strong judgments. One of the things about our current society is that the young graduates we're turning out don't like to make decisions based on values. I had lunch with a man who's vice-president of a very large corporation, and he said, "We have quit recruiting among certain colleges because the graduates that we get, and want to put in our executive training program, don't want to make a decision based on a value system; they have rebelled against it." Southern literature, regardless of how we categorize it, is tied up with a value system and a response to a value system. The system hasn't always been the same; there have been shifts of emphasis; but there has been a consistent response to a value system, and I think we can say there has been that continuity.

CALHOUN: One of the reasons that agrarianism or pastoralism as a theme in American literature and southern literature can be explored is that in our treatment of American literature for the last twenty years or so we have stressed a kind of dialectics, paired opposites—the light and the dark, yea-saying and nay-saying—and in southern literature this kind of study can lead to really pretty much the same sort of thing. We have the town *vs.* the wilderness, sectional values *vs.* national values, low-country *vs.* up-country, in some degree Old South ideas *vs.* New South ideas, romance *vs.* realism, innocence *vs.* evil. So it can lead into a discussion of the value system as it appears in southern literature in terms of the opposites which define that system, the positive values and the negative values.

INGE: Perhaps one of the reasons why Hemingway is not

being read in America much by young people is the fact that he places a good deal of emphasis on developing courage through physical conflict, and he demands that one take up the rifle and go into the wilderness to slay the beast. But in Faulkner, as Isaac McCaslin must do, he must leave aside these things and go into the wilderness to meet the beast face to face, and so in Faulkner you get an emphasis on responsibility and acquiescence, whereas Hemingway pits the young person against the environment. I think in line with what Norman Brown was saying that perhaps Faulkner would be more attractive to them for that reason. I do know that Hemingway is not terribly attractive to them for these other reasons.

CALHOUN: Where do you think James Dickey—his poetry and *Deliverance*—would fit into that? Which is it, as far as the wilderness is concerned? In *Deliverance* the Atlanta city people go into the wilderness and have to face a survival situation and not just face nature of course—they conquer nature—but also kill people. In a good deal of James Dickey's poetry, though, there is the idea of "the way of exchange," as Hal Weatherby has called it in his *Sewanee Review* article, entering into the animal, natural aspects and, of course, there's no element of killing or destruction in that aspect of the poetry.

YOUNG: I don't believe this is the time to analyze *Deliverance*, but it seems to me that the basic problem there is a group of men who are trying to discover an essential relationship to the natural forces around them; different people make different decisions. Some of them make the right decisions, some of them make the wrong ones. Some have right attitudes toward nature; some wrong. At least my students feel that the responsibility for the murder of the man with the bow and arrow is justified because of certain attitudes he's already exemplified towards nature, certain deviations that are involved. So I think it is basically, in one sense at least, a novel in which we are concerned with what is essentially an appropriate attitude toward nature in the twentieth century.

C. DAVIS: To move away from *Deliverance*, I should like to

point to a pattern of oscillation, to history as oscillation, history as swinging pendulum of some sort; it occurred to me that this may be so in the distinction that was made between Hemingway and Faulkner. I suspect that we do have sets of opposing ideas operating in our culture to which we can give different tags. One convenient tag, which has been used constantly through our history, is to call certain kinds of things more European, and other things less European. I remember articles by Tate in which he insists upon affirming the European aspects of our culture as opposed to those that are natively developed. This kind of swing occurs periodically in our culture.

HOLMAN: Could we shift for a moment from "continuity" to "southern," and step back to the earliest period? A great many people have insisted in writing about the South that it is not different, not in any significant sense distinctive, until somewhere in the 1820s or early 1830s when it begins to assume special characteristics. Therefore, they feel, we have a general American literature at least to Jackson, and at that time we begin to get a group of characteristics—whether we can agree on what they are or not—distinctive enough so that we need to talk about this region in terms different from those in which we have talked about the total nation. We've almost implicitly agreed this morning, as some of us did yesterday afternoon, that in the nineteenth century the course of American literary history and the course of southern American literary history have not always run parallel, that there are significant differences. How far back can we carry this sense of "southern"? Is it embedded in the earliest roots of the southern experience, in the colonial roots of the southern experience, or is it something that comes into being with the sense of political and economic separateness that begins to develop in the early decades of the nineteenth century?

BROWN: Perhaps Carl Bridenbaugh's thesis in his *Myths and Realities: Societies of the Colonial South* might be appropriately introduced here. Bridenbaugh suggests that before the Old South you have the "Old Souths," and he identifies several colonial

societies in the region that became the South—the Carolina society, the Chesapeake society, the Back Country, and he suggests
possibly a fourth society in seaboard North Carolina. He says
there was not even a southern accent, but that there were two
conditions which prefigured the Old South as we think of it, the
antebellum South. One was the rural nature of southern life—
except in Charleston and a few other seaboard towns you did not
have any developed town life—and the other was the presence of
the Negro.

R. B. DAVIS: I agree with hardly anything Carl Bridenbaugh's
ever written, but I do agree with these three divisions. Did any of
you see Alistair Cooke's second episode of his *America* last week,
with the New England *vs.* Jamestown beginnings of America and
particularly his characterization of the Massachusetts Bay Colony
as a pervasive influence in the dominion of New England as a
totalitarian state from beginning, he implied, to end—he didn't
get to the end—and the southern beginnings of representative
government? Here we get into politics. I would agree that we do
have those three or four Souths, but they have in common from
the first 1619 assembly at Jamestown on the individual's relation
to government, and Alistair Cooke gave a very interesting explanation of how they came into being, which I don't think is accurate but it is quite stimulating. It had to do with the individual's
relation to his local government and to his government in England, and the fact that the South, curiously for some people, was
the more tolerant section of the two colonial groups—tolerant of
all kinds and conditions of people, religions, national groups, and
so on. Cooke parallels New England with the Communist state in
which if you don't belong to the Communist party you can live in
the country but you have nothing to say, which of course was true
of Puritan New England, while in the South everybody had something to say. I can give some cases in point. There's an interesting
article in an early *Virginia Magazine of History* on George Brent,
an early Catholic in Virginia, with its established Church of England, yet he was attorney general, a member of the House of

Burgesses, and no one ever challenged him. Though he was a professed Roman Catholic, there was never any trouble. There were some minor persecutions of Quakers and so on in the South, but relatively speaking there has been a tolerance, except for the slave, and of course that came after the period I'm talking about. I would say the slave impact doesn't begin to be felt until the 1660s, and then it has channeled itself separately. I can't feel that it influences southern culture until well into the eighteenth century myself. But man's relation to his society—society being government in its various phases, both from abroad and within in little units such as vestries or parishes as in the South—was a concern from the beginning. The earliest records from the assemblies of Virginia, Maryland, North Carolina, South Carolina in the seventeenth century show this concern. Why does the king have the right? What are we going to do if we pass a law and it has to go to England before we can implement it or if we implement it and then it's thrown out? Such questions begin to appear on the floor of the assemblies by the 1680s at latest, and it comes right on through the colonial period. Here is politics, but it's a theme of literature. These men are speaking according to rhetorical principles and within rhetorical frames and we are getting a literature partly oral—if literature may be oral—and partly written. This is a very complex and involved matter.

BROWN: Carl Bridenbaugh suggested that there was no southern accent.

R. B. DAVIS: It's there by the eighteenth century; whether it's there earlier or not is very difficult to say, but you can tell it from the gazettes. As soon as we get the first southern gazettes you can see in their imitations of dialects and that in their attempt to write a dialect phonetically they're betraying how they speak; even though they're making fun of an Irish or a Welsh or a Scottish or an African dialect, they are showing how they themselves speak when they do that. But I don't know if you can find any proof of it before that. I haven't found any.

HOLMAN: You can also detect the beginnings of dialect, evidence for dialect pronunciations, from the letters, diaries, and other documents of semiliterate people.

R. B. DAVIS: I will take that back; that's right. As far back as the Virginia Company of London, the letters in those four great volumes that were published by the Library of Congress, the semiliterates do show dialects. Now whether you can classify them as southern or not I am not quite sure, but they are there.

BAIN: We can also see consciously developed differences between the North and South in writing in the South before 1720. Part of that difference may stem from the struggle between the king's party and the Puritans in England. But writers like George Alsop, William Byrd, and others caricatured Puritans frequently. We see this sometimes in the promotional tracts and in the histories. Someone has said that these early histories express Virginia's self-consciousness of its destiny, its history, and its possibilities. These promotional tracts and histories also express attitudes that are not New England attitudes at all.

CALHOUN: What you say is true and interesting; but when we talk about the characteristics of southern literature later, one thing that is mentioned is a religious sense of evil rather than an idealistic one of innocence. We have the southern attitude in the nineteenth century towards transcendentalism, for example, and we talk about southern Puritanism, southern Calvinism. If we're talking about continuity, when did this sense come in in the South, or have we overstressed it, and where is it reflected in the literature?

R. B. DAVIS: I don't think we can say when it came in. It's clearly evident by the second Great Awakening around the end of the eighteenth century and the beginning of the nineteenth. There is some evidence of it in the first Great Awakening, but when Whitefield went up and down the coast there are in the *South Carolina Gazette* and the *Virginia* and *Maryland Gazettes* reports of pro-Whitefield and anti-Whitefield things. This was one of the few issues that official printers to the government were allowed to give both sides of the question on. But it is not profoundly religious. I found plenty of colonial sermons from the South, but when I was trying to collect tracts I found no Whitefieldian tract ever published in the colony of Maryland during the whole Whitefield episode, as compared with the Philadelphia, New York, or New England areas in which there were simply scores, if not hundreds. That the South just wasn't much interested in religion then is one way of interpreting it; you may put it in other ways. But I can't see the evidence there in literature; it may be evident in some other things.

HOLMAN: Richard Beale Davis warned that he was simplifying when he was discussing the nature of the southern experience in the seventeenth century, and I'm going to simplify his simplification even more and ask if what we're talking about here is a sense of man in society and a concern with order and with social order beginning early, and raise the question as to whether it is one of the concerns that has persisted in southern writing?

R. B. DAVIS: That's one of our continuities. We have a sense of values in particular applied in this way.

HOLMAN: Is the sense of values based on the social structure, the social order?

R. B. DAVIS: Man in society—and the results of politics, government, and so on.

BAIN: The career of James Blair of Virginia demonstrates Mr. Davis's point. Blair was a member of the council of state; he was also commissary to the bishop of London from about 1690 to 1743. His influence was both secular and religious. He preached and published many sermons and was noted in England and America for his sermon style and delivery. But he was equally important in social and political affairs, and was almost single-handedly responsible for removing from office three colonial governors who, he felt, were ignoring the rights and wishes of the people of Virginia.

R. B. DAVIS: I agree with Robert Bain; if you take a look at James Blair's four-volume edition you will find that he has a "Preface" there in which he said, "In Virginia we don't have to write against Papists or atheists; we are concerned with men's manners and morals; we are writing of the concerns of everyday life and of men in relation to virtue" and, by implication, government. And these sermons are little moral and social homilies, a whole group of them. There's no chewing on a morsel of Calvin anywhere in Blair's sermons that I know of.

BAIN: There is another interesting point, too. Later writers—nineteenth- and twentieth-century writers—have criticized Blair. Many of these were church historians who criticized Blair for not keeping control of Virginia's Episcopal Church, as the Mathers had tried to control the church in New England. Their main criticism is that Blair failed to make Anglicanism as potent a force in Virginia as Puritanism was in the New England colonies.

HOLMAN: I think we are agreeing that if we were going to write the literary history of the South we should have to begin it in 1585, and that the region has had distinctive characteristics from the beginning which have made it possible to look at it differently—and not only made it possible to look at it differently but made it fruitful and almost obligatory that in certain respects it be looked at separately from the national experience. Then the question does arise about the continuity of this southern experience. Does it indeed survive, without enormous wrenchings, the kinds of events which occurred, the sudden awareness in moral and social terms of the issue of slavery, for example, which you're dating at the end of the seventeenth century, Richard Davis?

R. B. DAVIS: No, as far as it's being a conscious element probably the 1720s—that's where I'd put it.

HOLMAN: And then, of course, the Revolution, which we probably would all agree was a different kind of Revolution in the South if we measure it in class terms from what the Revolution was in New England, and then the second revolution, the Jacksonian election—all of these represent major historical experiences—and the Civil War, and Reconstruction. How well do these southern characteristics, if there are such distinctively southern characteristics, survive these different events? Many people would argue, for example, that—taking a different position from the one that Richard Beale Davis is taking—it is indeed the issue of race and slavery which has given to the southern experience its most distinctive characteristics.

c. DAVIS: I'm very much interested in the date, 1720, because it seems to me it's probably right that this is the time you find in the literature a certain awareness, a new consciousness. Is this a consciousness of slavery as an institution, or is this the consciousness of slaves as blacks in the society of that time? It seems to me we're talking about two different things.

R. B. DAVIS: We're talking about it as an institution, and long before that, in snatches of letters, in legislative records, and so on, there are grave misgivings. This I don't think has ever been sufficiently emphasized. There are grave misgivings scattered here and there—no unity which led to any movement, but personal expressions of misgivings, and then of course as soon as the gazettes get started in the 1720s you get plenty of these misgivings in print, as well as some defenses. I would say—maybe it's because I was conscious of it as I looked through gazettes—that there are more that express misgivings of slavery than ever defended it in the colonial period, as an institution. No, not blacks, because the Indian too, you see, was a slave in many sections, and they included both of them, and they're not thinking in terms of race or the place from which they came, but as a relation of man and man.

c. DAVIS: I'm convinced by your point, but then when does the awareness of the distinction of race become evident? When do you find signs of this, apart from misgivings about the institution, which obviously included not only blacks but Indians and touched in a tangential connection the whole system of indentured employment?

R. B. DAVIS: Leo Lemay is probably the best person in America to answer this question pretty precisely right now, because he has scoured all the American gazettes, especially the southern ones, with something of this kind in mind. Part of my answer is this: they become conscious of race and origin, as far as we can see it where the literature is concerned, pretty soon after the gazettes got started, probably by the 1730s, in their imitation of the dialects of Irishmen or Welshmen or Africans or something of that kind. Undoubtedly there are implications of social level there. The Welsh and Scottish and Irish dialects have the implication of indentured servants, for example—the semiliterate or the illiterate. The African, of indentured servants too to begin with; some of them were still indentured servants and not slaves at this period, but some were slaves. There may be implications in groups by then but it's primarily in use for humorous or literary effects that we see the differences in the races in these presentations of dialects, or sometimes for characterization in a tale or story which is included in the gazette. Now I confess that I don't remember the whole question, Charles; would you like to repeat the rest of it?

c. DAVIS: I asked a question that was not an innocent question, but I'll try to reconstruct it. I simply suggested that when we talk about the relationship in regard to slavery and awareness of it and consciousness of it, we are really talking about two things rather than one thing. One thing obviously involves a set of attitudes toward the institution of slavery itself, which included as we all know a number of different kinds of people, and the second thing has to do with the attitudes toward blacks, which indicate, as Richard Beale Davis has said, not only an awareness of differences in speech but differences in origin, differences in projected future, and presumably the beginning of justifications of various kinds of deviant patterns of behavior. Why should you behave toward a black any differently from how you behave toward anyone else? This is the kind of thing I was getting at, and I was trying to see when one found this awareness appearing in the literature itself.

LEARY: Could I add something to that? I wonder whether Charles Davis is asking this, when was there a sense that the Welsh, the Irish, and so on, could be assimilated into the society and the black could not?

c. DAVIS: That's another way of putting it.

R. B. DAVIS: That *is* another way of putting it. I would say that that does not come until after H. H. Brackenridge. That is, he's got at least seven different dialects in *Modern Chivalry*. As far as I can see through the eighteenth century the black and the Irish and the Welsh—particularly the black and the Irish—were the butts of jokes in the gazettes more than anything else. It looks as though they felt they never could assimilate in one sense. In another sense they were accepted—I don't know whether "assimilate" or "accept" or either is the right word—but I think we understand each other as to what we're getting at.

c. DAVIS: Norman Brown suggested to me certain kinds of evidence to indicate a somewhat earlier awareness of this. Do you want to repeat those, Norman?

BROWN: Well, I think that in Virginia within a half century of the arrival of the first blacks into the colony in 1619 that blacks were perceived as different and inferior. In some of the court records it shows. I mentioned a court case, I believe in the 1630s with this sentence: "Hugh Davis to be soundly whipped, before an assembly of Negroes and others for abusing himself to the dishonor of God and shame of Christians, for defiling his body lying with a Negro." Whether or not he was being punished simply for fornication, or was being punished especially for fornication with a black woman isn't clear. Would the word "defiling" have been used had he had a sexual relationship with a white woman? I don't know. It is even possible that the "Negro" may have been a male. You find in Elizabethan literature, in Shakespeare, for example, that blacks are perceived as different, as perhaps bestial. When the English started to trade on the coast of Africa, they perceived the blacks as different, inferior. The concept of blackness in medieval imagery is synonymous with evil and depravity, and it was natural to make this identification with the black man.

R. B. DAVIS: That is true. On the other hand, Hening's *Statutes at Large in Virginia* near the beginning of the colony lumped blacks, mulattoes, and Indians together in all the social legislation—those three. Now this is putting aside the Irish and Welsh questions.

C. DAVIS: Norman Brown, you started, it seems to me, on a sound basis and moved to one which is much less sound, when you were citing literary evidences. It seems to me that when you refer to this European tradition, essentially the characterization of blacks is perfectly true—but at the same time there is obviously a countertradition, the whole tradition of the noble savage, which sometimes involved as a very important factor the difference in color. In other words, you have, concurrently operating, two different traditions. It's very likely that the one you have indicated is the more dominant one, but the other one exists, too. And so when you have actually movement in the culture it means always the repression of something and the dominance of something else.

BROWN: You also have to point out that the English were aware of a century of experience of the Spanish in the Caribbean with Negro slavery. They had that precedent. And they moved very quickly in Virginia toward Negro slavery. It's evident (the court records are fragmentary) that about 1640 some Negroes were slaves in Virginia, though you don't get the first slave laws on that until the early 1660s.

TURNER: I was thinking of asking Norman Brown or Richard Beale Davis, one or the other, to comment on this: to what extent are you talking about a distinctively southern development in this connection, as against an American one? Your mentioning the English background for it suggests even more strongly that you have in mind an American development.

R. B. DAVIS: I don't think it is a distinctive southern one. We discussed this yesterday in regard to the ambivalent attitudes toward the Indian from the very beginning, within Captain John Smith himself, and I think Charles Davis is exactly right in pointing out that though the idea of slavery and enslavement may have been the dominant one, the inferiority idea, there was also the other. We get in legislative records occasionally accounts about some great African chief. Particularly we get, from the seventeenth century and growing stronger in the eighteenth, stories about the Mohammedan Negro who was already literate and who was translating various things into Arabic for his owner, who will hold him up as a noble savage, or the kind that we get in George W. Cable or in Melville's *Benito Cereno*.

BROWN: Do you think the colonials regarded these blacks who were being brought in manacles on slave ships from Africa as noble savages? The Indian on the frontier was a threatening presence—but the Negro was brought in as a captive, a person in chains. Was he perceived by the colonials as a noble savage?

R. B. DAVIS: I said this was not nearly as strong as the other tradition, but there were some who were conceived of in that way. They were exceptions rather than the rule.

YOUNG: Let me repeat Arlin Turner's question. Did you say, Dick, that the attitude that the black is inferior is not an exclusively southern attitude? Was this peculiarly southern at the time we're talking about, or would the same attitude toward the black be held in New England?

LEARY: I would say very much; Samuel Sewall's *The Selling of Joseph* argued that we should do away with slavery because the Negro could not produce soldiers for the military.

TURNER: I think of a sort of collateral question, related to the time in the nineteenth century when the Irish were coming in great hordes both to the South and to the North. Has there been a study of attitudes in this context of the people toward the Irish as they were coming in, the great unwashed illiterate?

BROWN: I believe that in the lower Mississippi Valley Irish workers were preferred on the more dangerous tasks of building the railroads, repairing the levees, unloading as stevedores, because if a Negro slave died that was a valuable piece of property lost, but if an Irishman died it didn't cost the employer anything.

LEARY: I was introduced in Boston once as—"He's Irish, but he's nice."

TURNER: Speaking of the Irish as they were introduced, was the attitude any different in New Orleans, for example, when they were coming off the ships from what it was up in Maine?

BROWN: I simply suggested that their lives were held to be

cheap, but beyond that, I'm afraid I don't know enough about the Irish in New Orleans to comment.

CALHOUN: You mentioned the noble savage, and something that has interested me in connection with southern literature, which we never have gone into, is what are the archetypes in southern literature? You mentioned the noble savage. How important is that? Is it an archetypal character? What about the garden, the virgin land? So much has been done with American literature in this respect. What about archetypal plots? The biggest in American literature, the initiation story—is there a continuity of that in southern literature? If not, why not?

BROWN: It seems to me there's a continuity of another social type, the southern poor white. I am thinking of Shields McIlwaine's book *The Southern Poor White: From Lubberland to Tobacco Road*: there is a continuity in that social type in southern literature.

CALHOUN: What about the initiation plot in southern literature? Where does it start? Where is it? It's a big theme in American literature.

C. DAVIS: I'm always troubled by the reference to initiation plots, and I'm troubled by people who talk about them, perhaps because I've heard so much about them. I'm tired of hearing about initiation plots, because it seems to me that you can see initiation plots in English literature very clearly. Maybe what we mean is that there's a difference in kinds of initiation. It's possible that the particular kind of initiation that we get in southern literature, perhaps in American literature in general, is rather more primitive and has to do with rites of passage, with acquisition of manhood in a more fundamental way than others. I'm willing to concede that possibility, but not much more.

YOUNG: I think I agree with Charles Davis. I was asked to read for a journal not too long ago an essay on *Swallow Barn* as an initiation novel. I'm being serious. The man was being introduced to the plantation system, and all this kind of thing; this was part of the maturity, he had to go through this.

WATKINS: I'd like to ask someone whether Faulkner's social and historical background for his four Indian stories—"A Justice," "A Courtship," "Red Leaves," and "Lo"—is fairly sound. Does anyone know?

R. B. DAVIS: I wish you'd look into it, Floyd. I'm interested in that myself, because of the early Indian . . .

TURNER: The initiation rites as a type of plot, and so on. . . . I've been wondering whether we're not in danger often—and perhaps in discussing southern literature as we're doing here—of starting with these phrases and concepts that are very hazy. I was on a dissertation committee examination recently in which the topic was "the myth . . ." and so on and so on, and one of the examiners asked at the end, "Couldn't you have left the word 'myth' out completely and had just as good a dissertation?" The student wasn't sure. . . . So I wonder again whether we sometimes don't try to take concepts and apply them when actually we need to look a little more to see what we have and then name it ourselves.

YOUNG: If you'll let me comment just briefly on Floyd Watkins's question, I think from what I have read, and I'm sure you've read the same things, there seems to be evidence that the biggest mistake Faulkner makes in his use of Indian lore is that he confuses Choctaws and Chickasaws, that basically his lore is correct but he's got the wrong tribe most of the time.

WATKINS: On one occasion he calls the same Indian a Chickasaw one time and a Choctaw later.

YOUNG: He changed it himself; someone had corrected him, and it's presumably a deliberate change on his part.

DOLMETSCH: I'm surprised in all this discussion of continuity in southern literature that nobody's introduced the topic of humor. It seems to me that this is one of the areas where there's a real chance to look at the development of a tradition and a continuity that's distinctive. A book that I have come across on this subject is one that I'm sure is familiar to everybody here—*Mark Twain and Southwestern Humor* by Kenneth Lynn, in which he traces the origins of Twain's devices of humor and attitudes back to William Byrd of Westover and his views in *The History of the Dividing Line*. What about that?

HOLMAN: I think we might very fruitfully inquire a little while again into the matter of what is distinctive about southern humor, that justifies us in saying that it's southern, as opposed to national, or simply humor.

GUILDS: Isn't it more of a frontier tradition rather than a southern one? Of course most of the frontier has been in the South or the Southwest. Of course it keeps moving further westward, but I wonder if it isn't the backwoods itself rather than where the backwoods is.

C. DAVIS: I don't think that even answers the problem. What seems to me clear—and it may be again the fact that I don't know—is that what is important about humor is that we become really aware of its existence in the early nineteenth century. This suggests the occurrence of particular phenomena in the culture that brings this to the fore. In short, the frontier existed, of course, from the first time a man put his foot on the soil here—there the frontier starts—but not the humor tradition. The humor tradition didn't come into being until much after that. There are other circumstances that bring the humor—if we think specifically of the southwestern humor tradition—into being at the beginning of the nineteenth century. We must avoid a search for a false continuity, ignoring perhaps the real one.

GUILDS: I can think of Simms, a Charlestonian, who when he visits the mountains of North and South Carolina was exposed to this frontier humor for the first time, and it was very new to him.

C. DAVIS: Exactly. You have to have a certain stratification in the culture, and in that way it resembles the pastoral, doesn't it? You have to have a certain complexity in the culture before you have the emergence of frontier humor. And when does that occur, at least to the extent that we have it?

YOUNG: It seems to me that there's another problem; it's not the emergence of the humor but that there's someone there to put it down. I think Southwest humor was around a long time before Joseph G. Baldwin and the other sophisticated outsiders came by and were impressed by it, as Simms was when he went to the frontier. I think there are almost always two things involved here. In Southwest humor we know there was someone from the outside who was impressed by what he heard and put it down, but the humor itself had been around for I don't know how long.

BROWN: Don't you think that the authors kept a certain distance between themselves and the characters? They didn't want their readers to think that they identified personally with them.

YOUNG: Quite true; this is one of the techniques, of course.

WATKINS: It seems to me that humor as a technique is the most difficult subject that we face in southern literature. Paschal Reeves has a good and amusing article in the *Southern Folklore Quarterly* about Thomas Wolfe's humor, and in Harry M. Campbell's and Ruel Foster's study of William Faulkner there is a study of humor, but they end up discussing how he's a Jungian in psychology. When I teach Faulkner's humor I can do only two things: one, read the jokes and try to get the class to laugh at them, or two, say that at the same time that it is very funny, it's also very serious. Then I start discussing the seriousness of it and again I've not been able to discuss the humor as an art. Can it really be done?

C. DAVIS: Walter Blair did it in *Native American Humor*—at least he taught me something about how it was done.

R. B. DAVIS: I wish Walter Blair had gone back farther.

BAIN: One reason we identify "humor" with the "South" is that New England's theological and polemical writings of the seventeenth century were almost humorless. When southern writers began to publish books at the end of the seventeenth and the beginning of the eighteenth century, we find Byrd, Beverley, Lawson, and others using humor as a literary device. This contrast may give us a false sense that there suddenly develops a special kind of humor that had really been present in the culture all along, and moves with the people as they moved South and West. The emphasis upon humor may also be part of the secularization that was occurring in New England, too, in the eighteenth century. Benjamin Franklin wrote comic pieces early and late in his career.

CALHOUN: I don't want to drop the subject of humor, but I'm glad that Carl Dolmetsch brought it up, because it seems to me we have sent Northrop Frye and archetypes back to the far north of Canada and I'm not sure what Floyd Watkins was doing with Jungian criticism, but I'm not so sure we're willing to do without Aristotle. It occurred to me that if we talk about continuity we could and should talk about continuity in terms of genres: for example, southern humor, or southern criticism, which interests me. Is there a continuity or are there changes from early Scottish Common Sense influence in the rhetorics, to romanticism, whether or not it's superficial, as Edd Parks and others have felt that Hayne and others were in their knowledge of romanticism, and then *to* the formalism of the New Criticism in the twentieth century? Or in southern fiction, from romance to *what*? What was the impact of naturalism on the southern romance, if any? I mean prior to Faulkner. Or in southern poetry, from the kind of occasional poems we have in the eighteenth century to poems about the death of beautiful women at the height of southern romanticism to Randall Jarrell and James Dickey. In short, if we talk about continuity, we need to talk about it in terms of genres. And humor is important there, to get back to humor.

GUILDS: One thing too I'm a little surprised that we haven't mentioned after yesterday is—in fact, I believe Charles Davis was the one who brought it up—the element of terror as a unifying theme in southern literature. Charles, would you initiate that again?

C. DAVIS: I'm not sure that I can. It has to do with the subject that Richard Davis was talking about earlier: the presence of blacks in a white society. Part of the awareness of the presence of blacks was the awareness of the fact that blacks would revolt, and that blacks represented a menace, a malignant force of some sort existing in the society. This makes for a peculiar condition, one that emerges at points in the writing. My own point, and one that I stole from Leslie Fiedler's *Love and Death in the American Novel*, is that the characterization of the natives of Tsalal in *The Narrative of Arthur Gordon Pym* owes something to the fact that Poe was aware of the presence of menacing blacks in Virginia and their hidden malignancy. You may remember that the natives of Tsalal were almost the most malignant creatures God ever . . . well, not God, but Poe ever created, because you remember they were all black, including their teeth. This kind of unpredictable malignancy owes something to more than soul, something to the conditions which exist, in this sense peculiar, in the society itself. That was the point, stated rather better yesterday than I've stated it here now.

BROWN: That novel was published within a decade after the Nat Turner insurrection in Southampton County, Virginia.

MOORE: Poe would certainly have known of it.

HOLMAN: One of the things that's generally present in the cliché statements about southern literature, and certainly related to what Charles Davis says about terror, is the persistence of violence in southern writing. Is this truly a characteristic of southern writing, and if so is it a function, as I think the humor may be, of the extent to which southern writing tends to see man in society rather than independently or individually? Are we willing to accept violence as more characteristic of the writing of the South than it has been of the writing of the rest of the nation?

YOUNG: It seems to me that if we would accept at least one of the basic propositions—that is, that southern writers, at least for some time, have agreed upon the nature of man as a depraved creature—then it would appear inevitable that violence would be associated with a man of that sort. If we're going to accept the first, it seems to me we have to accept the second as well. If you're talking about men in a social situation, depraved men in a social situation, the result of their poorly conceived and improperly conducted actions will be a violent situation.

CALHOUN: Professor Morse Peckham has a thesis in his book

Man's Rage for Chaos, as Jack Guilds knows, that in times of great order in society sometimes there's an outbreak of disorder and disconnected and disjunctive elements in art. I don't mean that I admire this thesis, but it's an interesting thing to apply when you have southern society as it was and you have violence at certain periods in southern literature.

C. DAVIS: The difficulty is that there is violence and violence, and when we speak about violence, do we speak about organized violence? Obviously the most profound organized violence in our history is the destruction of the Indian. We're really not talking about that; we're talking about forms of individual violence that occur within the society. Maybe one conditions the other; it seems to me very clear that present patterns of domestic violence are probably conditioned in part by the wholly irrational war that we are now conducting. I don't want to make a political speech, but the point is that what we are talking about when we talk about violence is domestic violence really—violence, in a sense, within the society—and maybe within a southern society there were possibilities for more of that. Again this is highly speculative and I can't really say. I would suspect that all over America there was a problem of order. It's a problem that you see early in the seventeenth century, and earlier, from the time, you remember, when the elder Richard Hakluyt drew up a set of rules for the founding of a colony. He was much concerned about problems of internal order.

INGE: There's probably no more violent a form of literature in the South than humor. I'm not just speaking of Sut Lovingood, where it reaches an epitome of some kind. To go back to the discussion of humor, probably the most fruitful way to study humor is not to anatomize it—the techniques of humor are universal; you find the same techniques no matter what country you go to—but there's something in the content, there's something in the state of mind. Violence is connected and probably a study of violence would tell us more about humor in society than to approach it in a formalistic way.

HOLMAN: We're moving toward the end of the time allotted for us, and I wonder if we feel that there is a need for a southern literary history. Do we feel that there is a need now for a study of the southern literary experience from its beginnings to the present on traditional or on something like traditional terms of literary history? Or do we feel that there's been enough done in this area?

GUILDS: I think it's already been said that if Jay B. Hubbell had been able to do the whole job we'd be in much better shape, but the fact that he did leave the twentieth century for someone else to do—no one has yet put the whole thing together—and I think there's a crying need.

R. B. DAVIS: There's a crying need, but we're not ready. Jay B. Hubbell, of whom I'm one of the greatest living admirers, simply didn't have the material to cover all the colonial period. It just wasn't available. That's got to be done first. We're not ready to write a literary history.

BROWN: Are we supposed to discuss whether or not there is material in the South, in the contemporary southern experience, for a continuing distinctive southern literature?

HOLMAN: Certainly I think it is a question that's within the general boundaries of our discussion. I am afraid that I was almost taking it for granted that with regard to the twentieth century there was not much debate, and that the real issue of a continuity resided in the relating of nineteenth-century and earlier experiences to the twentieth-century experience. If I'm wrong in that, then I may have carried us in a deceptive way.

BROWN: Floyd Watkins suggested earlier that the agrarian period was coming to an end, or agrarianism was winding down in the South. I wonder if we should discuss whether or not these distinctive elements that we have traced are going to continue to play a part in southern literature in the future.

CALHOUN: We did touch on the agrarianism aspect of that pretty thoroughly and down to the present, so that's one thing we did cover.

GUILDS: I'd like to come back to the point that Richard Davis made. I believe what he is saying is that we're not ready for any one man to write a literary history of the South. Is it possible to have a composite history of the South, *The Literary History of the United States* approach?

BROWN: You mean something comparable to the History of the South series that Louisiana State University is publishing, divided by periods?

GUILDS: Yes. Wouldn't we be ready for something like that? We'd let Richard Davis take the colonial.

CALHOUN: Well, where could we start? At the other end? If Hubbell did not go into the twentieth century, into the history of twentieth-century southern literature, do we have to wait for the materials in the colonial before we can start properly that way?

HOLMAN: If Richard Beale Davis is the greatest living admirer of Hubbell's work, I suppose I must be the second, but I would raise the question as to whether Hubbell's book actually is a literary history. It seems to me to be a collection of extremely useful essays on individual authors, grouped within a very loose historical frame, and if we're talking about a literary history I wonder if we aren't talking about approaching the whole issue with a totally different concept and organization from that in Mr. Hubbell's indispensable book.

TURNER: If someone were considering this kind of thing, there may be a pattern that would be useful in the history of Canadian literature that Carl Klink supervised. It has a chapter on scientific writing, a chapter on historical writing, and separate chapters on all sorts of writing. Northrop Frye wrote a conclusion or introduction which didn't seem to fit with the other chapters—it was a good essay, but he had a theory which wasn't borne out in the volume as a whole. That would be a possibility. The historical writing and other kinds of scholarly writing need to be surveyed, and a multiauthor undertaking might be the way to get it done. The Canadian literary history is less important, I believe, for what it says about the novel and poetry than for what it says in other parts.

HOLMAN: An enormous amount of what is valuable about the cultural history of the South still remains largely unexplored in letters and diaries and various things of this sort, which don't normally fall within the limits of a traditional literary history, and the kind of book that you're talking about would certainly give us an opportunity to explore these things and perhaps they do need to be explored in greater depth, as Richard Davis was suggesting, before the task of a synthesizing and organizing literary history of the South is attempted.

C. DAVIS: What Hugh said about Hubbell's book is evident even more clearly about *The Literary History of the United States*—we have a collection of essays by people with very different points of view. Some of them are good and some are not so good. The essay of Richard Blackmur on Henry James is superb, and there are other excellent essays of that kind. I should hope that when the history of southern literature is written that there would be some kind of agreement on the terms of the continuity. I think, as Jack Guilds does, that this is obviously an overwhelming and overpowering task. It is conceivable for one man to write about the colonial experience and another man to do the twentieth century, but the terms have to be agreed upon, so that there can be a genuine continuity of the sort that you do not get in *The Literary History of the United States*.

CALHOUN: I might point out the obvious, that the whole concept of literary history is now changing. I read the new journal *New Literary History*, out of the University of Virginia, to find out what the new literary history will be, and I try to read Roy Harvey Pearce on the new historicism. Of course there are matters of new historical approaches to be considered, too, as far as giving a unity of plan to a literary history of the South.

TURNER: Would Mr. Leary speak for the organization, the plan, the carrying out of the *LHUS* since it has been mentioned here? Is that feasible?

LEARY: I don't think it worked very well there, in spite of what Robert Spiller did; the first paragraph of each essay was usually written by Spiller in an attempt to make a bridge. I think I agree with Richard Beale Davis very strongly. I don't think we're ready; I don't think even in the history of the southern novel that there are very many people adequately informed. It seems to me that the study of southern literature is about where the study of American literature was in 1929 when Norman Foerster's *The Reinterpretation of American Literature* came out, and maybe what we need is a volume which calls for a reinterpretation and points out some of the problems which need to be looked into.

GUILDS: Well, isn't it true that a definitive history is never written anyway? If we wait until everything is just right, we'll be waiting for time eternal.

HOLMAN: That is true, but I wonder if Mr. Leary has not expressed a very good note for us to close this session on—that is, that what we need, and it is to be hoped one of the things which we have taken a small step toward accomplishing in this conference, has been to explore the implications of some of the things we do know, and try to find a direction to move in the future, and in a movement toward a reinterpretation. It seems to me that in actual fact there has been a very large element of reinterpretation involved in what we've been saying. It's not the old traditional way of looking at it. We've been asking some of the larger questions which we have tended, as scholars in southern literary study, not to ask, but instead to concentrate our work on very limited things. In this sense perhaps what we're doing is clearing the trees off before we plow the land, out of which we could raise a forest of literary history.

9. Thematic Problems in Southern Literature*

MODERATOR:

Louis D. Rubin, Jr.

PARTICIPANTS:

*Cleanth Brooks, George Tindall, Robert Jacobs,
George Core, Walter Sullivan,
Lewis P. Simpson, Philip Butcher,
Blyden Jackson, Charles Ray, Lewis Lawson*

RUBIN: Our topic today is thematic. We want to try to sketch out some of the thematic concerns in southern literary study. Questions of history and continuity are involved, but we would hope to get at some of the overriding topics, themes, patterns, concerns that have marked the literature of the South.

I think, for example, of race, and of community—the southern community. Eugene Genovese has said at various times that the Old South was preindustrial, and that the human relationships were not entered on the cash nexus of capitalism. The tie between master and slave was concrete, specific, human, not abstract. It was not very advantageous or attractive from the slave's point of view, but it was a human relationship. Cleanth Brooks, I wonder whether you would speak to this point.

BROOKS: It seems to me that one of the more striking differences between the South and New England was the fact that the South was, and still is, to a high degree anti-millennialist. The first settlers of New England were Protestant dissidents, indeed were

*Unlike all the other transcripts of conference sessions, this one has been recreated solely from notes.

[199]

of the left wing of Protestantism, who crossed the seas to set up the perfect church and the perfect state—a theocracy, no less, based upon the belief that the new world offered an opportunity to put into effect God's blueprint for the perfect church-state as recorded in the Holy Scriptures.

Later, when the older Calvinism began to fade away, and with it the doctrine of original sin, the belief that man was really perfectible and that the just and perfect society would be created on this earth increased rather than decreased in force. As the older Calvinism faded away, the idea of a utopian or millennial state was simply secularized and continued in full force. The Old South presented a contrast to this state of affairs: it was old-fashioned, rather orthodox, and in certain respects even feudal. The later waves of evangelical sects hardly changed this state of affairs, for the hot-gospelers preaching the "old-fashioned religion" still saw man as a guilty creature, a fallen creature, who could be saved, if at all, only by God's grace and at his good pleasure—not at all by his own human efforts. In fact, the South today, much more than the rest of the country, is in its notion of man still traditional, conservative, and religious—not secular, and not hopeful of utopian solutions. Read, for example, C. Vann Woodward's fine book entitled *The Burden of Southern History*.

TINDALL: We're getting into something that David Potter remarked on in an article entitled "The Enigma of the South." The key to the enigma, he suggested, was the background of a "folk society," which may be just another way of saying an "agrarian society," a society in which human relations are direct and personal, and it is the sense of that personalness that gives us a feeling of nostalgia about it from the perspective of a more complex society. It's of course not exactly an original observation that most of twentieth-century southern literature deals with the transition from one to the other, from gemeinschaft to gesellschaft.

JACOBS: So much has been made of the antebellum plantation society that we tend to forget the folk society of the Piedmont and points west, but some of the antebellum writers remind us of it.

Philip Pendleton Cooke, for instance, though he is usually thought of as a poet who wrote on subjects not too different from Poe's, published a number of tales of the frontier that support the concept of the South as a folk society.

RUBIN: We get something of this sense of the existence of a community in an image that one of the topics suggested for this conference brings up: the southerner in the North, or in Europe. When he gets away from the South he is forced into a position of having to try to understand and define the South that he has left. Being in a different kind of society seems to throw the southern background into perspective for him. This is true whether or not he's fleeing from it or merely stepping outside of it. I think of Quentin Compson's self-imposed obligation to "Tell about the South," and of Thomas Wolfe and what he has George Webber say about the South in *The Web and the Rock*. Or consider Ellison's *Invisible Man*. The thing that really triggers his anger and resentment and causes him to make the speech that so impresses the Brotherhood is the sight of human beings, an old couple, being *evicted*. At that point he goes into action. It's a violation of community.

BROOKS: It's quite true, as George Tindall has said, that there is, or was, a gemeinschaft society in the South. Because it's a very special kind of society, I would prefer to call it a "community"— that is, a group of people not brought together at random (a mere crowd) or a group of people related only by function—so many butchers, so many bakers, so many candlestick makers, that is, a mere society—but a community, a group of people held together by shared values. I use here the terms as W. H. Auden defines them in one of his essays.

Another, though a related way to look at the South, is to regard it as a kinship society. Some years ago in England I read a paper in which I tried to describe in concrete terms the kind of community that one found in Peter Taylor's story "Miss Leonora When Last Seen." I was delighted and surprised to have Mr. David Riesman, the Harvard sociologist, who was present, say to me a little later,

"Oh, yes, Mr. Brooks. You were describing in concrete terms what I would call more abstractly a kinship society." No wonder that the family bulks large in the southern "society." No wonder that in southern literature the family occupies so important a place. We see this in the work of a writer like Katherine Anne Porter, in her Miranda stories such as "Old Mortality." The heroine is often furious with her family; eventually, she tries to break away; but the family is there in the background, still very real and important to her.

I have argued in a book on Faulkner that his sense of the community is tremendously important for an understanding of his novels and stories. But, as one would expect, there are further complications. If Faulkner's Yoknapatawpha County possesses a community, that larger overarching community encompasses, of course, subcommunities. There are, in the first place, two obvious subcultures: the white culture and the black, sharing many of the same values, actually. Nearly all the black and the white citizens go to church and nearly all of them, black and white, are Protestant. But there are further subcultural differences: the subculture of the old planter stock and of the yeoman white farmers. Because Mississippi was a younger state—younger than the seaboard states, and closer to a frontier society—the world of Faulkner's novels shows a rather startling juxtaposition of Old South planter ideals and manners with a still robust frontier community. R. P. Warren has remarked to me on the fact that a good deal of the dramatic tension and interest in Faulkner's world comes from the fact that you have these poles of southern society (or community) much more sharply juxtaposed in the novels of Faulkner than in novels from South Carolina and Virginia—though Warren, I think, would point out that they are to be found in the older states to the east. I would insist on that fact. Mrs. Chesnut, for example, in *A Diary from Dixie*, records Sandhill "Tackies" coming to pay a call on her in her Mulberry Hill plantation. Ellen Glasgow's *Barren Ground* is focused upon the poor white stock who were certainly not country gentry, not even faded country gentry, though as a subculture they shared many of the basic values and interests of the overarching general southern culture.

CORE: This is a subject explored by Henry James not only in *The Bostonians* but also in *The American Scene* (from an entirely different vantage point, to be sure) twenty years later. After the war, as James points out, in the South the society is run by the female, and the male has become effeminate and useless in the way that Boston was when James satirized it.

JACOBS: Mr. Brooks's examples are modern, but the older writers also give us examples of this tension. The antebellum literary magazines are filled with accounts of Virginians who have gone west and have had to adjust themselves to the folk society of the frontier. Joseph Glover Baldwin's *The Flush Times of Alabama and Mississippi* (1853) shows us Virginians who as former Tidewater aristocrats were poorly equipped for the rough and tumble, catch-as-catch-can competition for land and power in the new states of Kentucky, Tennessee, Alabama, and Mississippi. As I remember, W. J. Cash in *The Mind of the South* quotes Baldwin as his chief authority on the predicament of the Virginia gentleman in the frontier states; but we also have the example of John Marshall Clemens, Twain's father, who moved through Kentucky, Tennessee, and on to Missouri, failing financially at each move simply because *as* a Virginian he couldn't cope with the frontier ethic, or, I should say, *lack* of ethics.

CORE: A later example of the same action and theme occurs in Andrew Lytle's *The Long Night*.

SULLIVAN: One of the problems has to do with the extent to which the planter hegemony actually existed. It doesn't seem to me that it will do merely to count noses, as Frank Owsley did in *Plain Folk of the Old South*, and show that there were very few planters who actually owned numbers of slaves. The point I want to make is that there seems to be some evidence that the planter dominated the society of the Old South in something of the same way that the capitalist dominated American society after the Civil War. He had power and influence beyond his mere numbers and his position was the goal toward which young men could work if they had sufficient energy. He represented success in a system that those much lower in the scale found satisfactory.

JACOBS: Turning again to Baldwin's *Flush Times*. He points out that the Virginian had to learn to be shifty in a new country. It was a totally different kind of society from what he was used to, yet, as Arthur Moore emphasizes in *The Frontier Mind*, tales were circulated in the East that the West was the great good place, the earthly paradise, the new place of creation. This myth is presented in many forms, but probably the most familiar version is in T. B. Thorpe's *Big Bear of Arkansas*, where the Arkansas hunter calls Arkansas the creation state and tells tall tales about the fertility of the soil and the superabundance of game. One comparison that I can't recall at the moment calls Heaven a "regular Kentucky of a place." This propaganda about the West attracted people like John Marshall Clemens, but when they actually arrived they found their neighbors were not gentlemen but speculators, landgrabbers, clay-eaters, eye-gouging alligator-horses—the "po'white trash" depicted in southwestern humor. The tension Mr. Brooks mentioned earlier is found in Faulkner, but it is predicted by the humorous writers of the nineteenth century, like Augustus Baldwin Longstreet, who in his "frame" stories in *Georgia Scenes* showed the consternation of the educated gentlemen at the antics of the frontiersmen.

SIMPSON: The question of whether or not the planter class actually existed as a hegemony certainly cannot, I agree with Walter Sullivan, be settled by statistical means. Nor do I think that it throws a great deal of light on the problem when we make a distinction between the Virginia planter and the frontier figure. The frontier society was assuredly different from that of the Tidewater world. But the planter went where the expanding southern economy called him, and everywhere he went, slavery went, of course. Slavery was his source of labor, and it was in a very fundamental way his source of political power. As I tried to indicate in my remarks at the Thursday evening session, I think a good deal must be said for Eugene Genovese's insistence on the southern community as a slave community ruled by a patriarchal and a paternalistic class. Accepting perhaps its own cliché images about itself—and even more images projected by romantic writers—we generally, especially those of us who are primarily students of literature, do not make much attempt to understand the historical reality of the slavery system and of the class of people who largely controlled the system. What were these people really like? Well, certainly they were individualistic and different. You can't sum them up easily. But I have been greatly impressed recently by a reading of the first volume of Edmund Ruffin's diary, which the Louisiana State University Press has brought out under the editorship of William Scarborough. Ruffin is often categorized as a "fire-eater," an eccentric Virginian, perhaps a little too eccentric for the truly elegant Virginia society. The diary, however, shows him to have been a man of letters of considerable discernment and an absolute and kindly gentleman. When he advocated the reopening of the slave trade on the grounds that slavery was a movement greatly beneficial to mankind, that it was in effect a progressive movement in a progressive age, was he speaking for his class? If he was, and there is actually no little reason to suppose that he was, he was depicting a class which advocated the "positive good" of slavery as compatible with the American ethos of moral progress—or of progress in general.

In reading a comment by David Donald in the *New York Times* on the Ruffin diary, I was struck by Donald's saying that Ruffin represents a class so different from the usual depiction of the planter class, and so different from the socially and politically powerful class in the North, that in this class we have a new type of man. I'm not quite sure what Donald has in mind. He does not elaborate on his statement, as I recall. But the suggestion that the southern planter was in some sense a version of the American as a new man, that he was connected in a vital way with the dynamics of American novelty—I think this suggestion is important. The idea that the community of the South in slavery consisted not in an anachronistic defense of the "peculiar institution" but at least partly in a commitment to its novelty under American conditions is an idea worth exploring. Possibly it would help in explaining the enigma of the Civil War—a war in which the South staked everything on the preservation of its slave society.

SULLIVAN: Did the South fight to preserve slavery? I raise this question not only in terms of the planter hegemony which I referred to earlier, but also in terms of the very complicated structure of the slave system. We have reason to believe, I think, that many people who found the practice of slavery abhorrent, nonetheless found the notion of sudden abolition even more abhorrent—so abhorrent, indeed, that they would fight to preserve a system they found disagreeable. This is merely a theory, of course, but it has the advantage of being rooted in a concrete situation. Could there not have been some intuition concerning what would happen to the whole sense of community once slavery was abolished? Still being highly theoretical, I should like to submit that the principal way the sense of community was maintained after the Civil War was by the paternalistic class system which virtually reenslaved the black man. And what could be more destructive to the sense of community than busing for racial balance? I think we need to stress the point that Cleanth has made more than once: the existence of a strong sense of community does not imply universal justice.

RUBIN: It seems to me that this idea of the community helps to explain the old dilemma. Why, after all, did the antebellum southerner, who for the most part wasn't a slaveholder, fight for the confederacy to preserve slavery? Remember the old remark about the War being a rich man's war and a poor man's fight. The argument that the southerner fought to preserve States Rights doesn't do it; that's too abstract. It's rather the idea of the community being under attack from outside.

BUTCHER: Is it proper, however, to take an overall, monolithic viewpoint on southern opinion, the southern community, and so forth? After all, in the Civil War South there were those who accepted the system. There were others who were alienated from the system but nevertheless loyal to the war effort. There were others who were loyal to the people—to the slaves who made up an important part of the community—but hostile to the system and the community insofar as the community represented the military effort. It seems to me that there was a great deal of inner tension in the society.

BROOKS: Yes. There were southerners who were torn two ways by their allegiance to the community and by their alienation from it because of slavery, which was incorporated in the general economic system by which the community lived. It reminds one of Yeats's famous statement: "We make out of the quarrel with others, rhetoric, but of the quarrel with ourselves, poetry."

SIMPSON: Yes, but that's us today, not the Old South. Cleanth has in mind, I think, Tate's essay, "A Southern Mode of the Imagination." Tate makes the point that one of the chief reasons the Old South did not develop a literature of any real power was that it was dominated by the rhetorical mode. That is, it was given to the mode of discourse inevitable in a society which gives itself up to politics and the law. The South in its quarrel with its outer enemies cultivated rhetoric and distrusted dialectic. But in the days when the South began to be free of the absolute necessity of rhetoric—save for Mark Twain, Tate says, not until after the First World War—the southern consciousness began to cultivate its inner drama. The quarrel with ourselves began. There wasn't, Tate says, very much of this in the Old South.

BROOKS: Yes, Allen Tate is quite right, and we could not get the deepest and most powerful literature as long as southern literature was simply a celebration of southern life without any questioning of its assumptions, or merely a defense of southern life against outside attack. But Allen, I believe, is assuming all along that unless you have a clearly defined self with which to quarrel—or a family meaningfully related to yourself, against which you feel the need to fight back, or a community that exerts real emotional claims on you, that you are forced to question—

you probably can't have a great literature. In other words, as in any dialectical argument, there have to be two terms. If the community breaks up completely, and it's simply every man for himself and the devil take the hindmost, you'll probably not get a very great literature. A fruitful quarrel with oneself implies not merely the fact of quarreling, but the fact of a self worth quarreling with, or a community worth rebelling against—and *hard* to rebel against. If it's easy, no tension is generated.

RUBIN: I think of something that Blyden Jackson has said. Blyden, would you summarize what you once remarked about the progression in Negro fiction?

JACKSON: Yes. In the earliest fiction by black Americans, the protagonists are mostly octoroons. What the author is saying is, "Look at me, I'm just like you, yet you mistreat me." Then comes the Harlem Renaissance, and the New Negro. What the black writer now tells his white audience is, "Look at me, I'm better than you. You're so inhibited by Puritanism and you love money so much that you can't enjoy with your senses." Then we get Wright, and *Native Son*. Remember the scene at the beginning, with the rat. He is saying that the social order kills the black in the same way. "Look at me," he says, "I am a threat to you." Then there is Baldwin's *Another Country*. This says, "Look at me. You have so traumatized me that I'm a threat to myself."

RUBIN: In other words, the social situation of the black writer has forced him into rhetoric—the argument with others. Then along comes Ellison and *Invisible Man*, and he turns it inward. He says, "Who knows but that, on the lower frequencies, I speak for you?" With this novel the protest novel moves inward; that is, the protagonist has moved out of the community and into an examination of himself, into dialectic. As we noted yesterday, the idea of community often runs into trouble because it seems to imply that because there was a community, this means that everyone in it was happy, when obviously the slaves, and the freedmen, and the black men in a segregated society, were far from contented with their role. The point is that a community can be a very unequal business, and many of the people within it can be very much upset over their situation. But it's still a community, and it offers a social identification. Could we hear from Cleanth Brooks on this?

BROOKS: I agree. Though we tend to praise the fact of community as a good thing (as in general we tend to praise unity or freedom as "good" things) its goodness is not a priori or absolute. If a community is a society which shares values, likings, and aversions, then the goodness of the community depends to some extent on what kind of values it shares. Thus, the unity (the fact of community in a Fascist nation) may render the Fascist nation more of a menace to mankind.

To apply this notion to the South: the South, as an authentic community, has held to some values that surely were, and are, questionable. The community of Faulkner's novels, for example, as Faulkner was careful to point out, holds to some false values and, at its worst, is guilty of hostility to all that is strange, and may even fall into mindless bigotry.

The real issue, I would insist, is this: surely we want more than a mere economically functioning "society"—cold, heartless, atomized society, in which the individual feels that he is merely anonymous and counts for nothing. As Western civilization moves more and more in that direction, it is a virtue that the South still represents a community in being—even if it is not at all points the community that we would like for it to be. (At least it exhibits a certain warmth and humanity and allows its people to be *human*.)

RAY: The idea of the search for community is a very important part of black writing. Alex Haley, who wrote the *Autobiography of Malcolm X*, finds a sense of the community in Africa, and he suggests that the southern community has African roots.

SULLIVAN: The great enemy of the writer and the community, it seems to me, is Abstraction. If I can be pardoned for repeating something that I was saying in yesterday's session, for the southern writer in the past, guilt over racial injustice couldn't possibly be an abstraction: it was there all around him, he was reminded of it every day. The sense of his own guilt was concrete, real. So he couldn't have a view of man as being perfectible; there had to be the conviction of original sin. But with the breakdown of the community, that sense goes. He doesn't have to confront all around him the human results of his ideas and attitudes. He loses the religious outlook, the conviction of original sin. I'd like to ask something else: to what extent, for the black writer today, is the idea of black brotherhood an abstraction?

RUBIN: As long as we're dealing with the matter of abstractions, let me bring up something else. I refer to the often-argued dispute as to whether Thomas Sutpen in *Absalom, Absalom!* is a "typical" southern planter, and whether or not the novel is thus "about" the South. The statement has been made, and I think rightly, that Sutpen's whole enterprise is based on an abstraction, that he builds his plantation house and sets up his family because it's a design, and that this makes him into something less than a typical southern planter. But I wonder whether the history of the Old Southwest into which Sutpen came doesn't give us the same sense of abstraction? This wasn't the Tidewater South, and the men who moved in to the virgin wilderness and created a planter society weren't for the most part the Virginians and the Tidewater Carolina aristocracy; they were new men, middle-class in origin. The career of Jefferson Davis is an example; Davis was born in a log cabin. Yet these people moved into the newly opened territories and in a matter of thirty years, within a single man's adult lifetime, created almost overnight a society of white-columned mansions. Now isn't there a sense of abstraction in that? Wasn't the plantation ideal of the Tidewater an abstraction for them?

BROOKS: Yes, you are right in saying that there was some sense of abstraction in the Mississippi planters' ideal of what a good life ought to be. Undoubtedly his notions of what kind of house he wanted to live in and what kind of life he wanted to lead derived in good part from plantation life in Virginia and the Carolinas. But this is probably always true of any civilization. Specifically, it was true of the Tidewater planters of the South, who undoubtedly took their ideal of culture and the good life from the English manorial tradition. That too was an abstraction for them. But ideals are always, to some extent, abstract, and tradition itself in its largest scope always has an element of abstraction in it. The difference between Thomas Sutpen's "abstraction" and that of the Compsons or the Sartorises or the De Spains, however, seems to me crucial. The planter ideal, for the Sartorises, was to a great extent lived, concrete, and personal. But as Faulkner makes thoroughly plain, Thomas Sutpen was concerned only with a surface and an appearance. Had he lived in New York in the 1870s, had he made a great deal of money, and had he aspired to live like a great millionaire, he would, like the robber barons, of that period and place, have built his design around a very different image. He would have built a palace at Newport, had a box at the opera, traveled in Italy, etc. But his impulse would have been the same, and in New York City in the 1870s he would have been just as "abstract" as he is "abstract" in Yoknapatawpha County. More than that, Sutpen was in his own special way, a kind of private "millennialist." Drusilla points out very clearly and correctly in "An Odor of Verbena" that Sutpen's dream, as opposed to John Sartoris's dream, was private and selfish. We may not think much of John Sartoris's dream—I don't—but Drusilla is quite right in making this distinction.

All of this bears on Sutpen as a "southerner." My argument is that his "southern" quality is derived and abstract, something that he wants to acquire and wear as he might a suit of clothes. In any case he certainly isn't the stereotyped southerner: lazing in the shade, drinking his toddy, wasting his time with cards and gambling, or talking about his family back in Virginia—or Worcestershire. He is not relaxed, but tense. He doesn't worship the past: he doesn't give a damn about it—only his future. He is indeed, as again Faulkner makes very plain, as single-mindedly "Puritan" and ascetic as any Connecticut Yankee righteously practicing the gospel of work and achievement.

RUBIN: I agree that Sutpen's ideal was different from the ideal of the early Compsons and Sartorises and De Spains and so forth. But I don't think you can simply write off Sutpen's dream of a plantation in the Mississippi wilderness as not southern, while saying that the Compson-Sartoris-De Spain ideal was southern. The history of the way that the Deep South was settled and made into a plantation society almost overnight, as it were—in a matter of no more than two decades—seems to me to have a certain resemblance to the performance of Thomas Sutpen. You get the feeling that those people went out there specifically in order to create a cotton version of the old Tidewater aristocracy, and what resulted was what the Virginians used to call "Cotton Snobs."

BROOKS: My point is not that there were no wicked, grasping people on the southern frontier. There certainly were in the 1830s and 1840s in Mississippi and Alabama. I expect there were also in Virginia and the Carolinas in the 1670s. Faulkner writes with some detail about at least one of them, Old Lucius Carothers McCaslin, who was ruthless and cruel, who acquired his plantation from the Indians in about the same way that Sutpen acquired his, and who actually begot a child on his own daughter. But McCaslin differs from Sutpen in some very important ways. McCaslin has no design—no abstract plan to which every human relation must be subordinated. We are told quite specifically by Faulkner that he cared nothing about his "get." He was certainly not trying to set up a dynasty. Yet this was the thing for which Sutpen lived and for which he actually sacrificed his children— finally, all of them. McCaslin was, in at least one aspect, a genuine aristocrat: he didn't give a damn about public opinion or for keeping up with the Joneses. He *was* the Jones, the laird, the manorial lord. Others could keep up with *him*—or not. It didn't matter to him. Thomas Sutpen, on the other hand, is the aspiring "new man," the person who must act in a certain way, because his hope to acquire prestige requires that he act in that way.

In some very important senses McCaslin is a much more wicked old man than Thomas Sutpen. Granted. Yet, in a curious way,

Sutpen is more "inhuman" than McCaslin. He is cold-blooded; his belief in abstraction and his belief in schedules, timetables and blueprints make him much closer to the go-getting "American" above the Mason-Dixon line or to the modern American who means to fulfill the millennial dream.

SIMPSON: I agree with Louis Rubin that there was abstraction in the Old South. I'd like to see more made of this in our study of the South, both antebellum and afterwards. I think, for instance, that slavery was an abstraction—the great overall abstraction of the southern mind. Not of course merely an abstraction. I don't mean that. But the defense of slavery as a beneficent, and as I said awhile ago, even a morally progressive institution, was based on the abstracting capacity of the mind. The southern dream of a great slave empire was an abstraction. There was a Great Southern Dream, and it was just as abstract as the Great American Dream. Every time I see the statement, so often repeated, that the southern mind was a "concrete" mind I am reminded that this maxim ought to be questioned—not necessarily discounted, but questioned.

LAWSON: I'd like to suggest a different way of looking at the southern community and southern life than has been brought up thus far. I wonder whether many of you have read a recent book, edited by Robert Manson Myers, entitled *Children of Pride*. This is a fascinating series of letters between members of a Georgia family in the nineteenth century. What struck me was the constant recurrence of illness and death. It was a continuing concern. Today people don't die in the bosom of the family, but in hospitals, set apart. We are ill individually, not as members of families. It seems to me that there was a kind of ritual about death, a ritual for dealing with it, that characterized family life before modern times, and that there are also other rituals. It might be very informative if we were to look at southern literature in terms of these rituals.

JACOBS: That's quite true. In Poe's time, for example, illness in women was considered attractive, and when Poe claimed in

"The Philosophy of Composition" that the death of a beautiful woman was the most poetic subject in the world he was very much in tune with his time. Edward Davidson argued in *Poe: A Critical Study* that Poe was popular in his own time because in a number of his poems he suggests elaborate funeral rituals—the mourner, the family vault, etc. But a great many other poets of Poe's time used the same subject—the proper celebration and mourning of the dead.

BROOKS: In part that is the general morbidity of the nineteenth century. But as for a concern with death, that has been a persistent concern throughout Western culture, and it has been eroded only in our time. It involves our symbolic underpinnings—our religious beliefs, and so on.

RUBIN: It ties in with the current concern for the violation of the dignity of death and old age, I think. I'm also reminded of something that Marshall McLuhan brings out in an early essay of his—back when he was still interested in literature—on "The Southern Quality." He speaks of the way that the southern writer doesn't burke the fact of mortality and of existence of decay and of evil. There's nothing antiseptic in the way that the southern writer looks at dying and the flesh.

JACKSON: I'd like to go back to the matter of abstraction, and the Old South. I wonder what you would say about Stark Young's fiction. Is his depiction of the old plantation realistic, or an abstraction?

BROOKS: I think the difference between the way that Stark Young and William Faulkner deal with the plantation is that where Young is building abstractions, Faulkner is criticizing them.

CORE: Isn't Young more or less sustaining illusions, where Faulkner is trying to get at what they mean?

JACOBS: If you think of Faulkner's *The Unvanquished*, you'll see how this works. In the final episode, "An Odor of Verbena," it's Drusilla who wants the abstraction carried out; she wishes Bayard to kill Redmond, because the ritual demands it. Bayard won't do it; he looks beyond the ritual demands to the human actualities.

SULLIVAN: Drusilla in that story is a priestess of violence. She wants the ritual carried out. Whereas John Sartoris is an anachronism. The time was past for his mode of operation. I am referring once more to Allen Tate here. The Old South was doomed anyway because it had no proper metaphysical foundation: it depended too much on style and not enough on substance. Or at least the John Sartoris type of southerner did.

RAY: What would you say of a character such as Hightower, in *Light in August*? What does abstraction have to do with his life?

BROOKS: Hightower is living for a dream—it displaces his own actuality. Faulkner is basically critical of people who live in dreams, and also—in the instance of the Snopeses—of people who are dreamless.

CORE: Despite the concrete elements in southern fiction and southern life, we need to remember that there is a strong element of abstraction. This element in the southern character is brought out by W. J. Cash, for instance. The clash between idealism (which is a kind of abstraction) and realism is a recurring theme in southern literature.

BROOKS: In many respects the ritual runs counter to the abstraction. We must be very careful in associating ritual with abstraction. I'm inclined to think that very frequently ritual is not abstract at all. A ritual is like a poem or a liturgy: it is highly concrete, even though symbolic. It is an "impractical" action, to be sure. Such an action is not designed to accomplish something in this world. Thus one's partaking of the morsel of bread and the sip of wine at the sacrament of communion is not designed to allay human hunger. But ritual runs counter to abstractions, just as concrete symbolic statement or action tends to be at the other pole from abstraction. As you will see, abstraction for me tends to be designed for action: we may describe it as stripped-down knowledge, schema and plan, not designed to provide "full knowledge" (in Allen Tate's sense) but to provide a recipe for action. For example, an oil painting of a landscape nourishes contemplation and aesthetic pleasure; a map of the same landscape shows one how to "use" it.

BUTCHER: I'd like to suggest something in line with this. I would say that as teachers of literature today, one of the things we must constantly remind our students of is of these rituals and of their importance in our lives. What has been said about the ritual involved in death and dying is quite relevant. We have to point out how this has changed nowadays. People die in hospitals now. In the past, dying was a ritual that took place at home, with the family assembled to witness it. Think how important this is with, for example, some of the poems of Emily Dickinson.

JACKSON: It might be well to think of *As I Lay Dying* in this light, as an illustration of the respect, if not reverence, for death.

SULLIVAN: There, it seems to me, abstraction and ritual get all mixed up. All the neighbors think what the Bundrens are doing is ridiculous, but it's a ritual, performed at the behest of an abstract command by Addie Bundren. One of the most abstract characters of all in Faulkner is Ike McCaslin. He has this notion of right and wrong. So when he confronts the fact of the corruption of innocence in his own family, his response is simply to get out, to refuse to play any more.

TINDALL: We have been talking about the sense of community. What about some of the themes of conflict in southern experience that are not represented in the literature? I think for example of the Populist impact on literature—is there one? Other than Warren's *All the King's Men* and *Night Rider*, which have to do with a later period anyway, where is the southern fiction that deals with this? Where is there a novel of the cotton mill?

JACOBS: Erskine Caldwell.

RUBIN: I think that a better way to put this question for our needs is, Why haven't these elements of the southern experience engaged the imagination of the southern writer in the way that other elements—race, for example—have?

TINDALL: Is it because the approach would necessarily be polemical? Rhetoric, rather than dialectic?

RUBIN: Of course, while it's true that topically these problems haven't been dealt with very much, the underlying issues have been dealt with often enough, in Faulkner for example.

TINDALL: But what of the real Populism of the 1890s? Why was there no southern equivalent of, say, Hamlin Garland? Several years ago, when compiling *A Populist Reader*, I looked all over for a southern piece that would evoke the life of the farmer and his problems imaginatively—something that would complement a selection from Garland on the Middle Border. I never found it. Where do you find this sort of thing in southern fiction?

RUBIN: George and I have a student who is writing a dissertation in history, on the New South in southern fiction. What he finds is that actually there isn't much there about it. The novelists weren't interested in it. Why is this?

LAWSON: Perhaps because in the mind's eye of the novelist the South is still bucolic: the myth of the agrarian South dominated the imagination and still perhaps does.

RUBIN: One factor is that the New South, industrialism, Populism, and so forth were issues of the late nineteenth and the early twentieth century, and the models for dealing with them in fiction were those of critical realism and naturalism. For some reason—and I'd like to know more about the reason—neither of these ways of writing fiction seem to have been compatible with the southern imagination. This I think is what largely accounts for the dearth of good southern writing between the death of the local-color period and the coming of the Renascence of the 1920s; the going modes, the creative discoveries, in American writing during those years were critical realism and naturalism, and the southern writer simply couldn't respond to them. All we got was Ellen Glasgow, and not even her best work.

JACOBS: This ties in, I think, with another characteristic of southern literature, which is the belief in the supernatural. All through southern writing there is a reliance upon and a strong conviction of the supernatural as something real, or at least as a constant point of reference. Obviously that wouldn't fit in very well with critical realism and naturalism.

BUTCHER: We might go at it in another way. Was a different

group drawn into writing in the South than in the North? Did they come from the same class structure?

RUBIN: Certainly as far as the twentieth century goes, almost all the leading southern writers have come from upper-middle-class families, from the leading elements of the community. The exception of course is Thomas Wolfe, who came from a lower-middle-class background, and who felt this keenly. Most of the others came from families in which the literary arts had a recognized role.

BROOKS: I should like to ask, though, just how many major English writers of the same period actually deal with industry and the factory? This omission may be true not just of the southern experience but of other places as well.

TINDALL: But if you think of the novels of Dickens, for example, and the way in which he was so concerned with urban life and factories and the like: these things *can* be made into literature, you know.

CORE: Yes, but in the next generation or so you have only Arnold Bennett.

RUBIN: Certainly Lawrence dealt with it.

BROOKS: That's true. But Lawrence's basic concern was with the dehumanizing impact of industry and the machine on what he felt to be the true matters of importance for the human being—the knowledge of the blood, the life force, the powerful energies of sex, etc. In other words, in this particular area, he tended to be as "reactionary as anybody" in rejecting the machine in the twentieth-century world—"worse" than the Agrarians.

JACOBS: Let me bring in the supernatural again, how apparently normal it was for a southern writer to count the supernatural instead of the natural as a resource. That approach of itself would make it a difficult matter. For instance, consider Tate's "The Last Days of Alice." After describing the predicament modern man faces because of the abstractions of modern science—the "theorem of desire" propounded by "drowsy cubes of human dust," he appeals to the supernatural, "O God of our flesh, return us to

Your wrath." It is interesting that his appeal is to a veritable Jehovah, an Old Testament God. One poem doesn't make a case, but I still argue that southern writers don't dwell on economic issues because they have been less concerned with the problems of making a living than with the condition of man's soul and heart. The human heart in conflict with itself, as I believe Faulkner says in his Nobel Prize speech.

LAWSON: What we face is the division between naturalism and the supernatural. The outlooks are mutually exclusive.

SULLIVAN: I'm afraid that you just can't get at literature in quite the way that George Tindall suggests. The writer doesn't approach the story in terms of subject matter that way. Dickens was *really* concerned with possession, avarice, what it does to the soul; the part of his work that is of least interest today is the explicit social and economic documentation. It's counterproductive to ask why you don't have a cotton mill novel. We just don't.

TINDALL: But we do have a novel about the Black Patch War. Why does that appear, but not the other? It doesn't have to be *about* the cotton mill or the problem of the cotton mill, but why don't we have a novel with that setting? Maybe just by chance no first-rate southern author ever came out of a textile community.

RUBIN: I think that's a legitimate question.

SULLIVAN: In a note at the beginning of *Night Rider*, Warren says that he is not writing a historical novel. I take this to be a warning against the sort of literary interpretation approach that we are trying to take here. The writer looks for the material in which he can discover the enduring theme, the ultimate human values he is searching for. The trouble with writing a novel about something is that the material gets rigid too quickly. The novelist is likely to have too many preconceived notions and what ought to be an exploration, a discovery, becomes a sermon.

RUBIN: One of the glories of twentieth-century southern writing, I think, is the way that it has come to grips with the actualities of the southern experience. It *has* dealt with race, and modernity, and so forth. Yet for some reason other, very important aspects of southern experience would seem not to have engaged the imaginations of the writers. Why?

CORE: It isn't correct to say that none of the southern writers has been very interested with the problems of making a living. Perhaps you know James Still's *River of Earth*, about just that, set in the hill country, and a good novel, too. And that brings up something else: the idea that innocence is in the hills, in the mountains, away from cities. There Still accomplishes what Jesse Stuart might have set out to do originally but never achieved.

RUBIN: Here we get into the function of the novel as pastoral. To use Empson's formulation, to what extent is the reliance on the small town, the agricultural milieu, the primitive, a kind of pastoral rebuke to an industrializing, urbanizing, complex modern society?

CORE: Katherine Anne Porter's "Holiday" is a good example of this.

BROOKS: I'd like to return to something that I brought up earlier. It has to do with the South as basically an antimillennial and antiutopian society, suspicious of rationality, against social engineering. This view is reflected in the literature. R. W. B. Lewis, R. P. Warren, and I have recently been working on a book, *American Literature: The Makers and the Making*. In the course of writing this book all three of us have been rather surprised, I in particular, with how powerful the strain of millennialism proves to be throughout American literature from its very beginnings to the present time. It shows up in all sorts of ways: it colors all sorts of treatments of history and the good life; it is associated always with a particular bias of mind and attitude. If it is, in many respects, the strength of the American character, it puts us up to solving problems long thought insoluble in which sometimes we succeed. It has also proved our bane. It has often blinded us to the difficulties of a particular course of action. It has allowed us to underestimate the cantankerousness of human nature, and the untidiness and final unpredictability of history.

Whereas it would probably be foolish to deny *any* millennialist element in the literature of the South, the contrast between southern literature and that of the rest of the country on this point is startling. Again, in this general connection, one might look again at Woodward's *The Burden of Southern History*. He touches on the problem, though he comes at it in his own way.

Millennialism can be traced back to the beginnings of the Christian era and, some scholars would say, further back still. But in historical terms, it may be convenient to think of it as a Christian heresy. St. Augustine pointed the contrast between the city of God and the cities of men. Though the city of God, the new Jerusalem, was to be the model for our earthly cities, it could never be realized by man's own effort but only with God's grace and in God's good time. In fact, when mankind entered the new Jerusalem, time would be at an end and he would live the life of the eternity in the eternal city. St. Augustine thus provided the classic statement of the relation of the two cities in terms of the Christian scheme.

In the course of the centuries, the millennialist dream did not die but grew and became stronger. But in Europe and in this country, it became gradually more and more secularized. We Americans, having put the errors of the old world behind us, planted on a new continent, and confident in our new powers and energies, have been peculiarly prone to take a millennialist stance. We fight wars to make the world safe for democracy or wars to end all war. Because in making such wars, we are virtuous and holy in our motives and ideals, actually acting for the good of the enemy, we demand—or nearly always demand—unconditional surrender. War is not an instrument of our national policy; we wage it only in order to make the world what it ought to be for everyone.

The American Civil War was fought in such terms. So were the First and Second World Wars. There is some reason to believe that our entry into the Vietnam War was occasioned, certainly encouraged, by these millennialist attitudes and expectations.

Yet I cite these wars simply as an illustration of our national attitudes, intended as no more than illustration. The millennialist characteristic in our culture is actually far more pervasive, more general, and more important than our war record suggests.

So much for an important element of American culture. I would argue that our southern subculture is to be distinguished from American culture generally as more realistic, more tough-minded, more aware of the darkness and difficulties of the historical process, less confident of man's perfectibility, still tinctured with some sense of "original sin." If such a distinction is even partially true, it might throw a good deal of light on the nature of southern culture and of the characteristic expression of that culture in southern literature.

EDITOR'S NOTE

The scholar who would undertake future study in southern literature will find much in this general discussion to suggest specific areas of needed inquiry. The nature of the southern community as revealed in fiction would seem to warrant investigation, including the relationship of the slave community to the plantation and to southern experience in general. What does southern literature reveal about the role of women—not only the lady of the plantation but southern women throughout the society? If antebellum society was, as seems agreed, not principally one of plantation lords and ladies and faithful slaves, but essentially a middle-class, folk society, how is this manifested in literature? Was southern society in the West importantly different from that in the older settled regions? If there was a plantation ideal that carried an influence out of all proportion to the actualities of southern economic, political, and social life, how did that ideal operate in fiction? To what extent did it function, both in the society and in the fiction, as an ideal, as an abstraction? Was, indeed, the whole notion of a slave society in the nineteenth century something of an ideal abstraction, as Lewis P. Simpson suggests? What can the literature show about this, and vice versa?

Slavery and the role of the black man in southern life have been often written about, and southern fiction has had much to say about it. There is need for much more thinking about the matter. What did the slave identity contribute to the southern community sense? What can be read, between the lines as it were, in writings by antebellum and postbellum southern white authors about the nature of slavery and of the relationship between blacks and whites? How much of the dynamics of the literature of black writers early and late has to do with black protest against the violation of human, community identity by whites?

It has long been accepted that in the small town and rural society of the preurban South, the family and the sense of "kin" was a powerful force for order and identity. How is this concept manifested in southern literature? And to what extent was the folk society of the South held together and organized in terms of certain rituals? What were these rituals? How do they function within literature? If ritual, as was suggested, is the antithesis of abstraction, how do such rituals serve to impede individual judgments and how do they serve to safeguard against dehumanizing processes? And how do religious belief and supernaturalism both condition and take form and meaning from such social rituals?

There was pretty general agreement that the southern literary imagination has for the most part not been attracted to specific economic and political problems, as such. Why not? What has this to do with religious attitudes, with the rituals of the community and the family, with the way that the southern community has functioned? Have such attitudes and assumptions acted to impede the writer's grappling with the human problems, black and white, of life in the South? Have they given strength and form to the southern literary imagination?

Again and again the discussion turned back to the nature of the southern community, both as revealed in literature and as it affected the form and shape of the southern literary imagination. What of the role of the arts in the community? How has the social status of the writer within the community organization affected the kind of literature written by southerners? Has the southern writer typically come out of an identifiable background of status and positions within that community? What, in the South, has been the relationship of the fine arts, including literature, with overall community concerns? Have the writer's status and expectations caused him to write about some things and not others? To adopt a role as rhetorical defender?

Clearly there is a great deal still to be learned about southern life from southern literature, and about how and why that literature has taken the forms it did in the South.

                                                        L. D. R.

APPENDIX

A List of Topics
Suggested for Further Study

General

Early myth and history, its survival and treatment in later southern literature—(Pocahontas-John Smith, Bacon's Rebellion, Francis Marion, Daniel Boone, the Kentucky Tragedy).

Early descriptions of southern nature and their effect on subject and image in later writing.

The historical novel.

The southern writer and the myth of the new world garden—The "wilderness" theme in William Faulkner, Robert Penn Warren, Andrew Nelson Lytle, Donald Davidson, Madison Jones, James Dickey, etc.

Negro slave revolts as a fictional theme—examples: Harriet Beecher Stowe's Dred, Arna Bontemp's Gabriel Prosser, William Styron's Nat Turner, John O. Killen's Denmark Vesey.

The novel of Appalachia.

The Populist impulse in southern fiction.

Texas-Oklahoma fiction as southern fiction.

A study of black writers who remained in the South.

A study of southern literary magazines—completion and publication of the series that the *Southern Literary Journal* has been publishing, plus identification and brief discussion of journals not important enough for detailed treatment.

Publication of correspondence of important southern writers.

A comprehensive study of agrarianism and its impact on southern thought and literature.

Cohesive factors that make the South still a region and thus justify a regional approach to its literature.

[227]

The extent to which southern literature has been dependent upon a clearly discernible value system.

The relationship of southern diaries, memoirs, letters, etc., to southern literature and literary studies: the diaries of Kate Stone, Mary Chesnut, Sarah Morgan, Edmund Ruffin, and similar records of life in the South that are outside "literature proper."

The role of *abstraction* in southern writing and literary thought. Is the assumption that the southern literary mind is "concrete" justified? What about the abstracting tendency of the southern mind in the creation of the image of the "Old South," the "New South," the image of slavery, of the plantation, etc.?

Comparative studies of New England and the South as literary cultures. The role of the writer in New England and the South.

An in-depth study of southern literary history in the making—a history of the history and criticism of southern literature.

The concept of "Progress" in the South.

A critical history of southern fiction from the 1820s to the 1960s. To be concerned especially with continuities.

The relationship of illiteracy to literacy in the South. Did illiteracy afford an advantage to the twentieth-century southern writer, giving him status in a world in which literacy still meant a special relation to life and society?

Literary societies in the South.

Literary (more broadly, cultural) relationships between Britain and the South at all periods, from the early Colonial onwards. Do these relationships differ significantly, either in quantitative or qualitative terms, from those between Britain and the northern states? An aspect of the larger question would be the reputation of southern authors in Britain—and vice versa—and the circulation in Britain of distinctively southern journals.

Regionalism in southern literature, as related to and compared with regional aspects of other literatures.

Pastoralism as a phenomenon in southern literature, with comparisons from further afield.

Dialect literature, and the use of dialect in "literary" fiction, again compared with nonsouthern and non-American examples.

Responses of various authors to changing attitudes on southern problems—Joel Chandler Harris, Ellen Glasgow, Faulkner, etc.

Nationalism and sectionalism at various periods—the 1830s, the 1930s, etc.

Death and ritual in selected southern literature.

Family reunions in southern literature.

A biography of Carson McCullers.

The Atlanta *Constitution* and its circle.

The slave owner in recent southern fiction.

The theological background of southern thought with particular reference to Calvinism in the South and evangelical Protestantism.

Felt differences between southerners and northerners, particularly in the nineteenth century. We have, for example, Henry Adams on the southern mind. Are there comparable expressions by southerners on the northern mind—in particular, expressions not directly political or connected specifically with slavery? (The latter tend to be polemical and defensive.) One would like analyses by southerners that are more detached and philosophical.

The British origins of southern pronunciation(s). Surely, someone ought to take advantage of recent and more rigidly scientific work on the English county dialects such as has been done by Professor Orton, of Leeds.

The effect of copyright law on the development of southern fiction.

Southern universities and the rise of southern letters.

A census of southern manuscript material in major libraries.

The relation of popular southern culture and southern art.

Southern writers and the reading public.

The "death" theme in southern literature.

A study of the literary ramifications of the southern sociopolitical hookup with the new West.

The southern writer and the minority mentality.

Sojourn in the South: revelation and trauma.

Varieties of southern ambivalence.

Source documents for the black southern experience.

A narrative history of southern writers and literature, especially since the Civil War and most especially on the southern renaissance.

Myth, stereotype, symbol in southern literature.

Religion in southern literature.

Race, class, and party in southern literature.

Colonial and Early National Period

Clues to the origins of southern rhetoric, written and oral, in seventeenth- and eighteenth-century legislative and executive oratory, Indian speeches (and treaties) in translations, and above all in reading tastes and fashions.

An assessment of southern verse and prose appearing in British and American journals and newspapers before the Revolution. Was there an appreciable body of belletristic or semibelletristic writing? Does it show "different" qualities? If so, what?

The southern colonial sermon and religious tract from Maryland through Georgia as a means of assessing the nature of the region's theological thinking, and as a body of literature.

French-German influences on early southern writing (Huguenots, Salzburgers, Moravians, Palatines, etc.).

The image of the Indian in early southern writing.

Southern letter writers of the seventeenth century—a collection of letters from the period designed to (1) show the major concerns of the southern colonials (2) demonstrate the range and diversity of the social classes of the writers (3) explore the form of the letter— one of the major literary "forms" practiced by southern writers of the period.

Southern letter writers, 1700 to 1775—same as above, but also to show the development of the form.

White consciousness of black art before 1830— a reevaluation of the works of white writers to discern any awareness of black art— folk art as well as others.

A reevaluation of white attitudes towards the American Indians before 1800.

A collection (with introductions) of southern sermons before 1775. An examination of these sermons for style and content, etc. Would include Anglican, Presbyterian, and other representative sermons from the period.

A reexamination of the "prose styles" of southern writing of the seventeenth and eighteenth centuries. Study of the impact of the "plain style" and of the beginnings and emergence of the high or grand style.

Character types in southern writing before 1800. Much in periodical literature that is derivative, but William Byrd's portraits of Old Capt. Hix and Epaphroditus Bainton suggest types that will become Cooper's Natty Bumppo. From Byrd's *Secret History.* There are others.

Reexamination of southern histories and reports for "mythmaking" that is both conscious and unconscious. Byrd, Beverley, Lawson, and others engage in this pastime.

A reexamination of the received assumptions about literacy in the South before 1800.

An edition of the writings of James Blair of Virginia.

Southern consciousness of British attitudes before the Revolutionary War. Since most southern books before the middle of the eighteenth century (and later) were published in England, how aware of the British audience were the early writers? What impact did this awareness have on their work?

A catalogue and a history of verse writing in the South before 1800.

Reevaluation of early southern writing for evidence of the beginnings of southwest humor and the appearance of the "grotesque."

Comparative studies of New England, Middle Colony, and southern writers, to identify likenesses and differences. For example, a study of the Mather dynasty of New England and that of James Blair of Virginia.

An edition of early periodical writings of southern newspapers and journals. Annotated, etc. The periodical essay and its impact on southern fiction before 1865 could be a by-product of such work.

Reevaluation of early writing for the development of sectional attitudes in southern writing—particularly of character types, such as the "Yankee," in the writing done before the Revolutionary War.

A history of *The Portico*—at least a monograph on this periodical.

The rhetorics and rhetorical theories taught at William and Mary (and other southern universities), and the impact of these teachings upon the South—especially Virginia.

A history of eighteenth-century Williamsburg based on the Tucker papers at the College of William and Mary.

A definitive biography of William Byrd.

The contribution of eighteenth-century southern historians.

Literary history of eighteenth-century Charleston: post Revolution.

Literary history of eighteenth-century Virginia.

A comprehensive literary history of the Colonial South (1607-1776). A great deal has been unearthed in the last two decades to "flesh out" and expand upon Jay B. Hubbell's treatment.

A collection of southern colonial newspaper verse (to about 1800).

Good, modern editions of important southern authors before ca. 1820.

A book on "The Virginia Wits": The Munfords, the Tuckers, William Wirt et al.—a group of neglected writers of the early national period who present some interesting parallels and contrasts to the much-studied "Connecticut Wits."

A comparative study of elements of style in the literature of the early South to determine whether there are significant differences between northern and southern styles in writing discernible before the antebellum period.

More publication of early records of the South where semiphonetic spellings may give a clue to how particular words were pronounced. Does, for example, Susie M. Ames's recently published *County Court Records of Accomack-Northhampton, Virginia, 1640-1645*, record such spellings?

Antebellum and Later Nineteenth Century

A collected edition of George Moses Horton.

The whole question of whether or not the antebellum and post-bellum South did in historical actuality constitute a "traditional" society or community, together with the problem of the relationship of the historical actuality to the literary interpretation of the South (which generally seems to hold that the element of tradition is a basic element in relationship of southern society and southern literature).

The extent to which antebellum southern writing indicates that southerners felt guilty about slavery and how valid is the evidence one way or the other in literary expression. (The topic may be confined possibly to fiction, or limited in some other way.)

The local colorist: insider or outsider.

Millennialism in the South (or the lack of it) as compared with other parts of the United States.

Southern writers and northern editors, esp. in the late 1800s.

A series of reevaluations of neglected early (pre-1920) "classics" of minor but continuing significance.

A study of the roles southern journals played in antebellum days in developing the elements of the Old South myth that was transmitted in postbellum days by writers from Thomas Nelson Page to Margaret Mitchell. A concerted effort was made by the few southern journals to get southern history rewritten and to portray "real" southern life and character as an answer to the "calumnies" of the North.

An up-to-date study of the literary taste of the antebellum (and postbellum, for that matter) South. The traditional line that southerners of the early period were totally addicted to Scott, Byron, and Moore needs to be qualified.

A reinvestigation of the connections between southern antebellum writers and periodicals with those of the North. In a number of cases these connections were closer than has been admitted, and the South was not totally deprived of avenues of publication and influence.

A reconsideration (and reevaluation) of dialect verse.

The artistic contribution of the antislavery narratives.

Charles Chesnutt and the genteel tradition.

The romantic verse narrative within the black literary tradition of the nineteenth century.

The literary debt of the New South to the Old.

Edition of Timrod's letters.

The influence of music on Lanier's poetry.

New edition of W. T. Thompson's Major Jones sketches.

A biography of Simms.

A biography of Timrod.

A biography of Irwin Russell.

Humor in Poe's work.

The Twentieth Century

Jean Toomer in Georgia.

A critical edition of Sterling Brown's *Southern Road*.

A critical biography of Elbert Sutton Griggs.

The "Second Reconstruction" and the writer. The modern civil rights movement as a thematic problem in southern literature.

Lone star mystique: Texas in fiction—such writers as Katherine Anne Porter, William Humphrey, William Brammer, Larry McMurtry, Edwin Shrake, etc.

The following authors merit further investigation: Caroline Gordon, Andrew Nelson Lytle, Madison Jones, George Garrett.

Southern urban fiction.

The terminal date of the southern literary renaissance, if it is not still continuing.

Discernible trends in southern writing of the 1960s.

Will the leveling effect of mobility and mass media produce contemporary writers who can no longer be considered southern?

A comprehensive critical history of southern writing from 1900 to about 1920.

A critical history of Southern writing from 1920 to 1970.

Recent southern magazines and various aspects of the South, *Sewanee Review, Southern Review, South Atlantic Quarterly, Virginia Quarterly Review,* etc. Also, these magazines in relation to southern authors.

Is writing by black authors improving, staying the same, or getting worse as a result of increased integration and greater opportunities for black intellectuals and artists?

Is writing about the black man by white authors improving, staying the same, or getting worse as a result of the white man's greater awareness of black rights and black ambitions?

Is the introduction of "alien" philosophical concepts into recent southern literature—O'Connor's Catholicism, Percy's existentialism—indicative of a significant change in the orientation and motivation of southern writing?

Generally speaking, are southern poets still readily identifiable as southern by their work?

A biography of W. N. Harben.

The periodical and the southern literary renascence—esp. the *American Review,* the first series of the *Southern Review,* the *Virginia Quarterly,* the *Fugitive,* and the *Double Dealer.*

The debt of the twentieth-century renaissance to previous southern writers.